RAND McNALLY

Classroom
Atlas
13th Edition

Author
Celeste Jones Fraser

Editors
Brett R. Gover
Joella M. Morris

Cartographic Project Managers
Rob Ferry
Marzee Eckhoff
Nina Lusterman

Cartography
Gregory P. Babiak
Justin Griffin
Marc Kugel

Research
Susan Hudson
Elizabeth Leppman, PhD
Felix Lopez
Raymond Tobiaski

Writing
Elizabeth Leppman, PhD
Joella M. Morris

Product Management Director
Jenny Thornton

Design
Michelle LeBlanc-Smith

Production
Carey Seren

Educator Review Board
Marianna Alho
Christine Brigham
Dr. Rhoda Coleman
Nicole Hardesty
Wendy Israel
Lynn Jeffries
Laurie Kotzen Miller
Kany Seck
Patricia Setze

Manufactured by RM Aquisition, LLC
9855 Woods Drive
Skokie, Illinois 60077

Printed in Madison, WI, U.S.A.
September 2015
1st printing
PO# 40357
ISBN: 0-528-01514-1
ISBN-13: 978-0-528-01514-4

If you have any questions, concerns or even a compliment, please visit us at randmcnally.com/contact or e-mail us at: consumeraffairs@randmcnally.com or write to:
Rand McNally
Consumer Affairs
P.O. Box 7600
Chicago, Illinois 60680-9915

For information about ordering the *Classroom Atlas* or the *Classroom Atlas Teacher's Guide*, call 1-800-333-0136 or visit our website at www.randmcnally.com/education.

TABLE OF CONTENTS

THE DISCOVERER'S TOOLS

Introduction

In this atlas, you will find maps, photographs, graphs, tables, and diagrams. Together, all these tools will give you a clear picture of the geography of regions, countries, and the world. The first section in this atlas, The Discoverer's Tools, will help you master the tools for unlocking a world of information. Each tool provides you a different perspective and different information. As you use this atlas, study all the tools—it will be a journey of discovery.

DID YOU KNOW?

Maps and globes show you pictures of the earth standing still. In real life, however, the earth is always moving. It spins on an imaginary line called an axis at about 1,000 miles per hour. It takes 24 hours to make one complete spin, or rotation.

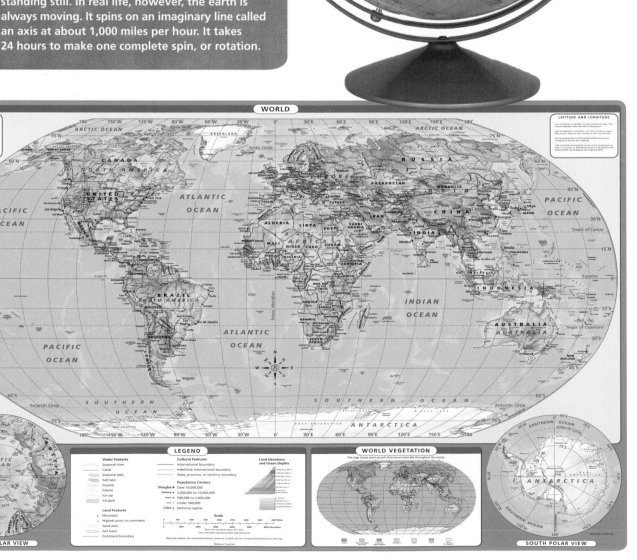

Globes vs. Maps

A **globe** is a model of the whole Earth. Because it is round like the Earth, a globe is an accurate representation of our planet. Shapes, sizes, distances, and directions are all shown correctly on a globe. A **map** is a flat picture of the whole world or just a part of it, such as a country, state, or city. Maps are drawn from an overhead perspective—from the view you would get looking down from above.

Different maps show different information. For example, a map might show the streets of a city, the shape of the land, weather patterns, or places where mining takes place. The size of the area shown on a map is determined by what the mapmaker wants to show. The top map on this page is a map of the whole world. The map below it is a map of the United States, without Alaska and Hawaii. Can you see how the map of the United States is just one small part of the map of the world?

Arctic Ocean

Arctic Ocean

North America

United States

Europe

Asia

Atlantic

Pacific Ocean

Pacific Ocean

Africa

South America

Ocean

Indian Ocean

Australia

Southern Ocean

Antarctica

©RMCN

DID YOU KNOW?

An atlas is a collection of maps. This atlas is a collection of more than 100 physical, political, and thematic maps.

Thematic Maps

Have you ever seen a weather map on television that uses different colors to show places with different temperatures? That map is a **thematic map**. It shows information about a **specific topic** and where a particular condition is found. The thematic maps in this atlas give you information about specific topics or themes.

This atlas has ten world thematic maps. These maps let you compare the same kinds of information for areas around the world. For example, you could use the World Climate Map to see what places in the world have a climate similar to the climate where you live.

This atlas also has thematic maps in the sections about each of the continents. Several different thematic maps often appear on facing pages. This allows you to compare different topics for the same area. For example, if you compare a climate map and a population density map for South America, what do you think you might discover?

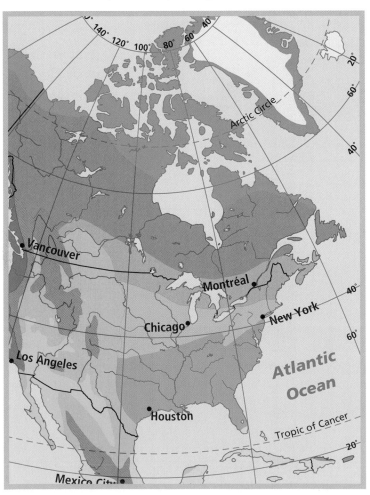

Physical Maps

On the physical maps, different **land elevations** and **ocean depths** are shown by different colors. Major **physical features**, such as the Rocky Mountains in North America, and major rivers, such as the Colorado River, are named. Countries and some cities are also named.

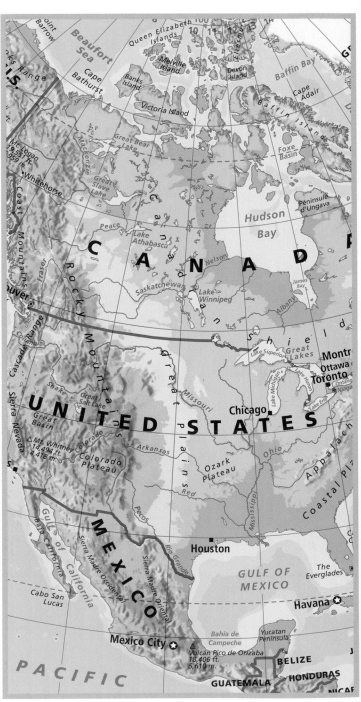

Political Maps

It would be impossible to show all the Earth's features on a single map. So, mapmakers create maps that show only a few things. For example, political maps show **political units**—areas under one government, such as countries, states, provinces, territories, and cities. Countries, states, and provinces are shown in different colors so that you can recognize type and have different symbols to show their populations.

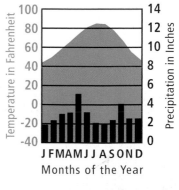

Canada Political Map

National capitals	Province capitals	Towns	Population
✪	✪	■	Over 1,000,000
✪	✪	▣	250,000 – 1,000,000
✪	✪	•	Under 250,000

━━━ International boundary
─── Province boundary

0   100   200   300   400 Miles
0   200   400   600 Kilometers

Climate Maps

Climate is the kind of weather a place has over long periods of time. Climates are measured by average temperature and precipitation. The term *precipitation* refers to moisture that falls to the earth in the form of rain, mist, hail, snow, or sleet.

On the climate maps in this atlas, each color represents a different climate region. Climate graphs accompany each climate map. Each graph shows the average monthly temperatures and precipitations for a specific city.

Climate Graph: Dallas, Texas

Climate Map

▢ Dry - very little rain

▢ Moderate - warm summer and mild rainy winter

▢ Continental - mild summer and snowy winter

▢ Highlands - varies with altitude

Environments Maps

Environments maps show what type of land is found in different areas. Each color represents a different type of **environment**, such as desert, forest, cropland, or **urban**. *Urban* refers to areas covered by cities and their suburbs.

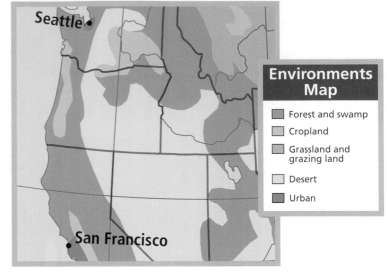

Environments Map

- Forest and swamp
- Cropland
- Grassland and grazing land
- Desert
- Urban

Economies Map

Land Use
- Little or no activity
- Forestry
- Agriculture
- Stock Raising
- Manufacturing
- Fishing

Economic Activity
- Cattle
- Dairy Cows
- Movies
- Oranges
- Petroleum
- Sheep
- Silver
- Tourism

Economies Maps

The purpose of economies maps is to show how people make a living in different areas. The colors show how the land is used. In the sample map shown, yellow stands for agriculture. The economies maps in this atlas also include symbols representing products and economic activities that are especially important in certain areas. In the sample map shown on the left, these products and activities include oranges, petroleum, and tourism.

Population Density Maps

Because people are not spread out evenly on the earth's surface, mapmakers have created **population density** maps. These maps show which areas have lots of people, which have a moderate number of people, and which have few people. The colors stand for the numbers of people per square mile. As you can see in the sample map, the darker the color, the more people there are per square mile. Population is densest in the regions with the darkest color.

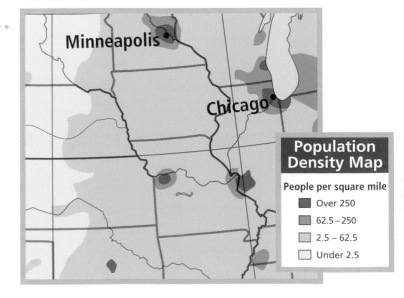

Population Density Map

People per square mile
- Over 250
- 62.5 – 250
- 2.5 – 62.5
- Under 2.5

Map Projections

The only way to make a flat map of the round Earth is by changing its shape. Mapmakers must stretch some areas and shrink other areas. For this reason, maps cannot show the world as it really looks.

Only a globe can do that. Mapmakers have developed many different methods of representing the round earth on a flat surface. These different methods are called **map projections**.

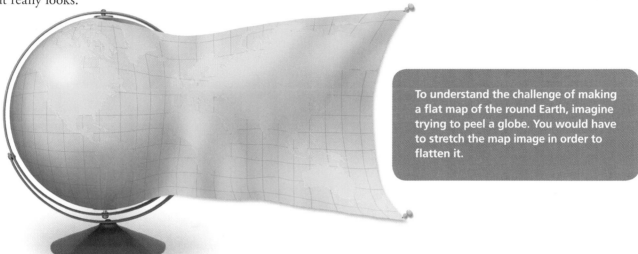

> To understand the challenge of making a flat map of the round Earth, imagine trying to peel a globe. You would have to stretch the map image in order to flatten it.

Types of Map Projections

Mapmakers choose different projections, depending on how the map will be used. Each map projection is different in the way it shrinks and stretches areas of the world. The maps on this page show three different kinds of map projections.

Mollweide Projection

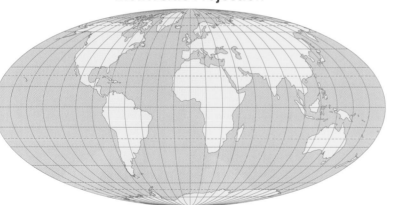

Robinson Projection

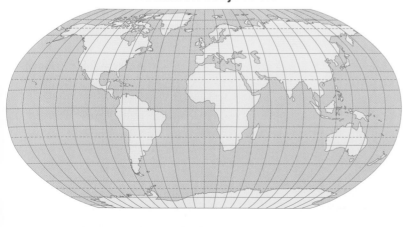

Mercator Projection

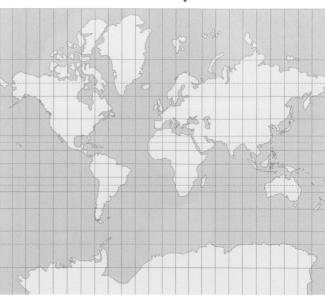

Orienting Yourself on the Earth

All directions on the Earth are based on the location of the **North and South Poles**. These are fixed points on the globe that never change. When you go north anywhere on the Earth, you are heading toward the North Pole. The same is true for going south and the South Pole.

This means that on the Earth and on maps, north and south are always opposite one another. West and east are always opposite one another, too. However, unlike the north and south directions, there is no east or west pole.

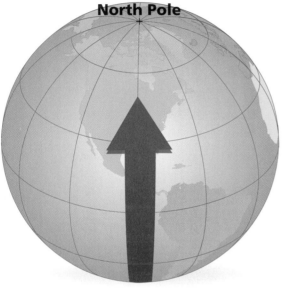

The arrow is pointing **north** towards the North Pole.

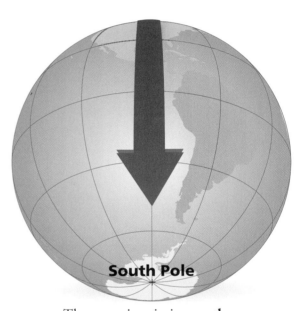

The arrow is pointing **south** towards the South Pole.

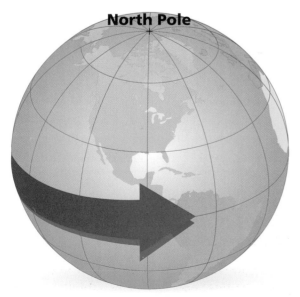

The arrow is pointing **east**.

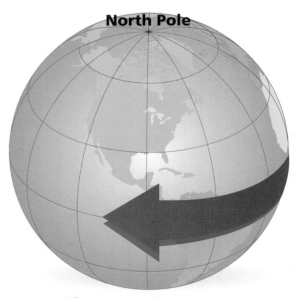

The arrow is pointing **west**.

Cardinal and Intermediate Directions

North, south, east, and west are called **cardinal directions**. The directions in between them, such as northwest, are called **intermediate directions**. Most maps include a **compass rose**, or direction symbol.

North Arrows

Some maps show only a **north arrow**. A north arrow indicates the direction toward the North Pole. What about the other directions? Once you know at least one direction, you can always figure out all the others. They never change in relation to each other.

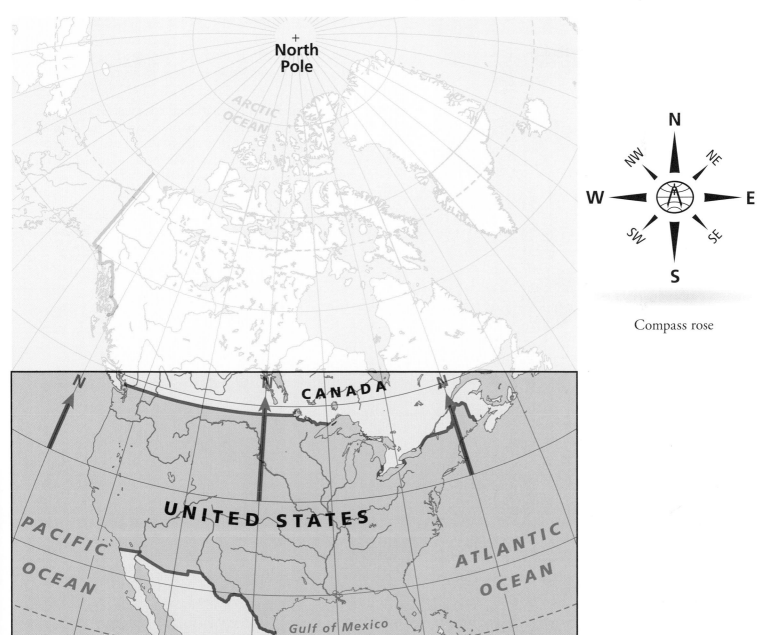

Compass rose

It is important to remember that north is not always straight up toward the top of the map. The United States map above has three north arrows. The map has been extended to show that each arrow points to the North Pole. The arrows are curved because this projection shows the roundness of the Earth.

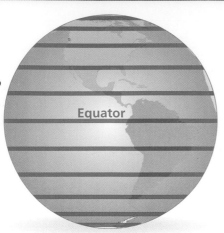

Lines of latitude, also called **parallels**, run east and west across globes and maps.

Lines of longitude, also called **meridians**, run north and south on globes and maps.

Latitude and Longitude

In order to identify any location on the Earth, people have invented a **grid system** of crisscrossing lines that circle the Earth.

Lines of **latitude** circle the Earth east and west. Latitude is the distance measured north or south of the Equator. The **Equator**, 0 degrees latitude, is halfway between the North Pole and the South Pole.

The North Pole is 90 degrees north latitude, and the South Pole is 90 degrees south latitude. Distance from the Equator can be expressed as any number between 0 and 90 degrees, north or south latitude.

Lines of **longitude** run north and south between the two poles. The line representing 0 degrees longitude is called the **Prime Meridian**. Longitude is the distance measured east or west of the Prime Meridian. Distance from the Prime Meridian can be expressed as any number between 0 and 180 degrees, east or west longitude.

Every location on the Earth has a **global address** made up of its latitude and longitude numbers. For example, the city of New Orleans, Louisiana, is located at 30 degrees north latitude, 90 degrees west longitude, so its address is 30° N, 90° W.

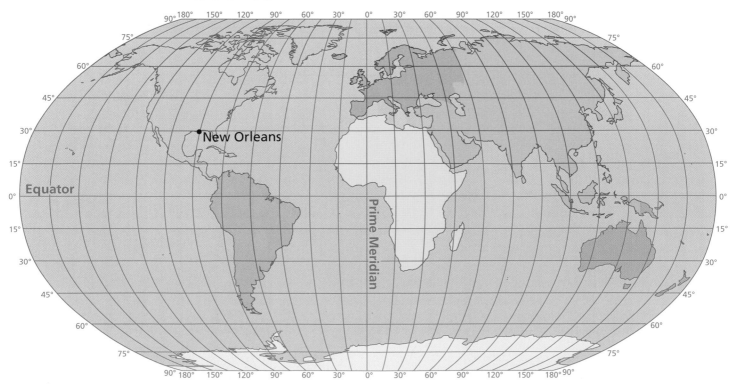

Letter-Number Grids

Some maps have **letter-number grids** to help people locate places. Letters run vertically down the sides of the map and numbers run horizontally across the top or bottom of the map, or vice versa. Each letter and each number corresponds to a band running vertically or horizontally across the map.

Let's say that you want to find the city of Pierre on the South Dakota map below, and you have been told that it is located at C-3. Using two hands, put your left index finger on C▶ and your right index finger on 3▼. Move the finger on C to the right and move the finger on 3 down until the two fingers meet. The square in which they meet can be identified as C-3.

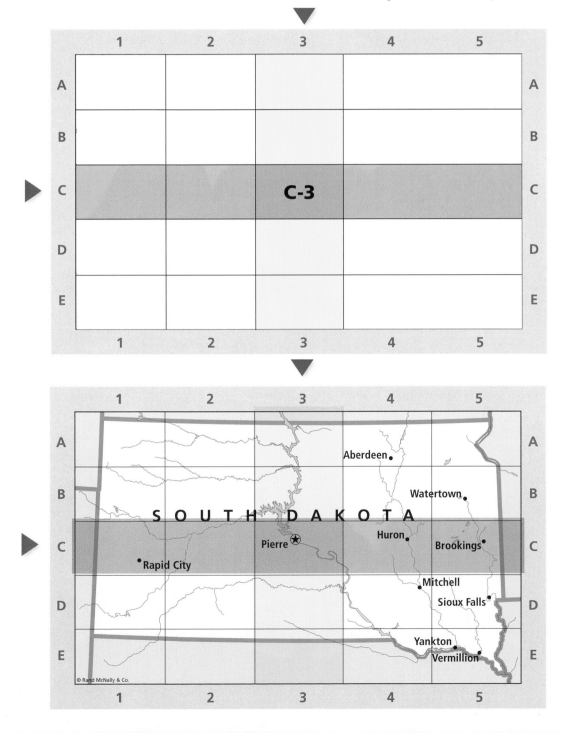

Halves of the Earth

People have invented ways to refer to different parts of the Earth. The Earth is round like a sphere, so people refer to half of the Earth as a **hemisphere**. The prefix *hemi* means "half."

The Equator divides the Earth into northern and southern halves. The half that is north of the Equator is the **Northern Hemisphere**. The half that is south of the Equator is the **Southern Hemisphere**.

Northern Hemisphere

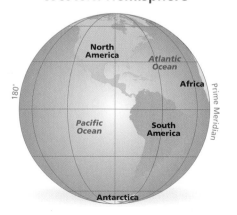

Northern Hemisphere

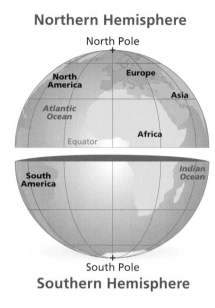

Southern Hemisphere

Southern Hemisphere

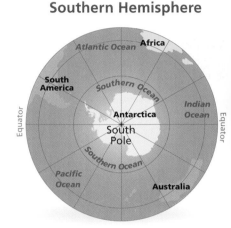

The Earth can be divided into eastern and western halves as well. We use the circle that is formed by the Prime Meridian and the 180th meridian as the dividing line between the two halves. The half that extends west from the Prime Meridian

to the 180th meridian is the **Western Hemisphere**. The half that extends east from the Prime Meridian to the 180th meridian is the **Eastern Hemisphere**.

Western Hemisphere

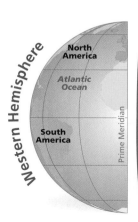

Eastern Hemisphere

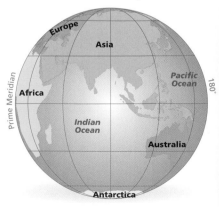

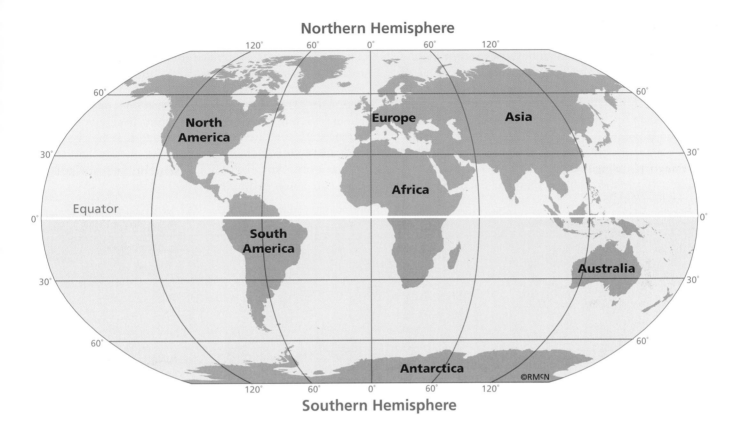

Northern Hemisphere

North America

Europe

Asia

Africa

Equator

South America

Australia

Antarctica

Southern Hemisphere

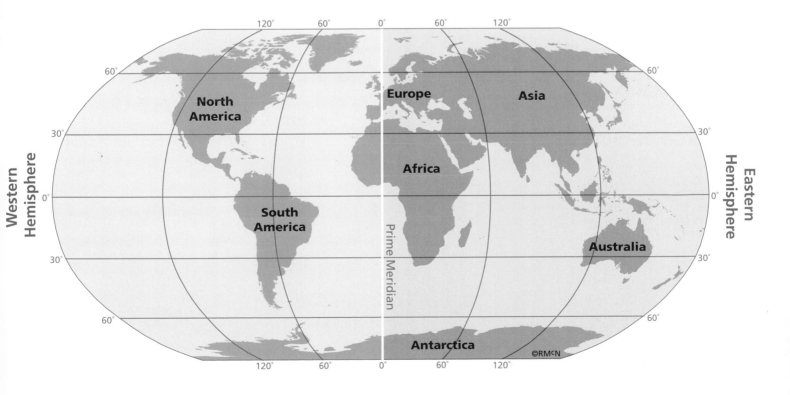

Western Hemisphere

Eastern Hemisphere

North America

Europe

Asia

Africa

South America

Prime Meridian

Australia

Antarctica

Map Legends and Symbols

The **legend** of a map explains the symbols used on the map. Map symbols can be lines, colors, patterns, or shapes. It helps you decode the information. In this atlas, the legends on the physical and political maps explain much of the map information. To keep the legends on the individual maps from getting too large, these legends include only a few key symbols. The complete legend for all information on the physical and political maps is on page 17. Take some time to get familiar with these symbols so that you can recognize them on the individual maps.

The **scale bar** tells how much smaller the map is than the real area it represents. The scale bar below is from the North America Political Map. To see how the scale bar works, place your ruler on the bar. You will see that one inch represents about 650 miles (one centimeter represents about 400 kilometers). Find two cities on the map that are about one inch apart (or two cities that are about one centimeter apart) on the North America Political Map. In the real world, these places are about 650 miles (or 400 kilometers) apart.

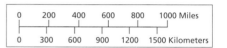

Measuring Distance

Suppose you wanted to measure the distance between Montgomery, Alabama, and Atlanta, Georgia.

Step 1 Place a small sheet of paper on the map. Line up its edge with Montgomery and Atlanta. Make a mark on the paper next to the dot symbol for each of the cities, as in Figure A.

Step 2 Place the sheet of paper with the marks beneath the bar scale, as shown in Figure B.

Step 3 By comparing the marks with the distances on the bar scale, you can see that the distance from Montgomery to Atlanta is about 150 miles.

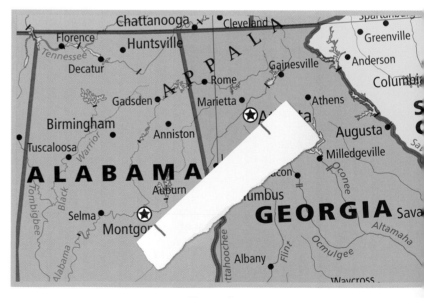

Figure A

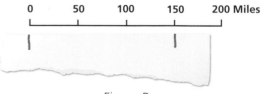

Figure B

Legend for Physical and Political Maps

Water Features

ATLANTIC OCEAN — Ocean or sea

Lake (physical map)

Lake (political map)

Salt lake (physical map)

Salt lake (political map)

Seasonal lake

Nile — River

Niagara Falls — Waterfall

Land Features

A S I A — Continent

Mt. Mitchell 6,684 ft. 2,037 m. △ — Mountain peak

Kilimanjaro 19,340 ft. 5,895 m. ▲ — Highest mountain peak

A l p s — Physical feature (mountain range, desert, plateau, etc.)

Borneo — Island

Cultural Features

———— International boundary

———— State, province, or territory boundary

EGYPT — Country

KANSAS — State, province, or territory

PUERTO RICO (U.S.) — Dependency

Population Centers

National capital	State, province, or territory capital	Town	Population
✪	✪	■	Over 1,000,000
✪	✪	▣	250,000 — 1,000,000
✪	✪	•	Under 250,000

Land Elevations and Ocean Depths

Land elevation

3,000 meters	9,840 feet
2,000 meters	6,560 feet
1,000 meters	3,280 feet
500 meters	1,640 feet
200 meters	656 feet
0 Sea level	0 Sea level

Water depth

0 Sea level	0 Sea level
200 meters	656 feet
2,000 meters	6,560 feet

Map A

Vallejo
San Pablo Bay
San Rafael
Concord
Berkeley
Golden Gate
San Francisco
Oakland
San Francisco Bay
Hayward
Fremont
Palo Alto
PACIFIC OCEAN
San Jose

0   10   20   30 Miles

Different Scales for Different Maps

Maps can be drawn to different **scales**. The three maps on this page all focus on San Francisco, California. The maps are the same size, but have different scales. On Map A, one inch represents about 30 miles. On Map B, one inch represents about 4 miles. On Map C, one inch represents about one-half mile.

Because of their different scales, the three maps represent different sizes of areas on the Earth.

DID YOU KNOW?

Map C shows the most detail of San Francisco as a city, such as its streets and parks.

Map B

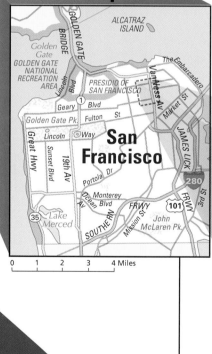

GOLDEN GATE BRIDGE
ALCATRAZ ISLAND
Golden Gate
GOLDEN GATE NATIONAL RECREATION AREA
PRESIDIO OF SAN FRANCISCO
The Embarcadero
Van Ness Av
Market St
JAMES LICK
Lincoln
Geary (1) Blvd
Golden Gate Pk. Fulton St
Great Hwy
Lincoln Way
San Francisco
19th Av
Sunset Blvd
Portola Dr
280 FRWY
IS puz
Monterey Blvd
35
Ocean Av
Lake Merced
SOUTHERN
Mission St
FRWY
101
John McLaren Pk.

0   1   2   3   4 Miles

San Francisco

Map C

Buchanan St
Laguna St
Octavia St
Vallejo St
Broadway St
Pacific Av
Jackson St
Washington St
Lafayette Park
Clay St
101
Sacramento St
California St
Gough St
Franklin St
Van Ness Av
Pine St
Bush St
Sutter St
Post St
Geary Blvd
Polk St
Larkin St
Cleary Ct

0   1/4   1/2 Mile

Index

The **index** is a list in alphabetical order of most of the places that appear on the maps. Each place entry in the index is followed by its map key, or alpha-numeric grid location, and the number of the page on which it appears.

Did You Know?

Each "Did You Know?" presents an interesting fact about the world.

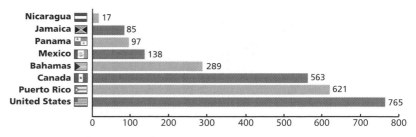

DID YOU KNOW?

Lake Michigan gets its name from an Algonquin Indian word, *michigami*, which means "big lake."

What If?

Each "What If?" asks you to use information from the atlas and other sources to answer a critical thinking question. There are no right or wrong answers, but be sure you can present facts to support your opinions.

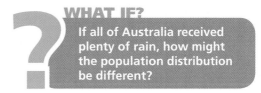

WHAT IF?
If all of Australia received plenty of rain, how might the population distribution be different?

Graphs, Charts, and Photographs

The graphs, charts, and photographs in the atlas help illustrate information from the maps. They may help you see the same information in a different way. They may also provide additional information about the themes of the maps. The photographs show you how the features shown on the map look in the real world.

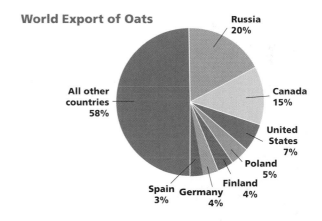

World Export of Oats

Russia 20%; Canada 15%; United States 7%; Poland 5%; Finland 4%; Germany 4%; Spain 3%; All other countries 58%

Automobiles per 1,000 people

Nicaragua	17
Jamaica	85
Panama	97
Mexico	138
Bahamas	289
Canada	563
Puerto Rico	621
United States	765

Geographical Terms

The large illustration to the right is a view of an imaginary place. It shows many of Earth's different types of landforms, bodies of water, and human-made features. The following vocabulary list defines many of the features on the map.

See if you can find an example of each feature on the maps in the atlas.

Archipelago
A group of islands

Canyon
A deep, narrow valley with high, steep sides

Coast
Land along a large lake, a sea, or an ocean

Desert
A large land area that receives very little rainfall

Forest
A large area covered with trees

Gulf
A large part of an ocean or a sea that lies within a curved coastline; a gulf is larger than a bay

Harbor
A sheltered body of water where ships can safely anchor

Hill
A small area of land that is higher than the land around it

Island
A piece of land that is surrounded by water

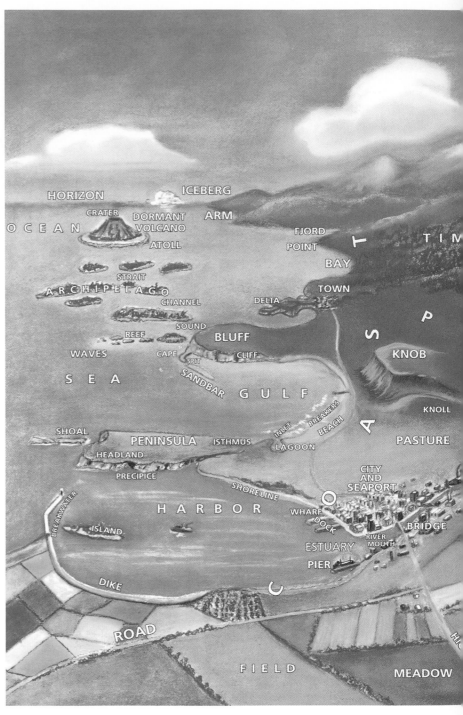

Isthmus
A narrow piece of land that joins two larger areas of land

Lake
A body of water completely surrounded by land

Mountain
Land that rises much higher than the land around it

Mountain range
A row of mountains that are joined together

Ocean
One of Earth's largest bodies of water

Plain
A large, flat land area

Plateau
A large area of land where the highest elevation is generally the same; a plateau may have deep valleys

River
A body of fresh water that flows from higher to lower land; a river usually flows into another river, a lake, a sea, or an ocean

Sea
A large body of salt water nearly or partly surrounded by land; a sea is much smaller than an ocean

Valley
Lower land between hills or mountains

Looking at the World

The Earth is an amazing planet. It has towering mountains, deep canyons, and pancake-flat plains. It has oceans and seas that spread across vast expanses, and rivers that stretch thousands of miles. It has deserts where rain almost never falls, and rain forests that get drenched by rain every day.

The map to the right shows some of the Earth's variety—places and physical features that rank above all others in their categories.

But even with all this variety, the earth has distinct patterns. The maps in this section will reveal the patterns in the Earth's physical and human-made features.

Largest Freshwater Lake
Lake Superior
(North America)
Surface area: *31,700 square miles*

Hottest Place
Al Aziziyah, Libya
(Africa)
Highest recorded temperature: *136°F*

Longest Cave System
Mammoth Cave
(North America)
Length: *365 miles*

Wettest Place
Mount Waialeale
(Hawaii)
Average yearly rainfall: *460 inches*

Largest Ocean
Pacific Ocean
Surface area: *63,800,000 square miles*

Longest Mountain Range
Andes
(South America)
Length: *4,500 miles*

Driest Place
Arica, Chile
(South America)
Average yearly precipitation: *0.03 inches*

Largest Rain Forest
Amazon Basin
(South America)
Area: *2,300,000 square miles*

Andes Mountains

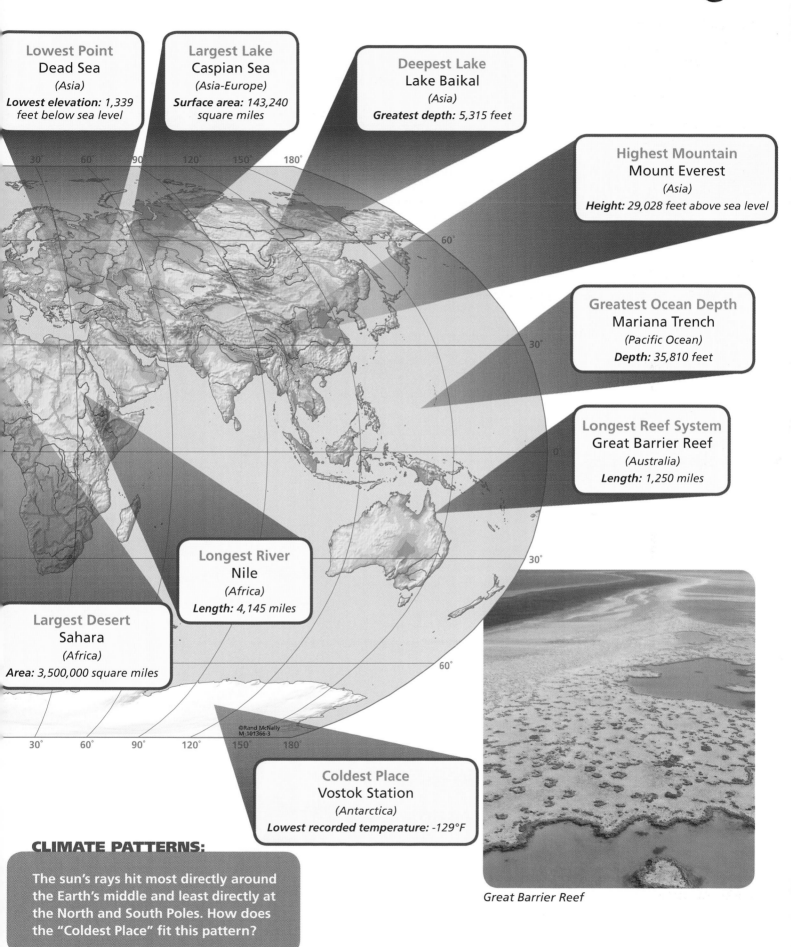

Lowest Point
Dead Sea
(Asia)
Lowest elevation: 1,339 feet below sea level

Largest Lake
Caspian Sea
(Asia-Europe)
Surface area: 143,240 square miles

Deepest Lake
Lake Baikal
(Asia)
Greatest depth: 5,315 feet

Highest Mountain
Mount Everest
(Asia)
Height: 29,028 feet above sea level

Greatest Ocean Depth
Mariana Trench
(Pacific Ocean)
Depth: 35,810 feet

Longest Reef System
Great Barrier Reef
(Australia)
Length: 1,250 miles

Longest River
Nile
(Africa)
Length: 4,145 miles

Largest Desert
Sahara
(Africa)
Area: 3,500,000 square miles

©Rand McNally
M-101366-3

Coldest Place
Vostok Station
(Antarctica)
Lowest recorded temperature: -129°F

CLIMATE PATTERNS:

The sun's rays hit most directly around the Earth's middle and least directly at the North and South Poles. How does the "Coldest Place" fit this pattern?

Great Barrier Reef

World Physical Map

This map shows the world's land elevations and ocean depths.

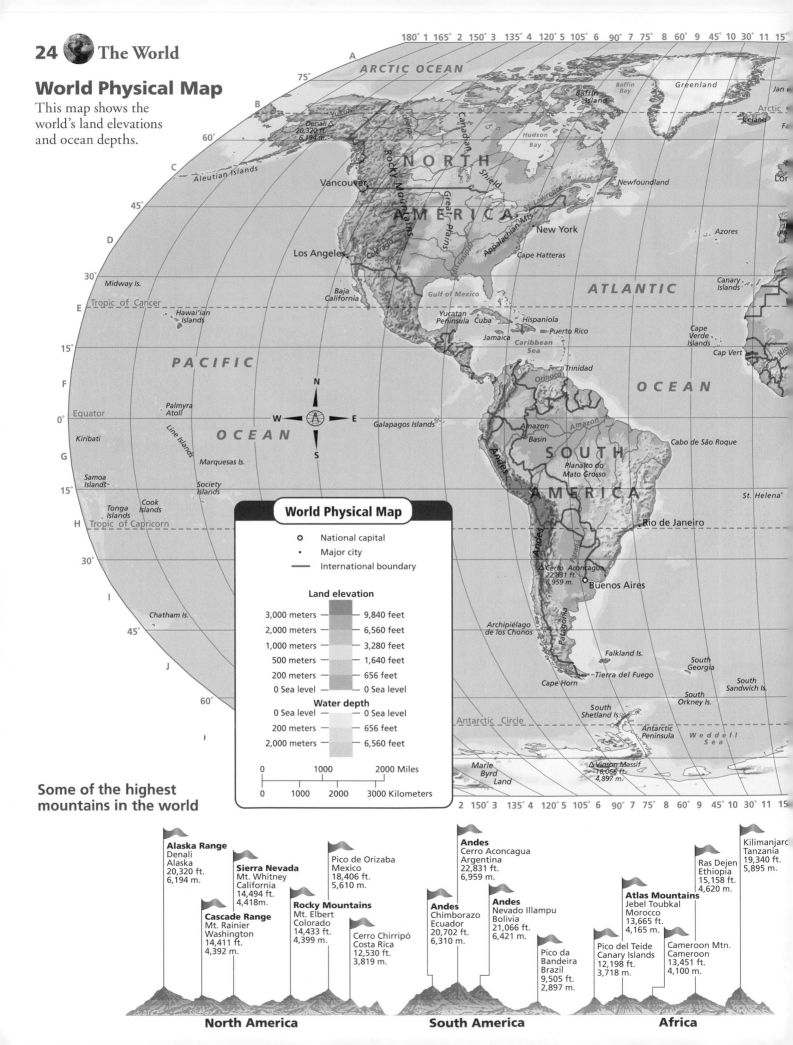

Some of the highest mountains in the world

World Political Map

People have divided up Earth's land into almost 200 countries. A few of these countries are more than a thousand years old, but most have been formed in the last 200 years.

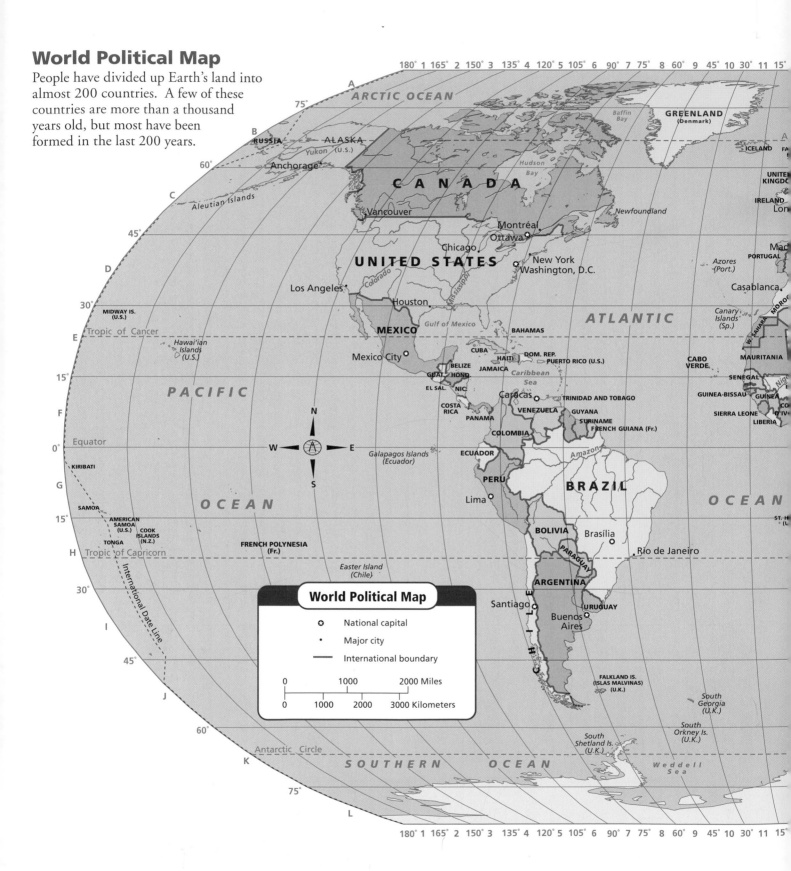

World Political Map

⊚ National capital

• Major city

— International boundary

0   1000   2000 Miles

0   1000   2000   3000 Kilometers

DID YOU KNOW?

The largest country in the world is Russia.

World Climate Map

This map shows climate conditions throughout the world. Climate is the average **weather conditions** over a long period of time. Temperature and precipitation together make up climate.

Climate Graphs

Each of the climate graphs below shows the average temperature and **precipitation** for every month of the year. Precipitation is rain, snow, sleet, or hail.

The 12 letters below each graph are the first letters of the twelve months, beginning with January (J) and ending with December (D). There is one climate graph for every type of climate region in the world.

Curved lines on the graphs show temperatures in degrees Celsius and degrees Fahrenheit. The numbers are to the left of the graphs.

Vertical bars on the graphs show monthly precipitation in inches and centimeters. The numbers are to the right of the graphs.

Colors on the graphs match colors on the map. The cities for the graphs are also shown on the map.

Climate Map

Tropical
- Hot with rain all year
- Hot with seasonal rain

Dry
- Desert
- Some rain

Moderate (Rainy Winter)
- Hot, dry summer
- Hot, humid summer
- Mild, rainy summer

Continental (Snowy Winter)
- Long, warm, humid summer
- Short, cool, humid summer
- Very short, cool, humid summer

Polar
- Tundra – very cold and dry
- Ice cap

Highlands
- Varies with altitude

© Rand McNally
Made in U.S.A.
M-102168-3

Temperature

Precipitation

°C	°F
38	100
27	80
16	60
4	40
-7	20
-18	0
-29	-20
-40	-40

in.	cm.
14	36
12	30
10	25
8	20
6	15
4	10
2	5
0	0

Jakarta, Indonesia
JFMAMJJASOND
Tropical
Hot with rain all year

Darwin, Australia
JFMAMJJASOND
Tropical
Hot with seasonal rain

Cairo, Egypt
JFMAMJJASOND
Dry
Desert

Tehran, Iran
JFMAMJJASOND
Dry
Some rain

Los Angeles, California, U.S.
JFMAMJJASOND
Moderate
Hot, dry summer

Buenos Aires, Argentina
JFMAMJJASOND
Moderate
Hot, humid summer

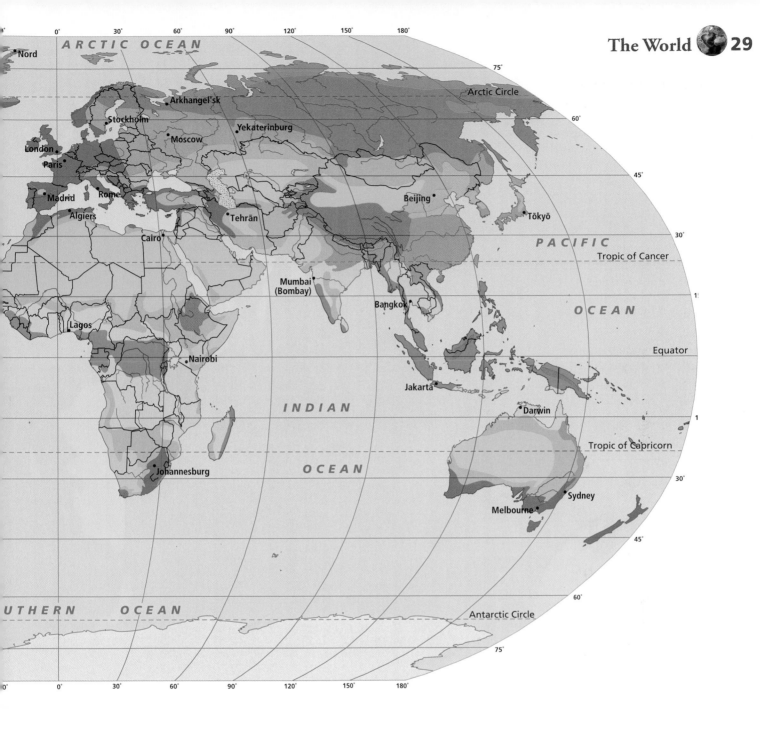

ARCTIC OCEAN

Nord
Arkhangel'sk
Stockholm
Moscow
Yekaterinburg
London
Paris
Madrid
Rome
Algiers
Cairo
Tehrān
Beijing
Tōkyō
PACIFIC
Tropic of Cancer
OCEAN
Mumbai (Bombay)
Bangkok
Lagos
Nairobi
Jakarta
INDIAN
Darwin
Equator
OCEAN
Tropic of Capricorn
Johannesburg
Sydney
Melbourne
UTHERN OCEAN
Antarctic Circle
Arctic Circle

Temperature

Precipitation

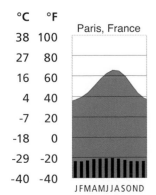

Paris, France
Moderate
Mild, rainy summer

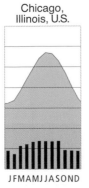

Chicago, Illinois, U.S.
Continental
Long, warm, humid summer

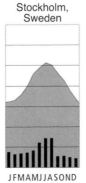

Stockholm, Sweden
Continental
Short, cool, humid summer

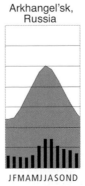

Arkhangel'sk, Russia
Continental
Very short, cool, humid summer

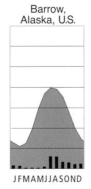

Barrow, Alaska, U.S.
Polar
Tundra—very cold and dry

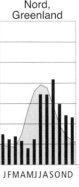

Nord, Greenland
Polar
Ice cap

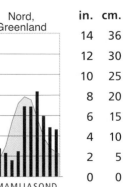

World Environments Map

This map shows different environments throughout the world. The environment of a place is its physical setting and conditions. Some environments, such as forest and tundra, are natural. Other environments, such as cropland and urban areas, have been created by humans. This map shows many of the world's largest urban areas.

The theme of this map is land environments, but approximately 75% of Earth's surface is covered by water. This causes Earth to look blue from space. For this reason, Earth is sometimes called the "blue marble."

Only 3% of the water on Earth is fresh water. The other 97% of Earth's water is salt water.

Environments Map

- Forest
- Swamp
- Crop & woodland
- Cropland
- Crop & grazing land
- Grassland
- Desert
- Tundra
- Barren
- Urban

© Rand McNally
Made in U.S.A.
M-102169-3

Earth as seen from space

Forest

This tropical rain forest in South America is green all year because the climate is hot and rainy. By contrast, forests in the middle latitudes lose their leaves when the weather turns cold.

Swamp

Low-lying, uncultivated land where water collects and certain types of trees and other vegetation may grow

Crop and woodland

Land made up of low-density forests; It is suitable for the cultivation of crops, such as grain, vegetables, or fruit.

Cropland

Flatter land where the climate is mild tends to be where most of the world's crops are grown. This farm is in Pennsylvania.

Crop and grazing land

Fields covered with grass or herbage, it is suitable for grazing livestock and cultivating crops.

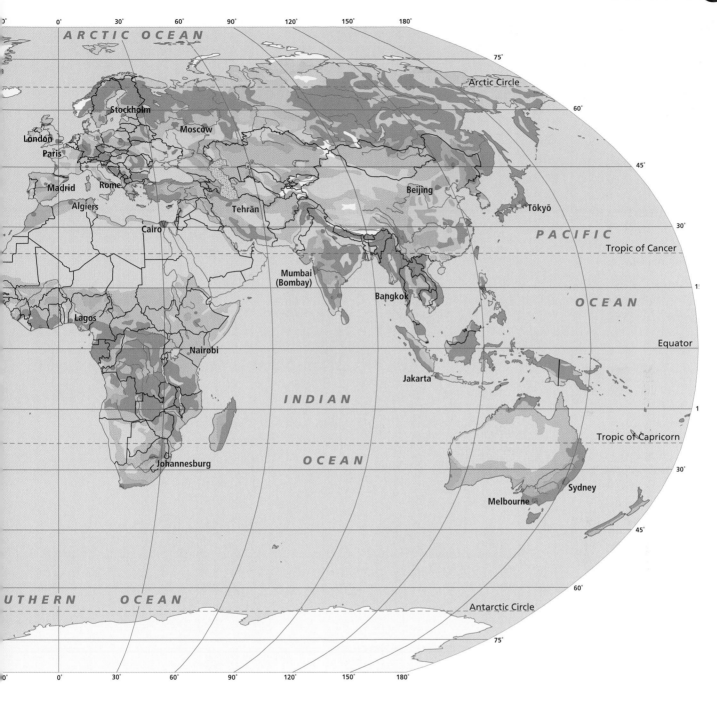

ARCTIC OCEAN

75°

Arctic Circle

60°

Stockholm

45°

London

Moscow

Paris

Madrid Rome

Beijing

30°

Algiers

Tōkyō

Tehrān

PACIFIC

Cairo

Tropic of Cancer

Mumbai
(Bombay)

OCEAN

Bangkok

Lagos

Equator

Nairobi

Jakarta

INDIAN

Tropic of Capricorn

Johannesburg

OCEAN

30°

Sydney

Melbourne

45°

60°

SOUTHERN   OCEAN

Antarctic Circle

75°

Grassland	Desert	Tundra	Barren	Urban

Natural grasslands, like this one in Oklahoma, are found where the climate is somewhat dry. These regions are not wet enough for growing crops, but perfect for grazing animals.	The Sahara is the largest desert in the world. With less than five inches of rain per year, it is a place with very few plants.	In tundra regions, like this one in Russia, the ground stays nearly frozen even in summer. The only plants that can grow there are low grasses and mosses.	Level land that is unable to support the growth of crops, trees, or vegetation	New York City is one of the world's great cities. Many of the urban areas on the map above have over one million people.

World Population Density Map

This map shows which parts of the world have many people and which have few people. Areas with many people living there have **dense** populations. The largest areas of dense populations are in East Asia, South Asia, and Europe. Vast areas of the world are too cold, too dry, or too mountainous for dense population.

World Population Growth

For most of human history, the world's population grew very slowly. About 250 years ago, it began to grow faster as people learned to control illnesses. However, today people in many parts of the world are having smaller families, and the rate of growth may be slowing down.

Population Density Map

People per sq. mile
(People per sq. km)

- Over 1,250 *(Over 500)*
- 250 – 1,250 *(100 – 500)*
- 62.5 – 250 *(25 – 100)*
- 25 – 62.5 *(10 – 25)*
- 2.5 – 25 *(1 – 10)*
- Under 2.5 *(Under 1)*

© Rand McNally
Made in U.S.A.
M-102170-2

World Population Growth

Year: 1500, 1600, 1700, 1800, 1900, 2000

Population

Children Around the World

North America

North America

Middle America

South America

Europe

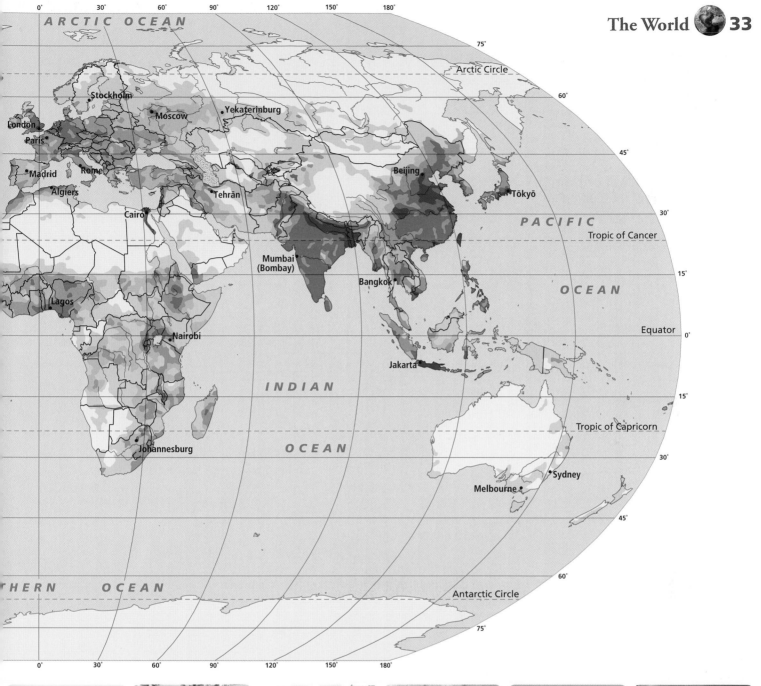

ARCTIC OCEAN

Arctic Circle

Stockholm

Moscow
Yekaterinburg

London

Paris

Madrid
Rome

Algiers

Tehrān

Cairo

Beijing

Tōkyō

PACIFIC

Tropic of Cancer

Mumbai
(Bombay)

Bangkok

OCEAN

Lagos

Nairobi

Equator

Jakarta

INDIAN

OCEAN

Johannesburg

Tropic of Capricorn

Sydney

Melbourne

THERN   OCEAN

Antarctic Circle

Hong Kong, China, is a city with a very high population density.

This street market is in India. India's population is one of the densest in the world.

La Paz, the capital of Bolivia, is a medium-size city. It has a density of 62.5 to 250 people per square mile.

The surrounding area of a village in Africa has an average density of 2.5 to 62.5 people per square mile.

In the Australian Outback, settlements such as this cattle ranch are separated by miles of open land.

Some regions of the world have very few people. One such region is the Sahara, a vast desert in northern Africa.

Africa

Middle East

Asia

Asia

Australia

World Patterns of Economic Activity

This map shows the kinds of jobs people have around the world. Each color on the map shows the most important economic activity for that area.

Look at the bright yellow area of Canada and the United States. According to the map legend, agriculture is the most important economic activity there. If you went to this area, you would see farm fields, orchards, and farm animals such as dairy cows and pigs. You would probably see grain elevators, feed stores, and other businesses that support farming. Of course, you would see banks, office buildings, stores, and factories, but not as many as you would see in the areas colored red.

According to the map legend, the most important economic activities in the red areas are manufacturing and commerce. Manufacturing is making goods. Automobiles, computers, clothing, and skateboards are examples of goods.

Commerce is the buying and selling of goods. Commerce also includes the buying and selling of services. Medical care, banking, education, and cable television are examples of service industries. In Canada, the United States, Europe, and Japan, more people work in service industries than in manufacturing or agriculture. If you went to the areas shown in red, you would see a concentration of banks, office buildings, factories, and stores. Many of the world's largest manufacturing and commerce areas are shown on this map.

According to the map legend, hunting, forestry, and subsistence farming are the most important economic activities in the brown areas. In these areas you would find people working on small farms, growing food for themselves and their families. You would find people hunting and fishing to get food for themselves and their families.

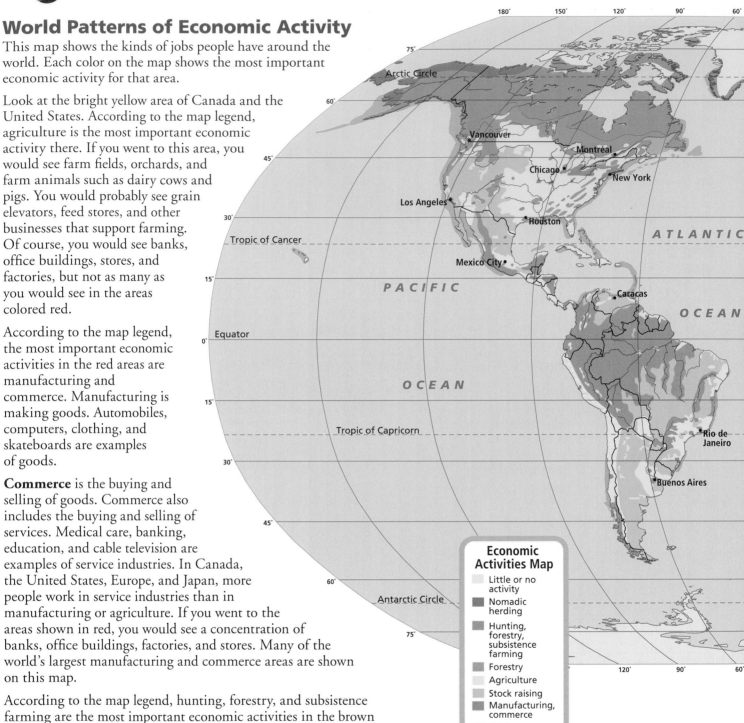

Economic Activities Map

- Little or no activity
- Nomadic herding
- Hunting, forestry, subsistence farming
- Forestry
- Agriculture
- Stock raising
- Manufacturing, commerce
- Fishing

Nomadic herding

Hunting

Subsistence farming

Forestry

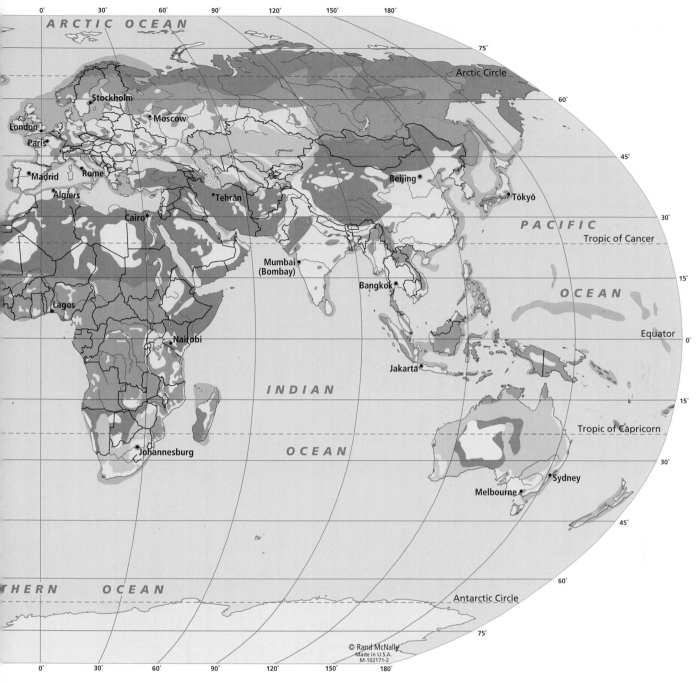

ARCTIC OCEAN

75°

Arctic Circle

60°

Stockholm

Moscow

45°

London

Paris

Beijing

30°

Madrid   Rome

Tōkyō

Algiers

Tehrān

PACIFIC

Cairo

Tropic of Cancer

15°

Mumbai
(Bombay)

OCEAN

Bangkok

Lagos

Equator   0°

Nairobi

INDIAN

Jakarta

15°

Johannesburg

OCEAN

Tropic of Capricorn

30°

Sydney

Melbourne

45°

THERN   OCEAN

60°

Antarctic Circle

75°

© Rand McNally
Made in U.S.A.
M-102171-2

0°   30°   60°   90°   120°   150°   180°

Agriculture   *Stock raising*   *Manufacturing*   *Commerce*   *Fishing*

World Mineral Fuel Deposits

Deposits of coal, petroleum, and natural gas are found in very limited parts of the world. What types of deposits does the United States have? Which continents have many coal deposits?

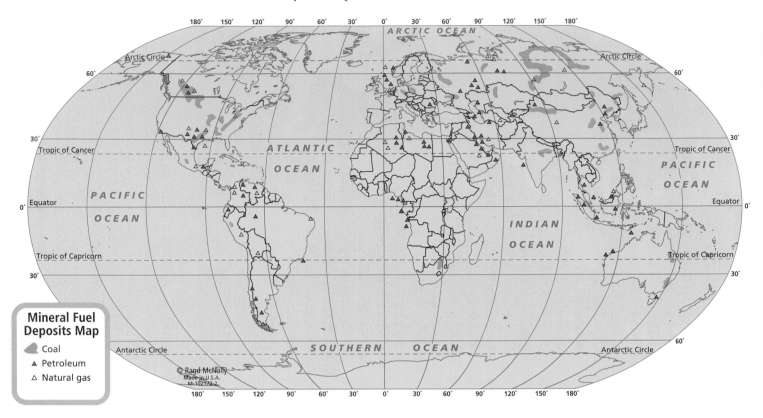

Mineral Fuel Deposits Map

- Coal
- ▲ Petroleum
- △ Natural gas

© Rand McNally
Made in U.S.A.
M-102192-2

World Coal Production

China and the United States, which have extensive deposits of coal, lead the world in coal production.

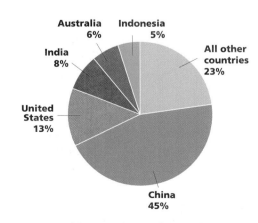

Australia 6%
Indonesia 5%
India 8%
All other countries 23%
United States 13%
China 45%

World Petroleum Production

Saudi Arabia, Russia, and the United States produce more than one-third of the world's oil.

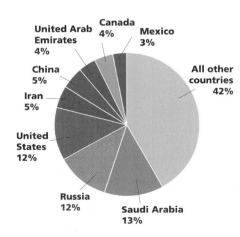

United Arab Emirates 4%
Canada 4%
Mexico 3%
China 5%
Iran 5%
All other countries 42%
United States 12%
Russia 12%
Saudi Arabia 13%

World Uranium Production

Australia and Kazakhstan lead the world in production of uranium, which is used as a fuel in nuclear energy plants.

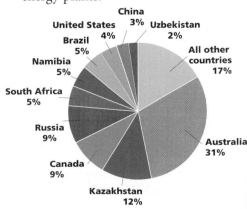

China 3%
United States 4%
Uzbekistan 2%
Brazil 5%
Namibia 5%
All other countries 17%
South Africa 5%
Russia 9%
Australia 31%
Canada 9%
Kazakhstan 12%

World Energy Consumption

Manufacturing, heating, and transportation are the three main ways that people use energy. This explains why the largest users of energy are industrialized countries that have large populations and relatively cold climates.

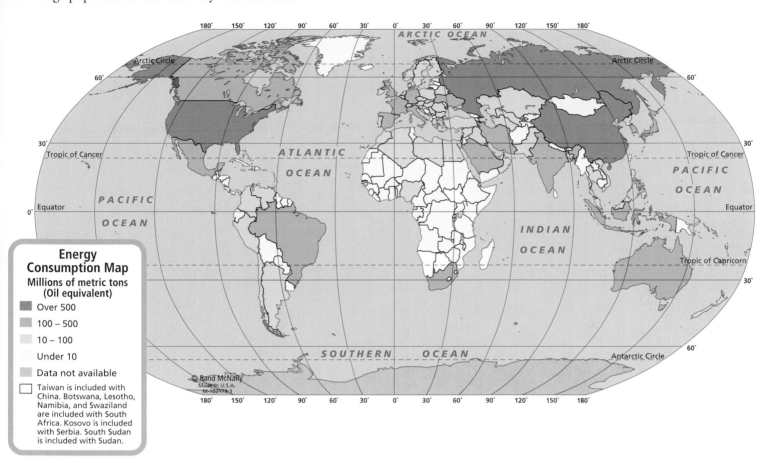

Energy Consumption Map
Millions of metric tons (Oil equivalent)

- Over 500
- 100 – 500
- 10 – 100
- Under 10
- Data not available

Taiwan is included with China. Botswana, Lesotho, Namibia, and Swaziland are included with South Africa. Kosovo is included with Serbia. South Sudan is included with Sudan.

© Rand McNally
Made in U.S.A.
M-102174-3

Energy Terms

Coal

A rock created from ancient plant life under enormous pressure; It is burned to produce heat and create steam for running machines or making electricity. Most coal, when burned, emits sulfur, a major component of acid rain.

Geothermal power

Uses water heated naturally beneath the earth's surface; The steam that results powers engines that create electricity. Geothermal power is a clean source of energy, but it is available only in very limited areas.

Fossil fuels

Formed from remains of plants and animals over millions of years; Fossil fuels are not renewable sources of energy, because it takes vast amounts of time to create them. Coal, oil, and natural gas are fossil fuels.

Hydroelectricity

Generated by fast-moving water that is used to power generators; Dams on rivers provide sources of rapidly moving water. Hydroelectricity is a clean source of power, but the dams can have negative effects on their surroundings.

Natural gas

A form of petroleum; This flammable gas is used mainly as fuel for stoves, furnaces, and hot-water heaters. Natural gas is a clean-burning fuel.

Nuclear energy

Created by splitting atoms; The energy is used to heat water that makes steam to drive electricity generators. The safety of nuclear plants and the hazardous wastes they create are of great concern.

Petroleum

A liquid, also called oil; Petroleum is the most widely used source of energy in the world. It is used to produce gasoline, kerosene, and fuel oil. It is also used to manufacture plastics and other products.

Wind power and solar energy

Two sources of renewable energy; They are not in wide use today, but in some places the use of wind to make electricity is increasing.

Plate Tectonics

According to the theory of plate tectonics, Earth's surface is divided into more than a dozen plates. These plates move very slowly—just a few inches a year. As they move, they collide or grind past each other. Most of the world's volcanoes and earthquakes occur at the places where plates meet.

Many plates collide with or grind past the Pacific Plate. Find the Pacific Plate on the Plate Tectonics map. The Ring of Fire is the name given to the band of earthquakes and volcanic activity around the Pacific Ocean.

225 million years ago: *Most of the world's land was together in a single "supercontinent." Scientists call this giant continent Pangaea.*

180 million years ago: *Pangaea split up into separate landmasses.*

65 million years ago: *The oceans as we know them today began to take shape. South America and India moved away from Africa.*

The present day: *India has joined with Asia, Australia has moved away from Antarctica, and North America has separated from Europe.*

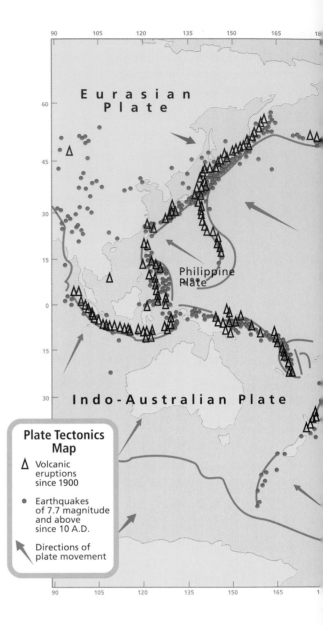

Plate Tectonics Map

Δ Volcanic eruptions since 1900

• Earthquakes of 7.7 magnitude and above since 10 A.D.

→ Directions of plate movement

Some Notable Earthquakes

Year	Magnitude (Richter Scale)	Place	Estimated Deaths
2011	9.0	Near Honshū, Japan	20,352
2010	7.0	Near Port-au-Prince, Haiti	316,000
2004	9.1	Sumatra, Indonesia	227,000 killed by earthquake and tsunami
1990	7.4	Iran	50,000 killed by earthquake and landslides
1976	7.5	Tangshan, China	255,000
1970	7.9	Peru	66,000
1964	9.2	Prince William Sound, AK	128 killed by earthquake and tsunami
1948	7.3	Turkmenistan	110,000
1927	7.9	Qinghai, China	200,000
1923	7.9	Japan	143,000 killed by earthquake and fire
1908	7.2	Italy	70,000 killed by earthquake and tsunami
1906	7.8	San Francisco, CA	3,000 killed by earthquake and fire

Damage from the 1906 San Francisco earthquake

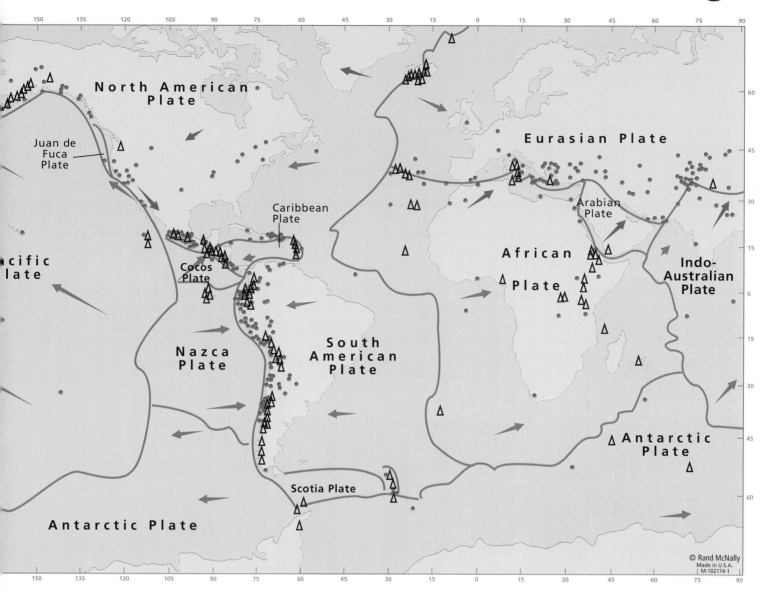

North American Plate

Juan de Fuca Plate

Caribbean Plate

Cocos Plate

Pacific Plate

Nazca Plate

South American Plate

Scotia Plate

Antarctic Plate

Eurasian Plate

Arabian Plate

African Plate

Indo-Australian Plate

Antarctic Plate

© Rand McNally
Made in U.S.A.
M-102174-1

Some Notable Volcanic Eruptions

Year	Volcanic Explosivity Index (VEI)	Name (location)	Estimated Deaths
2010	4	Eyjafjallajökull (Iceland)	Disrupted air travel for 20 countries
1991	6	Mt. Pinatubo (Philippines)	900
1985	3	Nevado del Ruiz (Colombia)	25,000
1980	5	Mt. St. Helens (Washington, U.S.)	57
1963	3	Surtsey (Iceland)	Volcano creates new island
1902	4	Mt. Pelée (Martinique)	30,000
1883	6	Krakatoa (Indonesia)	36,000 killed, most by tsunami
1815	7	Gunung Tambora (Indonesia)	92,000
79	5	Vesuvius (Italy)	16,000 killed in Pompeii and Herculaneum

Eruption of Mt. St. Helens in 1980

World Time Zones

The world is divided into 24 standard time zones. As Earth turns on its axis each day, the sun is overhead at different places at different times. Each time zone is based on the place where the sun is overhead at noon. The boundaries are adjusted so that people whose activities are connected live in the same time zone.

You can figure out the standard time for any time zone in the world. Add one hour for each time you count as you go east. Subtract one hour for each time zone you count as you go west.

Prime Meridian

The Prime Meridian is also called the Greenwich Meridian, because it is centered on the Royal Greenwich Observatory near London in the United Kingdom. It represents 0° longitude. Time around the world is counted from the Prime Meridian.

International Date Line

The International Date Line is halfway around the world from the Prime Meridian, at 180° longitude. Like time zone boundaries, the International Date Line is adjusted from 180° so that people in the same country have the same day. The time is the same on both sides of the International Date Line, but the day is different. West of the International Date Line it is one day later than it is east of the International Date Line.

New Zealand, which lies just west of the International Date Line, is one of the first places in the world to greet each new day.

The precise location of the Prime Meridian is marked at the Royal Greenwich Observatory near London.

Examples of Time Changes

Auckland, New Zealand

12 midnight
June 26

Los Angeles, California, United States

4 a.m.
June 25

Montréal, Québec, Canada

7 a.m.
June 25

Rio de Janeiro, Brazil

9 a.m.
June 25

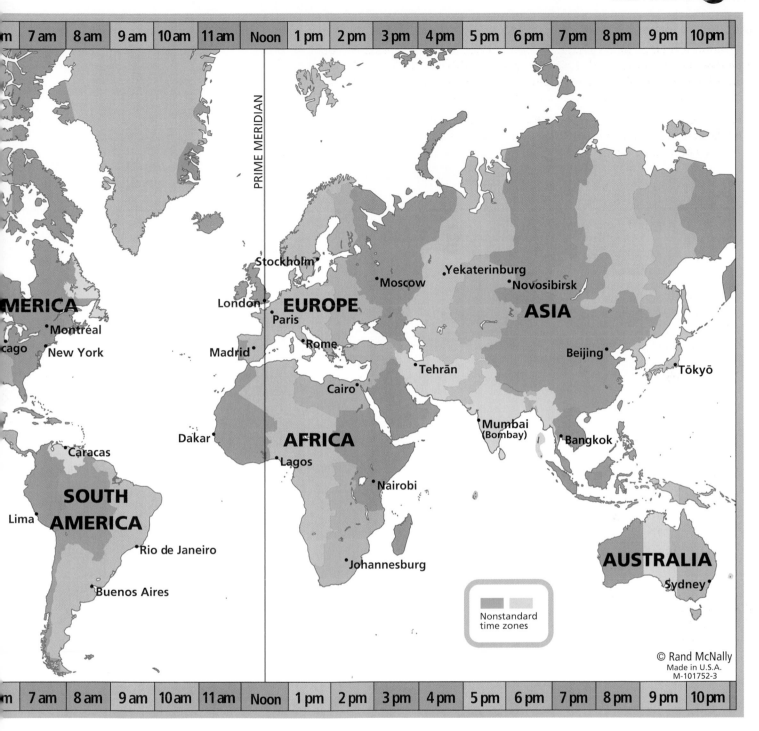

| m | 7am | 8am | 9am | 10am | 11am | Noon | 1pm | 2pm | 3pm | 4pm | 5pm | 6pm | 7pm | 8pm | 9pm | 10pm |

PRIME MERIDIAN

AMERICA

Montréal
cago New York

Stockholm

London EUROPE
Paris
Madrid Rome
Cairo

Dakar

AFRICA
Lagos

Nairobi

Moscow Yekaterinburg
Novosibirsk

ASIA

Beijing

Tehrān Tōkyō

Mumbai
(Bombay) Bangkok

Caracas

SOUTH
AMERICA

Lima

Rio de Janeiro

Buenos Aires

Johannesburg

AUSTRALIA

Sydney

Nonstandard
time zones

© Rand McNally
Made in U.S.A.
M-101752-3

| m | 7am | 8am | 9am | 10am | 11am | Noon | 1pm | 2pm | 3pm | 4pm | 5pm | 6pm | 7pm | 8pm | 9pm | 10pm |

| Paris, France | Moscow, Russia | Novosibirsk, Russia | Tōkyō, Japan |

1 p.m.
June 25

3 p.m.
June 25

6 p.m.
June 25

9 p.m.
June 25

NORTH AMERICA

Denali, Alaska, United States

North America is the third-largest continent. About 506,000,000 people live there.

It stretches more than 5,400 miles (8,700 kilometers) from northern Canada to the Panama-Colombia border.

Three countries—Canada, the United States, and Mexico—make up most of North America. The Caribbean island countries, the countries of Central America, and the island of Greenland make up the rest of the continent.

Central America is a region within North America. It is made up of the countries of Belize, Guatemala, Honduras, El Salvador, Nicaragua, Costa Rica, and Panama.

Central America is part of a larger region of North America called Middle America. This region consists of Central America, Mexico, and the Caribbean countries.

Generally, the people of North America have used its rich natural resources to great advantage. But not everyone has benefited. There are people throughout the continent who struggle with poverty, particularly in Central America and some Caribbean countries.

Toronto, the largest city in Canada

San Francisco, California, United States

Pyramid of the Sun, Mexico

Caribbean starfish

A Historical Look At North America

About 20,000 years ago
First inhabitants of North America may have arrived from Asia across a land bridge that has since disappeared.

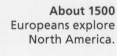
About 1200-1500 C.E.
Aztec civilization is dominant in Mexico.

About 5000 B.C.E
Corn (maize) is first cultivated in Middle America.

About 1500
Europeans explore North America.

Urbanization in North America

In the late nineteenth century and early twentieth century, many new factories were built in the United States and Canada. People moved from farms to cities to take jobs in factories and offices. They were joined by immigrants from many countries. After World War II, many people in cities moved to suburbs, and urbanized areas began to grow, especially along the East Coast between Boston and Washington, D.C. Today, people in Mexico are moving to cities and to suburbs. Some of them cannot find steady jobs, and the cities have trouble providing water, sewers, and schools for the rapidly growing populations.

DID YOU KNOW?
Greenland, which is part of North America, is the largest island in the world.

Yellow represents densely populated areas.

Pacific Ocean

Atlantic Ocean

© Rand McNally

Rising Urban Population
Urban population as a percentage of total population, 1900-2000 (shown in 25-year increments)

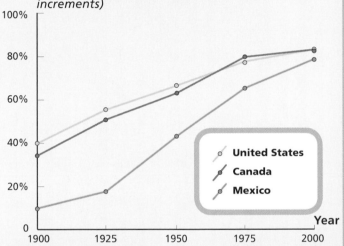

Legend:
- United States
- Canada
- Mexico

Year: 1900, 1925, 1950, 1975, 2000

New York City, the largest city in the United States

An abandoned farm on the Great Plains

Zachatecas, a city in Mexico

Suburban sprawl in Colorado

1776
The United States declares independence.

1821
Mexico becomes independent.

1867
Canada forms a confederation of four provinces.

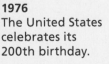

1976
The United States celebrates its 200th birthday.

1994
Canada, the United States, and Mexico sign the North American Free Trade Agreement, creating the largest free trade area.

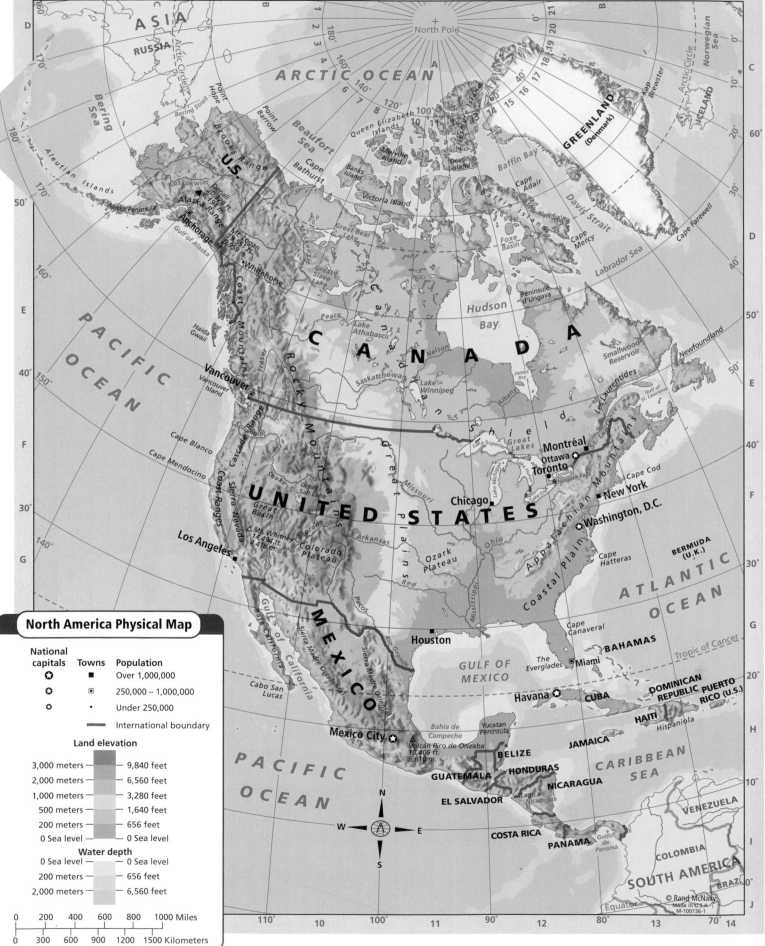

North America Physical Map

National capitals   **Towns**   **Population**

✪	■	Over 1,000,000
✪	▣	250,000 – 1,000,000
✪	·	Under 250,000

——— International boundary

Land elevation

3,000 meters	9,840 feet
2,000 meters	6,560 feet
1,000 meters	3,280 feet
500 meters	1,640 feet
200 meters	656 feet
0 Sea level	0 Sea level

Water depth

0 Sea level	0 Sea level
200 meters	656 feet
2,000 meters	6,560 feet

0   200   400   600   800   1000 Miles

0   300   600   900   1200   1500 Kilometers

© Rand McNally
Made in U.S.A.
M-100136-1

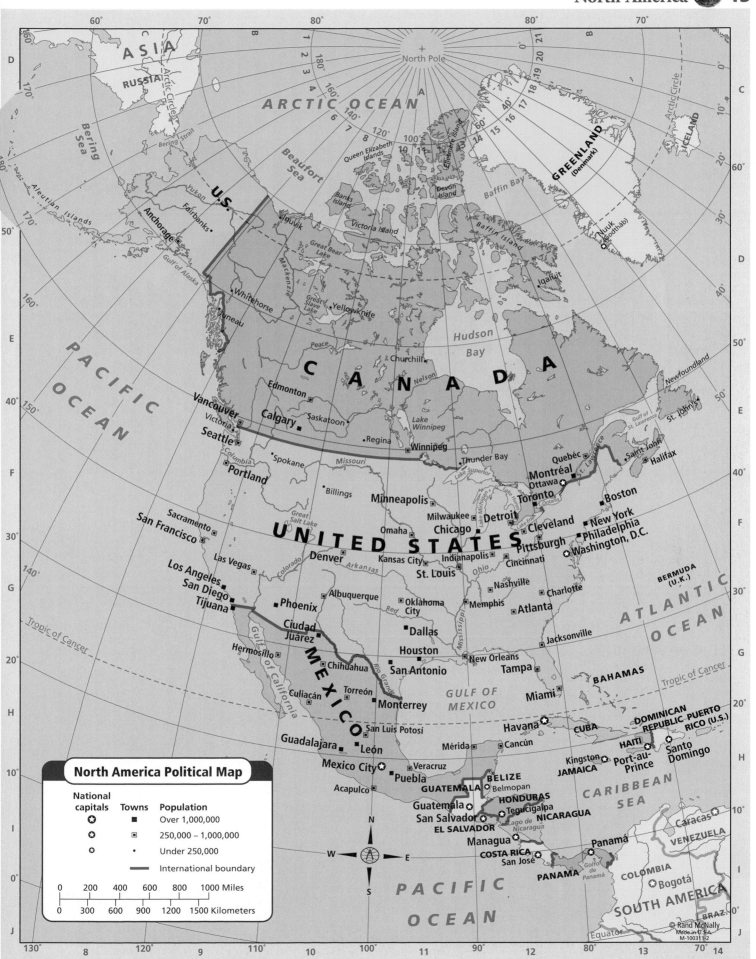

North America Political Map

National capitals
- ⊛ Over 1,000,000
- ⊕ 250,000 – 1,000,000
- ⊙ Under 250,000

Towns   Population
- ■ Over 1,000,000
- ▣ 250,000 – 1,000,000
- • Under 250,000

— International boundary

```
0    200   400   600   800   1000 Miles
0   300   600   900  1200  1500 Kilometers
```

ASIA
RUSSIA
ARCTIC OCEAN
North Pole
Bering Sea
Bering Strait
Aleutian Islands
Arctic Circle
U.S.
Anchorage
Fairbanks
Yukon
Gulf of Alaska
Whitehorse
Juneau
Beaufort Sea
Inuvik
Banks Island
Victoria Island
Great Bear Lake
Mackenzie
Yellowknife
Great Slave Lake
Queen Elizabeth Islands
Devon Island
Ellesmere Island
Baffin Island
Baffin Bay
GREENLAND (Denmark)
Nuuk (Godthåb)
Iqaluit
ICELAND
Arctic Circle

PACIFIC OCEAN

CANADA
Hudson Bay
Churchill
Peace
Nelson
Edmonton
Vancouver
Calgary
Saskatoon
Victoria
Seattle
Regina
Spokane
Portland
Billings
Winnipeg
Lake Winnipeg
Thunder Bay
Lake Superior
Newfoundland
St. John's
Lake Huron
Lake Ontario
Lake Erie
Lake Michigan
Québec
Ottawa
Montréal
St. Lawrence
Gulf of St. Lawrence
Saint John
Halifax
Boston
New York
Philadelphia
Washington, D.C.

UNITED STATES
Sacramento
San Francisco
Las Vegas
Great Salt Lake
Denver
Colorado
Arkansas
Minneapolis
Milwaukee
Omaha
Chicago
Kansas City
Indianapolis
St. Louis
Detroit
Cleveland
Cincinnati
Pittsburgh
Nashville
Charlotte
BERMUDA (U.K.)
Los Angeles
San Diego
Tijuana
Phoenix
Albuquerque
Red
Oklahoma City
Memphis
Atlanta
ATLANTIC OCEAN
Tropic of Cancer
Ciudad Juárez
Dallas
Hermosillo
Gulf of California
Chihuahua
Rio Grande
Houston
San Antonio
New Orleans
Mississippi
Jacksonville
Tampa
Miami
BAHAMAS
Tropic of Cancer
MEXICO
Culiacán
Torreón
Monterrey
San Luis Potosí
GULF OF MEXICO
Havana
CUBA
DOMINICAN REPUBLIC
PUERTO RICO (U.S.)
Guadalajara
León
Mérida
Cancún
Kingston
JAMAICA
Port-au-Prince
HAITI
Santo Domingo
CARIBBEAN SEA
Mexico City
Puebla
Veracruz
Acapulco
GUATEMALA
BELIZE
Belmopan
Guatemala
HONDURAS
Tegucigalpa
San Salvador
EL SALVADOR
NICARAGUA
Lago de Nicaragua
Managua
COSTA RICA
San José
PANAMA
Panamá
Golfo de Panamá
Caracas
VENEZUELA
COLOMBIA
Bogotá
SOUTH AMERICA
BRAZIL
Equator

N
W   E
S

PACIFIC OCEAN

© Rand McNally
Made in U.S.A
M-100311-2

Climate

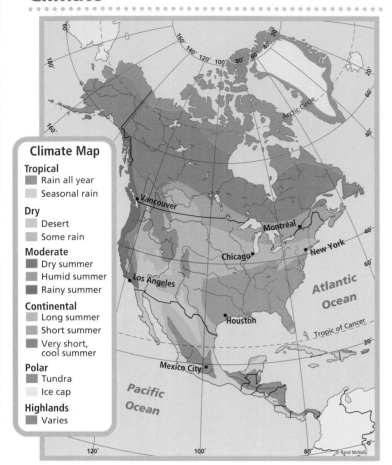

Climate Map

Tropical
- Rain all year
- Seasonal rain

Dry
- Desert
- Some rain

Moderate
- Dry summer
- Humid summer
- Rainy summer

Continental
- Long summer
- Short summer
- Very short, cool summer

Polar
- Tundra
- Ice cap

Highlands
- Varies

Environments

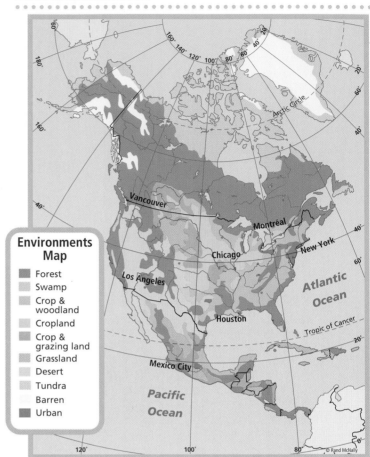

Environments Map
- Forest
- Swamp
- Crop & woodland
- Cropland
- Crop & grazing land
- Grassland
- Desert
- Tundra
- Barren
- Urban

Population

More than one-half of North Americans live in the United States. Canada is the continent's largest country in area, but it is home to only six percent of the continent's population.

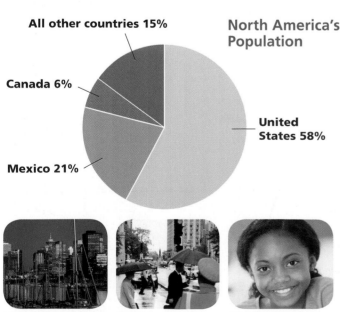

North America's Population

All other countries 15%

Canada 6%

Mexico 21%

United States 58%

Vancouver, British Columbia, Canada

Street scene in Chicago, Illinois

Girl in Haiti

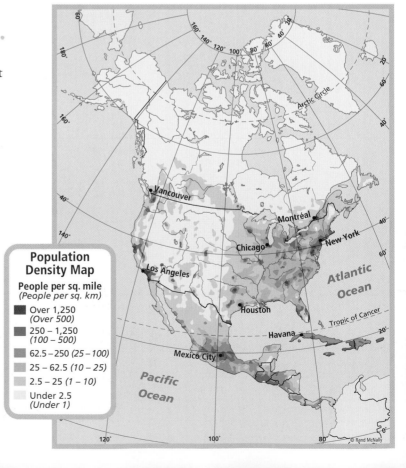

Population Density Map

People per sq. mile
(People per sq. km)

- Over 1,250 *(Over 500)*
- 250 – 1,250 *(100 – 500)*
- 62.5 – 250 *(25 – 100)*
- 25 – 62.5 *(10 – 25)*
- 2.5 – 25 *(1 – 10)*
- Under 2.5 *(Under 1)*

The Great Lakes

The Great Lakes lie along the border between the United States and Canada. Canals and rivers allow ocean-going ships to travel to the lakes and between them. Together, the lakes, canals, and rivers form a huge waterway that connects cities far inland with the ocean.

Size rank	Lake	Area sq. miles / sq. kilometers	Greatest depth feet / meters
1	Superior	31,700 / 82,100	1,332 / 406
2	Huron	23,000 / 59,570	750 / 229
3	Michigan	22,300 / 57,757	925 / 282
4	Erie	9,910 / 25,667	210 / 64
5	Ontario	7,320 / 18,960	802 / 244

Lake Superior is the largest of the Great Lakes.

The Welland Canal in Ontario, Canada, connects Lake Erie and Lake Ontario.

DID YOU KNOW?

Lake Michigan gets its name from an Algonquin Indian word, *michigami*, which means "big lake."

Relative Depths of the Great Lakes

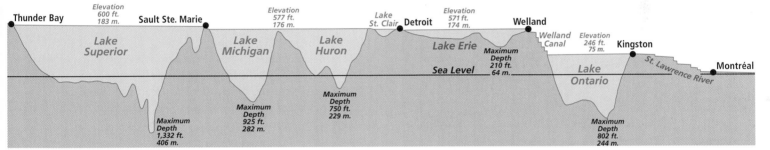

Thunder Bay
Elevation 600 ft. 183 m.
Sault Ste. Marie
Lake Superior
Maximum Depth 1,332 ft. 406 m.

Lake Michigan
Elevation 577 ft. 176 m.
Maximum Depth 925 ft. 282 m.

Lake Huron
Maximum Depth 750 ft. 229 m.

Lake St. Clair
Detroit
Elevation 571 ft. 174 m.

Lake Erie
Sea Level
Maximum Depth 210 ft. 64 m.

Welland
Welland Canal
Elevation 246 ft. 75 m.
Kingston
Lake Ontario
Maximum Depth 802 ft. 244 m.
St. Lawrence River
Montréal

Economic Activities

The map at right shows that agriculture is the most important economic activity for a large part of North America. Much of the continent's manufacturing and commerce is concentrated in a wide band between Chicago and New York.

In 1994, Canada, the United States, and Mexico enacted the North American Free Trade Agreement (NAFTA) to remove all trade restrictions between the three countries.

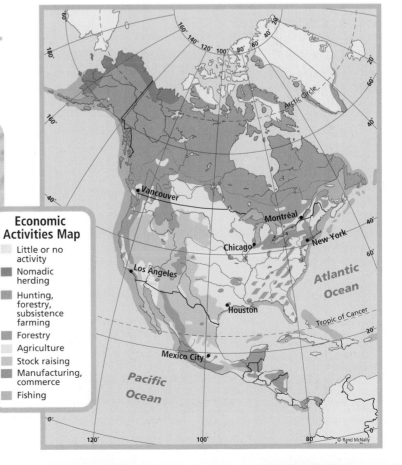

Economic Activities Map
- Little or no activity
- Nomadic herding
- Hunting, forestry, subsistence farming
- Forestry
- Agriculture
- Stock raising
- Manufacturing, commerce
- Fishing

Vancouver
Montréal
Chicago
New York
Los Angeles
Houston
Mexico City
Atlantic Ocean
Pacific Ocean
Tropic of Cancer
Arctic Circle

© Rand McNally

Fishing trawlers in California

Grain elevators in Alberta, Canada

Factory in Mexico

Natural Hazards

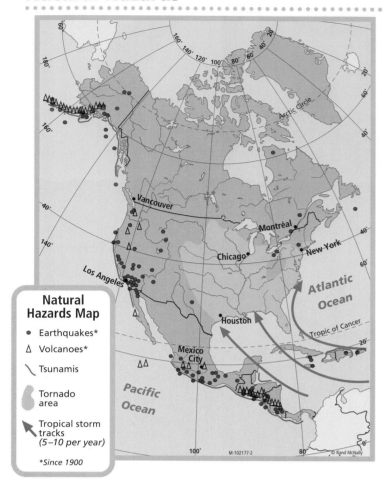

Natural Hazards Map

- Earthquakes*
- Volcanoes*
- \ Tsunamis
- Tornado area
- Tropical storm tracks (5–10 per year)

*Since 1900

This satellite image shows a hurricane approaching the Atlantic coast of Florida.

Twister!

Tornadoes are rapidly rotating columns of air. They are usually funnel-shaped, and their winds may reach 200–500 miles per hour (320–800 kilometers per hour). They are usually less than one-quarter mile (400 meters) wide, but they can be extremely destructive. Texas has more tornadoes than any other state. Oklahoma ranks second in number of tornadoes, and Kansas ranks third.

Transportation

Automobiles in Mexico City add to the severe pollution problem there.

Automobiles per 1,000 people

More people in wealthy countries—especially those countries that do not offer much public transportation—own cars.

Country	Automobiles per 1,000 people
Nicaragua	18
Panama	73
Bahamas	81
Jamaica	84
Mexico	147
Canada	420
United States	439
Puerto Rico	582

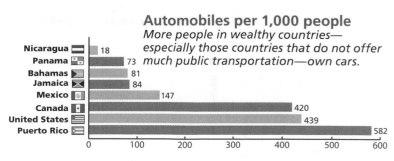

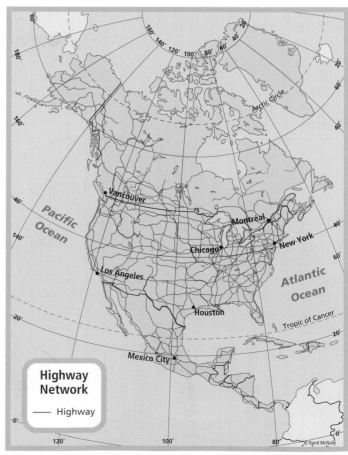

Highway Network

— Highway

Energy

Most nuclear power plants in North America are in the eastern and central United States.

The Hoover Dam in Nevada provides hydroelectric power to three states.

Wind power is a promising alternative energy source.

Electricity Production by Type

More than two-thirds of North America's electricity is produced by power plants that burn coal, oil, and natural gas. This is called thermal energy. Most of the remaining electricity comes from nuclear plants and hydroelectric, or waterpower, plants. Less than one percent of the continent's electricity is produced by geothermal plants, which tap into the heat of Earth's molten interior.

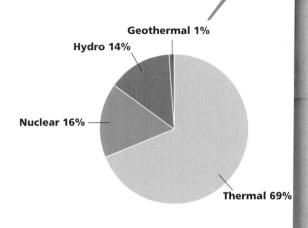

Geothermal 1%
Hydro 14%
Nuclear 16%
Thermal 69%

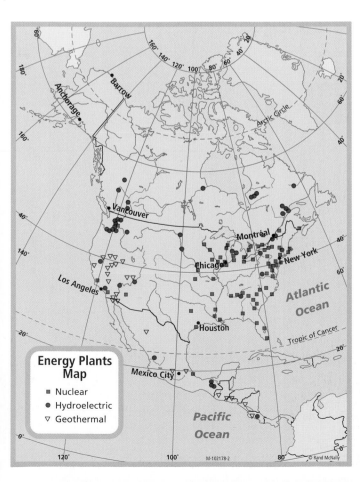

Energy Plants Map

- ■ Nuclear
- ● Hydroelectric
- ▽ Geothermal

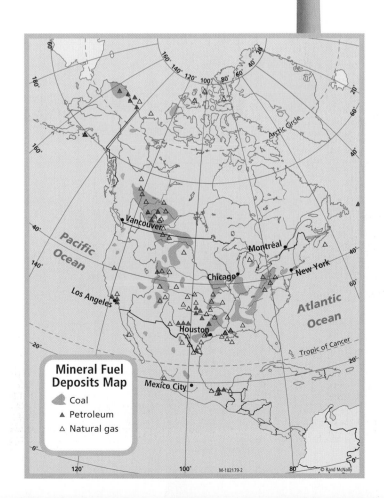

Mineral Fuel Deposits Map

- ◣ Coal
- ▲ Petroleum
- △ Natural gas

M-102178-2   © Rand McNally

M-102179-2   © Rand McNally

Looking at the United States

The United States stretches over great distances. The map to the right shows the points of land that lie farthest to the north, south, east, and west. The map also shows some of the country's extremes—places that rank at the top of their category.

Most maps of the United States show 48 of the states accurately, with Alaska and Hawaii dropped in as inset maps—usually off the coast of Mexico.

The other maps in this section will give you a new view of our country. They show all 50 states in their true locations and sizes.

Crater Lake, Oregon.

Mount Waialeale, Hawaii.

Westernmost Point
Cape Wrangell, Attu Island, Alaska
Longitude: 172° East

Coldest Place
Prospect Creek, Alaska
Lowest recorded temperature: -80°F

Highest Point
Denali, Alaska
Height: 20,320 feet above sea level

Deepest Lake
Crater Lake, Oregon
Greatest depth: 1,932 feet

Snowiest Place
Blue Canyon, California
Average yearly snowfall: 241 inches

Wettest Place
Mount Waialeale, Hawaii
Average yearly rainfall: 460 inches

Southernmost Point
Kalae, Hawaii
Latitude: 18° North

© Rand McNally
M-101368-1

THE SOUTHERNMOST POINT:

The southernmost point in the United States is found in Hawaii. Using latitude and longitude, explain its location in relation to southern Florida.

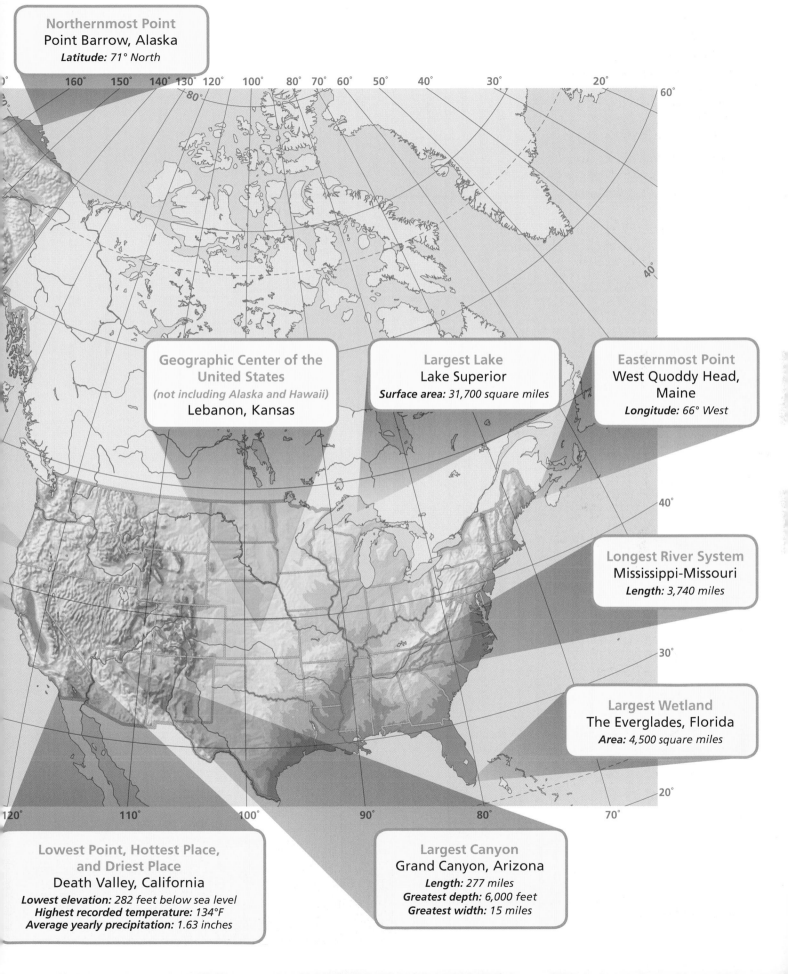

Northernmost Point
Point Barrow, Alaska
Latitude: 71° North

Geographic Center of the United States
(not including Alaska and Hawaii)
Lebanon, Kansas

Largest Lake
Lake Superior
Surface area: 31,700 square miles

Easternmost Point
West Quoddy Head, Maine
Longitude: 66° West

Longest River System
Mississippi-Missouri
Length: 3,740 miles

Largest Wetland
The Everglades, Florida
Area: 4,500 square miles

Lowest Point, Hottest Place, and Driest Place
Death Valley, California
Lowest elevation: 282 feet below sea level
Highest recorded temperature: 134°F
Average yearly precipitation: 1.63 inches

Largest Canyon
Grand Canyon, Arizona
Length: 277 miles
Greatest depth: 6,000 feet
Greatest width: 15 miles

United States Physical Map

National capitals	State capitals	Towns	Population
✪	✸	■	Over 1,000,000
✪	✸	▣	250,000 – 1,000,000
✪	✸	•	Under 250,000

International boundary

State boundary

Land elevation

3,000 meters	9,840 feet
2,000 meters	6,560 feet
1,000 meters	3,280 feet
500 meters	1,640 feet
200 meters	656 feet
0 Sea level	0 Sea level

Water depth

0 Sea level	0 Sea level
200 meters	656 feet
2,000 meters	6,560 feet

0   100   200   300 Miles

0   100   200   300   400 Kilometers

95°   7   90°   8   85°   9   80°   10   75°   11   70°   12   65°

ONTARIO

ADA

Lake of the Woods

Lake Nipigon

QUÉBEC

NEW BRUNSWICK

B

Lake of the Woods

Isle Royale

Lake Superior

Keweenaw Peninsula

Whitefish Point

Ottawa

St. Lawrence

Mt. Katahdin 5,268 ft. 1,606 m.

MAINE

Moosehead Lake

Kennebec

45°

NNESOTA

Upper Peninsula

MICHIGAN

Great Lakes

Georgian Bay

Ottawa

Montréal

Lake Champlain

VERMONT

White Mts.

△Mt. Washington 6,288 ft. 1,917 m.

Gulf of Maine

C

Minneapolis

Chippewa

WISCONSIN

Lake Winnebago

Wisconsin

Green Bay

Lake Michigan

Lake Huron

Saginaw Bay

Muskegon

Lower Peninsula

Grand

Toronto

Lake Ontario

Niagara Falls

Adirondack Mountains

NEW YORK

Green Mts.

Catskill Mts.

NEW HAMPSHIRE

MASS.

Boston

Cape Cod

CONN.   R.I.

Martha's Vineyard   Nantucket Island

nesota

IOWA

Des Moines

Iowa

Mississippi

Illinois

Chicago

Detroit

Lake Erie

Allegheny Plateau

PENNSYLVANIA

Appalachian Mountains

Hudson

New York

Long Island

40°

Cleveland

OHIO

Wabash

White

Scioto

Ohio

Allegheny

Philadelphia

NEW JERSEY

Susquehanna

Delaware Bay

DELAWARE

St. Louis

Lake of the Ozarks

Missouri

INDIANA

ILLINOIS

WEST VIRGINIA

Washington, D.C.

MARYLAND

Potomac

James

VIRGINIA

Chesapeake Bay

D

MISSOURI

Green

Lake Barkley

Lake Cumberland

KENTUCKY

Cumberland

Appalachian

Blue Ridge

Roanoke

Albemarle Sound

70°

Neosho

Ozark Plateau

Boston Mts.

White

Kentucky Lake

Cumberland

Cumberland Plateau

△Mt. Mitchell 6,684 ft. 2,037 m.

NORTH CAROLINA

Cape Hatteras

Pamlico Sound

35°

Ouachita Mts.

ARKANSAS

Missouri

Arkansas

Ouachita

TENNESSEE

Tennessee

Piedmont

Cape Fear

Coastal Plain

Cape Lookout

Cape Fear

ATLANTIC OCEAN

E

Yazoo

J. Strom Thurmond Reservoir

SOUTH CAROLINA

Santee

Savannah

Sea Islands

Atlanta

MISSISSIPPI

ALABAMA

GEORGIA

Pearl

Alabama

Tombigbee

Chattahoochee

Flint

Altamaha

Suwannee

N

W   E

S

30°

Sam burn Res.

Toledo Bend Res.

Red

ine

nity

LOUISIANA

Lake Pontchartrain

Mississippi

Cape San Blas

Apalachee Bay

FLORIDA

Cape Canaveral

F

Houston

New Orleans

Atchafalaya Bay

Mississippi Delta

Tampa Bay

Lake Okeechobee

GULF OF MEXICO

The Everglades

Miami

BAHAMAS

25°

Cape Sable

Florida Keys

© Rand McNally
Made in U.S.A.
M-101115-2

G

95°   7   90°   8   85°   9   80°   10   11

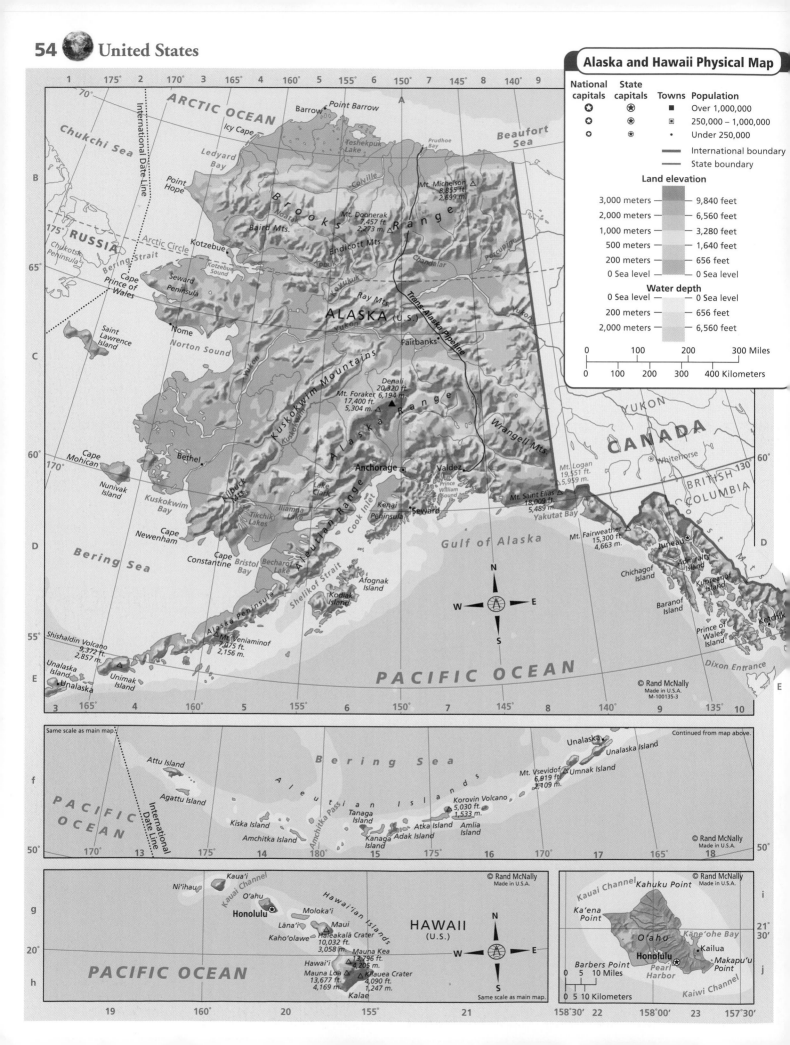

Alaska and Hawaii Physical Map

	National capitals	State capitals	Towns	Population
	⊛	⊛	■	Over 1,000,000
	⊛	⊛	▣	250,000 – 1,000,000
	⊕	⊛	•	Under 250,000

International boundary
State boundary

Land elevation

3,000 meters	—	—	9,840 feet
2,000 meters	—	—	6,560 feet
1,000 meters	—	—	3,280 feet
500 meters	—	—	1,640 feet
200 meters	—	—	656 feet
0 Sea level	—	—	0 Sea level

Water depth

0 Sea level	—	—	0 Sea level
200 meters	—	—	656 feet
2,000 meters	—	—	6,560 feet

0   100   200   300 Miles
0   100   200   300   400 Kilometers

Main Map (Alaska)

ARCTIC OCEAN
Chukchi Sea
Beaufort Sea
RUSSIA
International Date Line
Arctic Circle
Bering Strait
Chukotsk Peninsula
Cape Prince of Wales
Saint Lawrence Island
Nome
Norton Sound
Cape Mohican
Nunivak Island
Cape Newenham
Bering Sea
Bristol Bay
Cape Constantine

Barrow
Point Barrow
Icy Cape
Teshekpuk Lake
Prudhoe Bay
Point Hope
Ledyard Bay
Brooks Range
Mt. Michelson 8,855 ft. 2,699 m.
Kotzebue
Baird Mts.
Noatak
Mt. Doonerak 7,457 ft. 2,273 m.
Endicott Mts.
Kobuk
Kotzebue Sound
Seward Peninsula
Colville
Chandalar
Porcupine
Koyukuk
Yukon
Ray Mts.
ALASKA (U.S.)
Trans-Alaska Pipeline
Fairbanks
Yukon
Denali 20,320 ft.
Mt. Foraker 6,194 ft. 17,400 ft. 5,304 m.
Alaska Range
Kuskokwim Mountains
Bethel
Kilbuck Mts.
Lake Clark
Iliamna Lake
Tikchik Lakes
Kuskokwim Bay
Anchorage
Valdez
Kenai Peninsula
Cook Inlet
Seward
Prince William Sound
Wrangell Mts.
Mt. Logan 19,551 ft. 5,959 m.
Mt. Saint Elias 18,009 ft. 5,489 m.
Yakutat Bay
Mt. Fairweather 15,300 ft. 4,663 m.
CANADA
Whitehorse
BRITISH COLUMBIA
Gulf of Alaska
Aleutian Range
Becharof Lake
Shelikof Strait
Afognak Island
Kodiak Island
Alaska Peninsula
Mt. Veniaminof 7,075 ft. 2,156 m.
Shishaldin Volcano 9,372 ft. 2,857 m.
Unalaska Island
Unalaska
Unimak Island
PACIFIC OCEAN
Juneau
Chichagof Island
Admiralty Island
Baranof Island
Kupreanof Island
Prince of Wales Island
Ketchikan
Dixon Entrance

© Rand McNally
Made in U.S.A.
M-100135-3

Aleutian Islands Inset

Same scale as main map.
Continued from map above.
PACIFIC OCEAN
International Date Line
Attu Island
Agattu Island
Kiska Island
Amchitka Island
Aleutian Islands
Amchitka Pass
Tanaga Island
Kanaga Island
Adak Island
Atka Island
Amlia Island
Korovin Volcano 5,030 ft. 1,533 m.
Bering Sea
Unalaska
Unalaska Island
Mt. Vsevidof 6,919 ft. 2,109 m.
Umnak Island
© Rand McNally
Made in U.S.A.

Hawaii Inset

© Rand McNally
Made in U.S.A.
Ni'ihau
Kaua'i
Kauai Channel
O'ahu
Honolulu
Moloka'i
Lāna'i
Kaho'olawe
Maui
Haleakalā Crater 10,032 ft. 3,058 m.
Mauna Kea 13,796 ft. 4,205 m.
Hawai'i
Mauna Loa 13,677 ft. 4,169 m.
Kīlauea Crater 4,090 ft. 1,247 m.
Kalae
Hawaiian Islands
HAWAII (U.S.)
PACIFIC OCEAN
Same scale as main map.

O'ahu Inset

© Rand McNally
Made in U.S.A.
Kauai Channel
Kahuku Point
Ka'ena Point
Kāne'ohe Bay
O'ahu
Honolulu
Kailua
Barbers Point
Pearl Harbor
Makapu'u Point
Kaiwi Channel
0 5 10 Miles
0 5 10 Kilometers

Location of Alaska and Hawaii

The states of Alaska and Hawaii are separated from the 48 conterminous states. Canada lies between Alaska and the other states. Hawaii is a chain of islands in the middle of the Pacific Ocean.

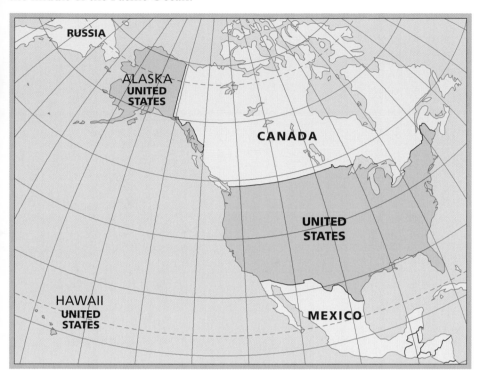

The coast of Maui is the second largest of the Hawai'ian islands.

The United States purchased the vast territory of Alaska from Russia in 1867. When Alaska became the 49th U.S. state in 1959, it increased the size of the country by nearly one-fifth.

Indian Reservations of the Conterminous United States

About 3 million Native Americans, or American Indians, live in the United States. About 22% live on or near reservations.

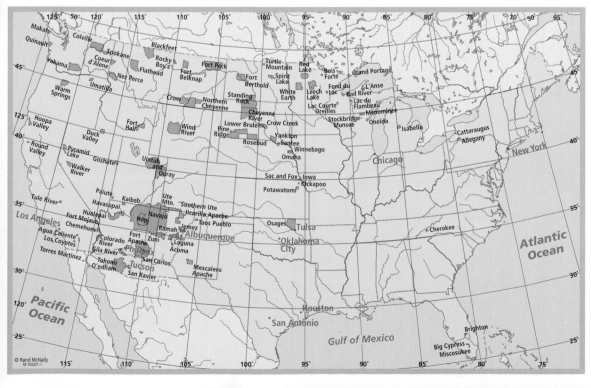

Pueblo Indian ruins in New Mexico reflect an ancient culture.

Navajo Reservation in Gallup, New Mexico.

Ceremonial clothing at a powwow in North Dakota.

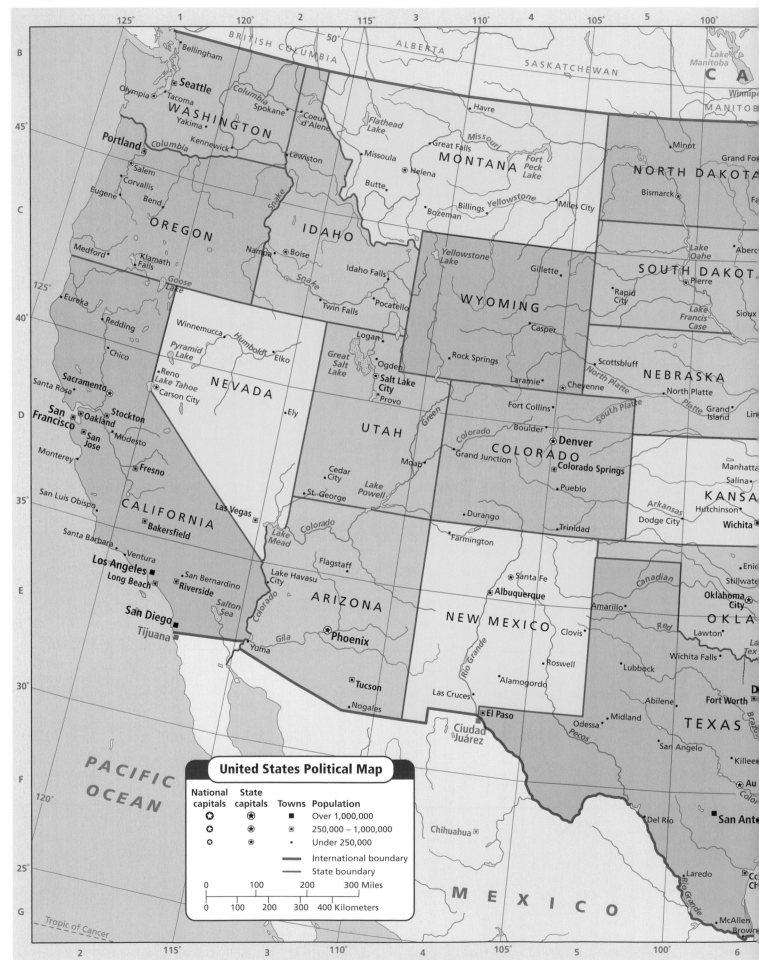

United States Political Map

National capitals	State capitals	Towns	Population
⊛	⊛	■	Over 1,000,000
⊛	⊛	▣	250,000 – 1,000,000
⊛	⊛	•	Under 250,000

International boundary
State boundary

0   100   200   300 Miles
0   100   200   300   400 Kilometers

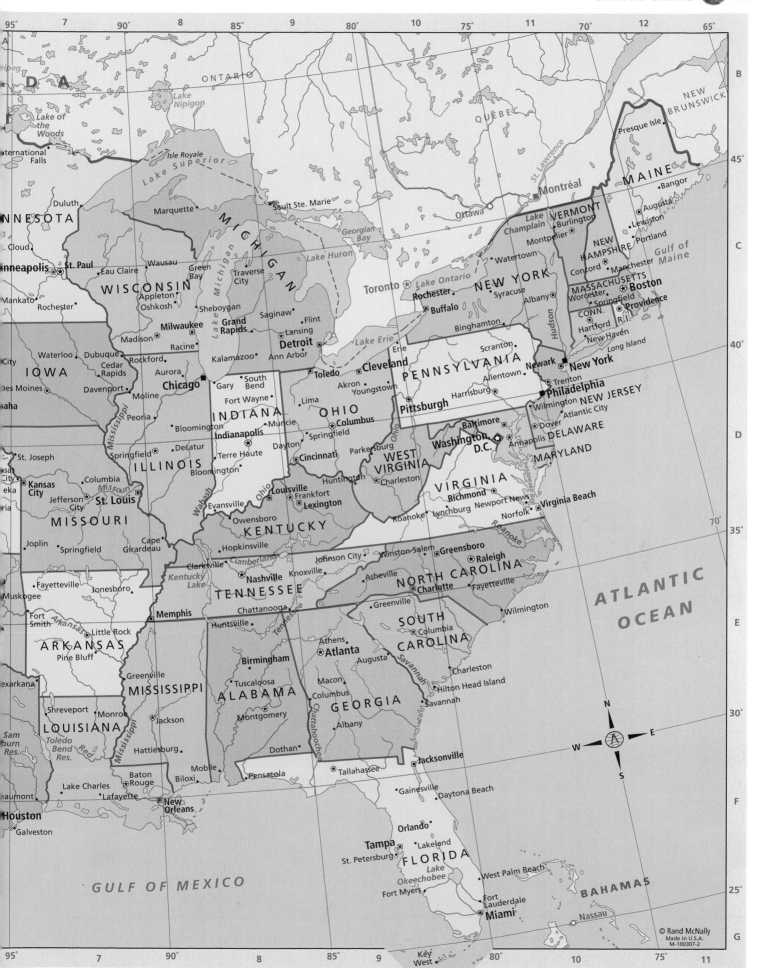

ONTARIO

Lake of the Woods

Lake Nipigon

QUÉBEC

NEW BRUNSWICK

MINNESOTA

. Cloud

Duluth

Marquette

Isle Royale

Sault Ste. Marie

MICHIGAN

Georgian Bay

Lake Huron

Toronto

Lake Ontario

Ottawa

St. Lawrence

Montréal

MAINE

Presque Isle

Bangor

Augusta

Lewiston

Portland

Gulf of Maine

Lake Superior

Minneapolis   St. Paul

Mankato

Rochester

Eau Claire

Wausau

WISCONSIN

Green Bay

Traverse City

Lake Michigan

Saginaw

Flint

Lansing

VERMONT

Burlington

Montpelier

NEW HAMPSHIRE

Concord   Manchester

Watertown

NEW YORK

Syracuse

Albany

MASSACHUSETTS

Worcester   Springfield

Boston

Providence

CONN.

Hartford   R.I.

New Haven

Long Island

Appleton

Oshkosh

Sheboygan

Milwaukee

Madison

Racine

Grand Rapids

Kalamazoo

Ann Arbor

Detroit

Lake Erie

Cleveland

Erie

Rochester

Buffalo

Binghamton

Scranton

PENNSYLVANIA

Allentown

Newark

New York

Hudson

IOWA

Waterloo

Dubuque

Cedar Rapids

Rockford

Aurora

Chicago

Gary

South Bend

Fort Wayne

INDIANA

Toledo

Lima

Akron

Youngstown

OHIO

Columbus

Harrisburg

Pittsburgh

Trenton

Philadelphia

Wilmington   NEW JERSEY

Atlantic City

Dover

City

Des Moines

maha

Davenport

Moline

Peoria

Bloomington

Indianapolis

Muncie

Springfield

Dayton

Cincinnati

Parkersburg

Baltimore

Washington, D.C.

Annapolis   DELAWARE

MARYLAND

St. Joseph

as City

eka

ria

Kansas City

Columbia

Missouri

Jefferson City

St. Louis

MISSOURI

Springfield   Decatur

ILLINOIS

Terre Haute

Bloomington

Evansville

Wabash

Ohio

Louisville

Frankfort

Lexington

Huntington

WEST VIRGINIA

Charleston

VIRGINIA

Richmond

Newport News

Norfolk   Virginia Beach

Chesapeake

Roanoke

Joplin

Springfield

Cape Girardeau

KENTUCKY

Owensboro

Hopkinsville

Cumberland

Kentucky Lake

Nashville

Johnson City

Winston-Salem

Greensboro

Raleigh

Roanoke

Fayetteville

Clarksville

Knoxville

Asheville

NORTH CAROLINA

Charlotte

Fayetteville

Muskogee

Fayetteville

Jonesboro

Memphis

TENNESSEE

Chattanooga

Tennessee

Greenville

Wilmington

Fort Smith

Arkansas

Little Rock

Huntsville

SOUTH CAROLINA

Greenville

Columbia

ARKANSAS

Pine Bluff

Birmingham

Athens

Atlanta

Augusta

Savannah

Charleston

Hilton Head Island

exarkana

Greenville

MISSISSIPPI

Tuscaloosa

ALABAMA

Macon

Columbus

GEORGIA

Savannah

ATLANTIC OCEAN

Shreveport

Monroe

Jackson

Montgomery

Albany

Sam burn Res.

LOUISIANA

Toledo Bend Res.

Red

Mississippi

Hattiesburg

Dothan

N

W   E

S

Beaumont

Houston

Galveston

Lake Charles

Lafayette

Baton Rouge

New Orleans

Biloxi

Mobile

Pensacola

Tallahassee

Gainesville

Daytona Beach

GULF OF MEXICO

Orlando

Tampa

Lakeland

St. Petersburg

FLORIDA

Lake Okeechobee

West Palm Beach

Fort Myers

BAHAMAS

Fort Lauderdale

Miami

Nassau

Key West

Population

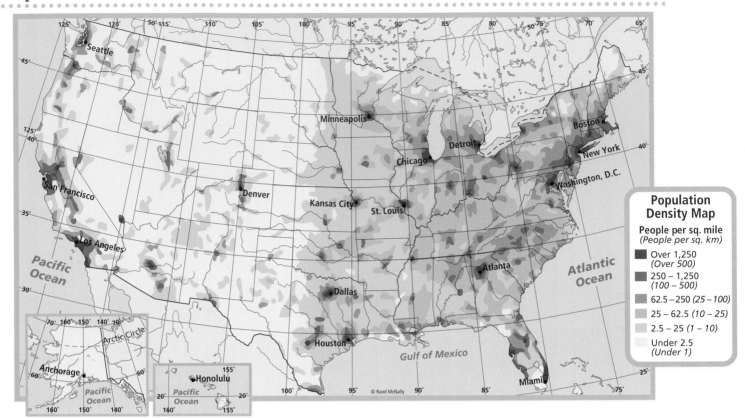

Population
Density Map

People per sq. mile
(People per sq. km)

⬛	Over 1,250 *(Over 500)*
⬛	250 – 1,250 *(100 – 500)*
⬛	62.5 – 250 *(25 – 100)*
⬛	25 – 62.5 *(10 – 25)*
⬛	2.5 – 25 *(1 – 10)*
⬜	Under 2.5 *(Under 1)*

The United States has always been a nation of immigrants. It is one of the most culturally diverse countries in the world.

Approximately 81% of all Americans live in cities and towns.

Urban and Rural Population in the United States

1920

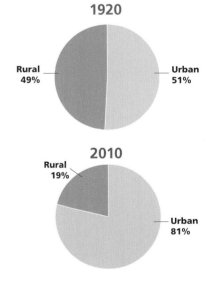

Rural 49%   Urban 51%

2010

Rural 19%   Urban 81%

City Landmarks

Many cities have famous landmarks, such as buildings, bridges, and monuments. How many of these landmarks and their cities can you name? The answers are at the bottom of the page.

1

2

3

4

5

6

Answers: 1. The Gateway Arch in St. Louis, Missouri 2. The Space Needle in Seattle, Washington 3. The Alamo in San Antonio, Texas 4. The Golden Gate Bridge in San Francisco, California 5. The Empire State Building in New York, New York 6. The Corn Palace in Mitchell, South Dakota

Environments

Everything that surrounds you is your **environment**. The environments map shows the different types of environments found in the United States—what you would likely see if you visited any particular place.

Imagine that you could go back in time and see what the land looked like a few hundred years ago. You would find that many areas had different environments than they do now. For example, many areas that are now cropland were once grassland or forest.

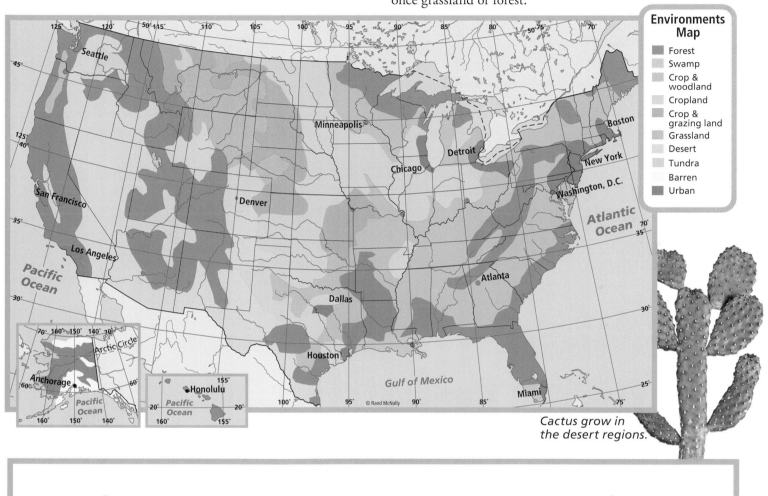

Environments Map

- Forest
- Swamp
- Crop & woodland
- Cropland
- Crop & grazing land
- Grassland
- Desert
- Tundra
- Barren
- Urban

Cactus grow in the desert regions.

Annual Precipitation Map

- Under 10 inches
- 10-20 inches
- 20-40 inches
- 40-60 inches
- 60-80 inches
- Over 80 inches

©Rand McNally
N-FOR24000-D1- -1-1-1

United States Regions

The United States can be divided into regions or areas with common characteristics. A single place can be part of several regions. For example, one city could be part of a mountain region, a cold region, and a forest region. The maps in the previous section show different kinds of regions. They show physical regions, political regions, and population regions, to name a few.

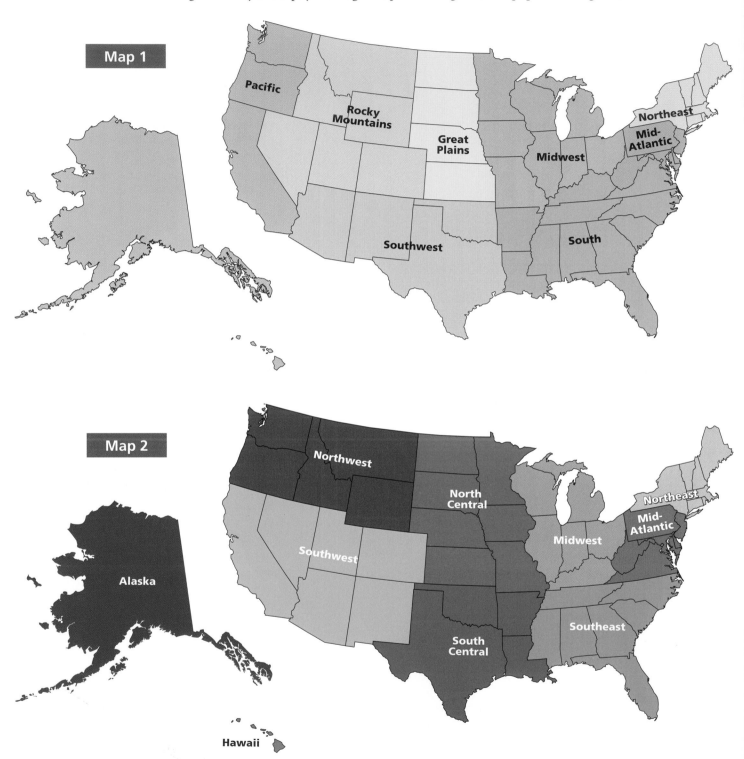

The 50 states can be grouped together into regions in many different ways. There are many opinions about what to call the different regions. There are also many opinions about where the boundary lines between regions belong. The pages that follow show information about the regions shown on Map 2. The regions are based on population, climate, landforms, land use, and location. Alaska and Hawaii are treated as two separate regions, because they are located apart from the other states and because they are so different from the other states, especially in their physical geography.

Comparing the Regions

The bar graphs below compare the 10 regions in two different ways. The graph on the left compares the regions by land area, or size. The graph on the right compares the regions by population. As you can see, some of the larger regions have relatively small populations. Similarly, some of the smaller regions have relatively large populations.

Land Area

Population

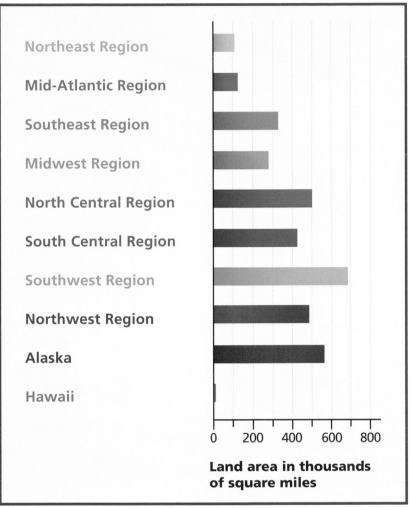

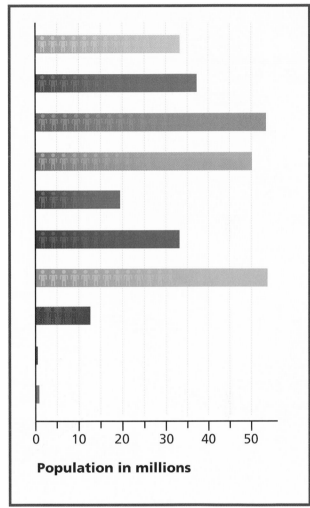

In the Northeast Region, New York City has a very large population compared to its small land area.

Looking at the Northeast Region

The Northeast Region is small in area but huge in population. It was settled by people from Western Europe. In fact, the six states east of New York are known as New England. The Northeast was the site of five of the original 13 American colonies. Most of the people live in an area that forms a broad band along the Atlantic coast, from Boston to New York City. This is called a **megalopolis,** a continuous urban area where the population centers all run together.

From early in the United States' history, people in this region have looked to the sea to meet their needs. Because much of the land is not suitable for farming, manufacturing has always been important in this region. Large cities are centers of business and trade. Today, ships from all over the world dock in the busy harbors of New York City and Boston, carrying goods to and from the country.

Vermont is known for its brilliant fall colors and its abundant dairy farms.

New York, New York, is the most populous city in the Northeast and in the United States.

Every state in the Northeast Region except Vermont borders the Atlantic Ocean. This lighthouse is in Maine.

States of the Northeast Region

State	Land Area (square miles)	Population	Capital
Connecticut	4,842	3,574,097	Hartford
Maine	30,843	1,328,361	Augusta
Massachusetts	7,800	6,547,629	Boston
New Hampshire	8,953	1,316,470	Concord
New York	47,126	19,378,102	Albany
Rhode Island	1,034	1,052,567	Providence
Vermont	9,217	625,741	Montpelier

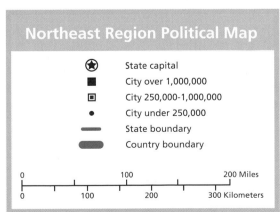

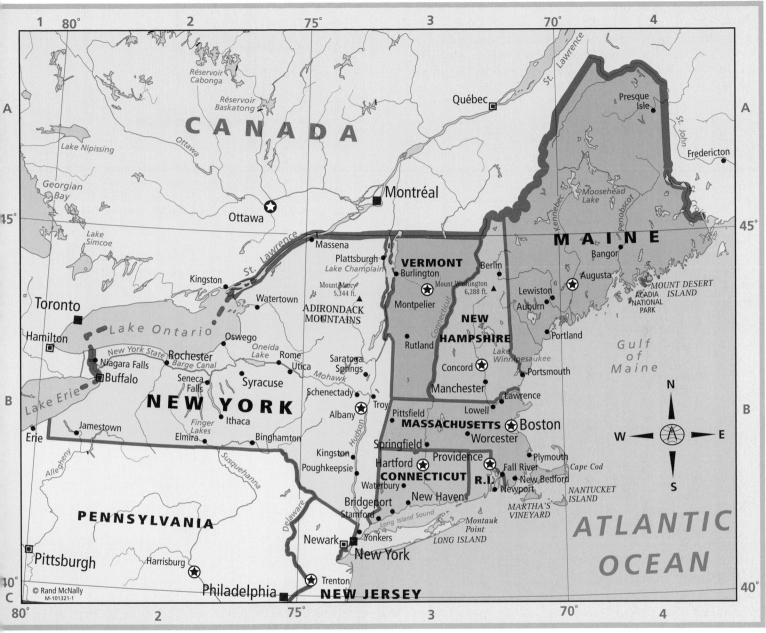

1 80° **2** 75° **3** 70° **4**

A

CANADA

Réservoir Cabonga

Réservoir Baskatong

Lake Nipissing

Ottawa

Georgian Bay

Lake Simcoe

Québec

Montréal

Ottawa

Presque Isle

Fredericton

M A I N E

St. John

Moosehead Lake

Bangor

Augusta

MOUNT DESERT ISLAND

ACADIA NATIONAL PARK

45°

15°

Lake Erie

Toronto

Hamilton

Niagara Falls

Buffalo

Jamestown

Erie

Allegheny

Kingston

St. Lawrence

Lake Ontario

New York State Barge Canal

Rochester

Oswego

Oneida Lake

Rome

Utica

Seneca Falls

Syracuse

Mohawk

Saratoga Springs

Schenectady

Massena

Plattsburgh

Lake Champlain

Mount Marcy 5,344 ft.

ADIRONDACK MOUNTAINS

VERMONT

Burlington

Montpelier

Rutland

Berlin

Mount Washington 6,288 ft.

NEW HAMPSHIRE

Concord

Lewiston

Auburn

Portland

Lake Winnipesaukee

Portsmouth

Gulf of Maine

N

W E

S

B

NEW YORK

Finger Lakes

Ithaca

Elmira

Binghamton

Kingston

Poughkeepsie

Hudson

Albany

Troy

Pittsfield

Springfield

Hartford

CONNECTICUT

Waterbury

New Haven

MASSACHUSETTS

Worcester

Boston

Lowell

Lawrence

Manchester

Connecticut

Providence

R.I.

Fall River

Newport

New Bedford

Plymouth

Cape Cod

NANTUCKET ISLAND

MARTHA'S VINEYARD

B

C

PENNSYLVANIA

Pittsburgh

Harrisburg

Philadelphia

Allegheny

Susquehanna

Delaware

Newark

Yonkers

New York

Trenton

NEW JERSEY

Bridgeport

Stamford

Long Island Sound

Montauk Point

LONG ISLAND

ATLANTIC OCEAN

40°

10°

80° **2** 75° **3** 70° **4**

© Rand McNally
M-101321-1

The original Mayflower *ship brought 102 passengers from England to Massachusetts in 1620. Today, visitors can tour this replica in Plymouth, Massachusetts.*

Northeast Region Political Map

⊛ State capital

■ City over 1,000,000

▣ City 250,000-1,000,000

• City under 250,000

— State boundary

— Country boundary

0		100		200 Miles
0	100	200	300 Kilometers	

The People of the Northeast

Most of the people in the Northeast live within 100 miles of the Atlantic coast. This is flatter land, so as cities grew, they were able to spread out in all directions. In some parts of the region, you can hardly tell where one city ends and another begins. New York City has the largest population of any city in the United States.

Comparing State Populations

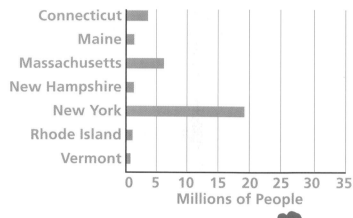

Climate Map

- ▨ Tropical - hot and rainy
- ☐ Dry - very little rain
- ▨ Moderate - warm summer and mild rainy winter
- ▨ Continental - mild summer and snowy winter
- ▨ Highlands - varies with altitude
- — Region boundary

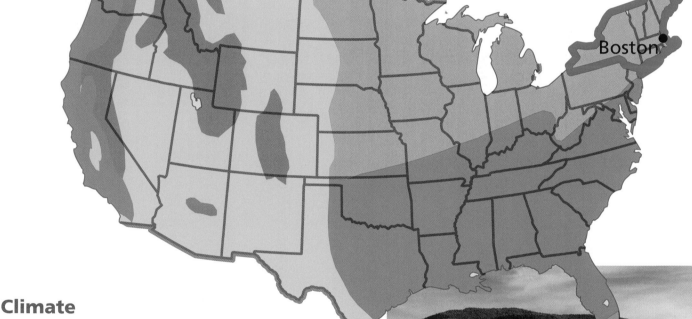

Boston

Climate

As the climate map shows, the Northeast has a continental climate. Winters are cold and snowy and summers are mild. At any time of the year, the Northeast can be hit with powerful storms. Sometimes snow falls for days, clogging roads and closing schools. A lot of precipitation falls during every month of the year!

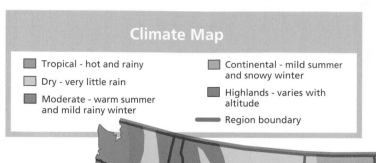

Boston, Massachusetts: Continental Climate

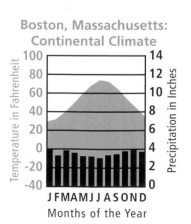

Small towns, like this one in Vermont, dot the Northeast Region. The sugar maple trees of this region turn brilliant red with the cold temperatures of fall.

Working in the Northeast Region

Because of its rocky soil, the Northeast is not a major farming region. Instead, it has grown into a huge center for business. Many companies have their offices in the tall skyscrapers of New York City and Boston. Factories in the region produce goods such as helicopters and computers.

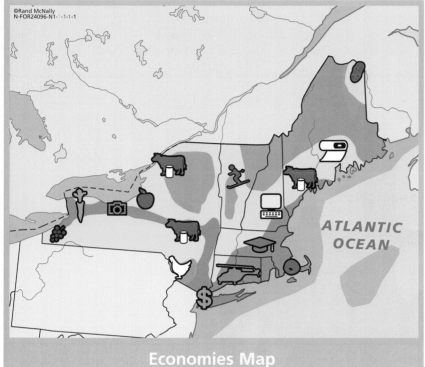

©Rand McNally
N-FOR24096-N1- -1-1-1

ATLANTIC OCEAN

Economies Map

Land Use

- ◻ Agriculture
- ◻ Fishing
- ◻ Forestry
- ◻ Manufacturing

Economic Activity

- 🍎 Apples
- 📷 Cameras
- 🫐 Cranberries
- 🐄 Dairy cows
- 🎓 Education
- 💻 Electronics
- 💲 Financial services

- 🍇 Grapes
- 🚁 Helicopters
- 📄 Paper
- 🥔 Potatoes
- 🐔 Poultry
- ⛷ Ski area
- 🌱 Vegetables

Lobster traps and buoys sit on a pier in Maine. Many people along Maine's coast make their living in the lobster industry.

The Boston area is a center of business and education. It is home to some of the country's top universities, including Harvard University and the Massachusetts Institute of Technology.

Land

A senator from Massachusetts once said, "The Northeast has a harsh climate, a rocky soil, a rough and stormy coast, and we love it." The Appalachian Mountains run through the region like a giant spine. Most of the land is very hilly. Rivers race down wooded slopes. Lakes are sprinkled across the lowlands. If you take a drive through the region, you can see why the Northeast is known for its beauty.

The moose is the state animal of Maine.

Dense forests blanket many of the mountainous areas of the Northeast Region, as shown in this photo of the Adirondack Mountains in New York.

The land and climate make skiing possible in the Northeast.

Maine is not heavily populated, but its scenery draws visitors from all over the world.

Niagara Falls, in New York and Canada, provide hydroelectric power to the Northeast.

A Threat to the Environment

Acid rain has become a problem in the Northeast. **Acid rain** refers to pollution in the air that falls as rain.

As you can see on the map, the Northeast is especially hard hit by acid rain. This is because of its factories and dense population. Cars and smokestacks in the Northeast spew out pollutants. Prevailing winds bring pollutants from cities in the Midwest, too. Over time, acid rain harms soils and lakes, which in turn harm forests and fish.

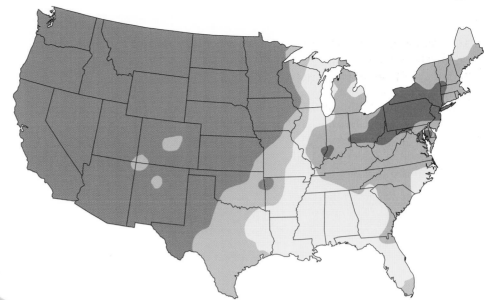

©Rand McNally
N-FOR24000-X7- -1-1-1

Cars can contribute to acid rain.

Acid Rain Map

less acidic ⟷ more acidic

Source: Environmental Protection Agency

How Acid Rain Occurs

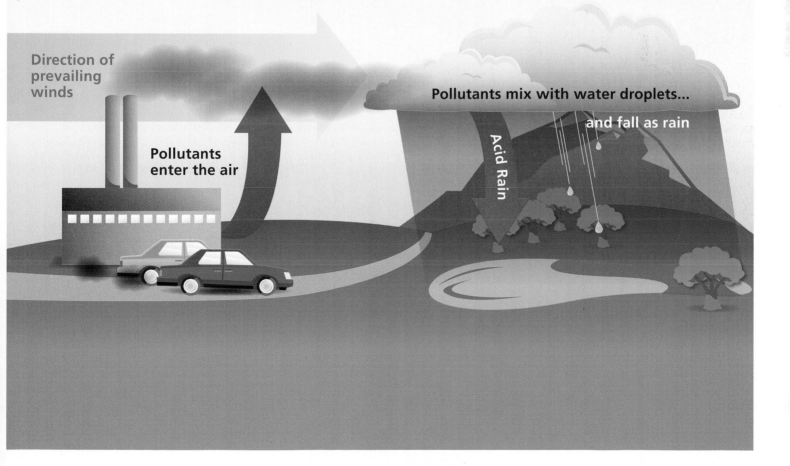

Direction of prevailing winds

Pollutants enter the air

Pollutants mix with water droplets...

and fall as rain

Acid Rain

Looking at the Mid-Atlantic Region

The Mid-Atlantic Region is small in size, but large in population. Most of the region's people live along or near the Atlantic Coast. The population thins out in the western part of the region. Oil, steel, and coal from this region fueled America's industry and power for many decades.

The Mid-Atlantic Region is home to the nation's capital, Washington, D.C., or the District of Columbia. The capital is not in any state. Instead, it is considered a federal district sandwiched between Maryland and Virginia. Many people in this area work in government offices.

The Senate and House of Representatives meet in the U.S. Capitol Building in Washington, D.C.

Atlantic City, Cape May, and other resort cities draw millions of visitors to the New Jersey shore each year.

Philadelphia, Pennsylvania, is the most populous city in the Mid-Atlantic Region.

West Virginia is the most rural state in the Mid-Atlantic Region. This quaint scene is in Babcock State Park.

States of the Mid-Atlantic Region

State	Land Area (square miles)	Population	Capital
Delaware	1,949	897,934	Dover
Maryland	9,707	5,733,552	Annapolis
New Jersey	7,354	8,791,894	Trenton
Pennsylvania	44,743	12,702,379	Harrisburg
Virginia	39,490	8,001,024	Richmond
West Virginia	24,038	1,852,994	Charleston
Washington, D.C.*	61	601,723	— —

* The District of Columbia is not a state but a federal district.

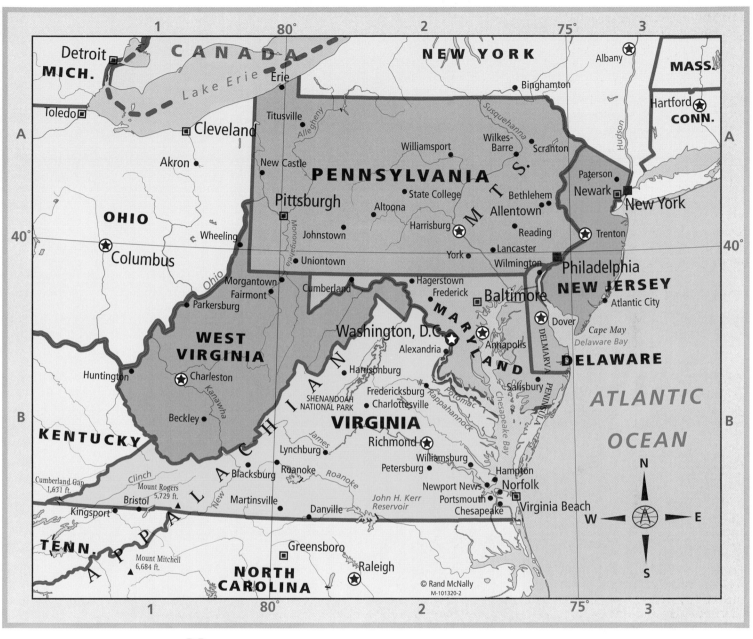

CANADA

Detroit
MICH.
Toledo
Lake Erie
Erie
Cleveland
Akron
OHIO
Columbus
Wheeling
Titusville
New Castle
Pittsburgh
Johnstown
Uniontown
PENNSYLVANIA
Williamsport
State College
Altoona
Harrisburg
NEW YORK
Albany
Binghamton
Wilkes-Barre
Scranton
Bethlehem
Allentown
Reading
Lancaster
York
Wilmington
Paterson
Newark
New York
Trenton
Philadelphia
MASS.
Hartford
CONN.
M T S.

40°

NEW JERSEY
Atlantic City
Dover
DELAWARE
Cape May
Delaware Bay

Morgantown
Fairmont
Parkersburg
Cumberland
Hagerstown
Frederick
Baltimore
Washington, D.C.
Alexandria
Annapolis
MARYLAND
DELMARVA PENINSULA
Chesapeake Bay
Salisbury

WEST VIRGINIA
Huntington
Charleston
Beckley

KENTUCKY

Harrisonburg
Fredericksburg
SHENANDOAH NATIONAL PARK
Charlottesville
VIRGINIA
Richmond
Lynchburg
Roanoke
Petersburg
Williamsburg
Hampton
Newport News
Norfolk
Portsmouth
Chesapeake
Virginia Beach

ATLANTIC OCEAN

Cumberland Gap 1,631 ft.
Clinch
Mount Rogers 5,729 ft.
Bristol
Kingsport
Blacksburg
Martinsville
Danville
John H. Kerr Reservoir

APPALACHIAN

TENN.
Mount Mitchell 6,684 ft.
Greensboro
Raleigh
NORTH CAROLINA

© Rand McNally
M-101320-2

N
W   E
S

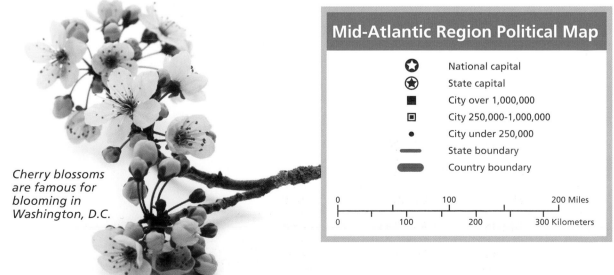

Cherry blossoms are famous for blooming in Washington, D.C.

Mid-Atlantic Region Political Map

⭑ National capital
⭑ State capital
■ City over 1,000,000
▣ City 250,000–1,000,000
• City under 250,000
━ State boundary
━ Country boundary

0   100   200 Miles
0   100   200   300 Kilometers

The People of the Mid-Atlantic

Early in the United States history, settlements grew up along the Atlantic Coastal Plain. These factory towns could trade goods, along the rivers that flow into the Atlantic Ocean. Population patterns reflect that history today. Most people in the region still live east of the Appalachian Mountains.

Comparing State Populations

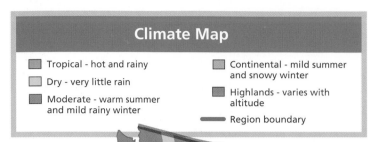

Millions of People

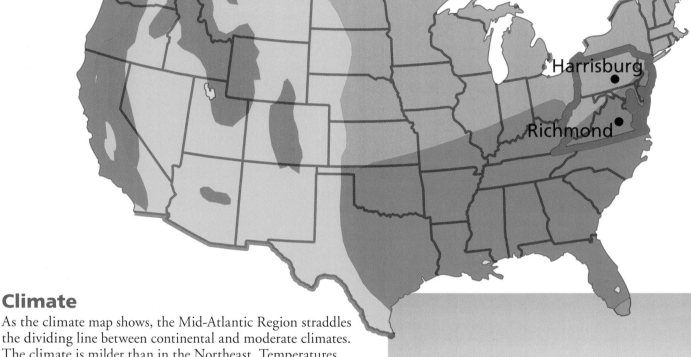

Climate Map

▦ Tropical - hot and rainy	▦ Continental - mild summer and snowy winter
▦ Dry - very little rain	▦ Highlands - varies with altitude
▦ Moderate - warm summer and mild rainy winter	▬ Region boundary

Climate

As the climate map shows, the Mid-Atlantic Region straddles the dividing line between continental and moderate climates. The climate is milder than in the Northeast. Temperatures often stay above freezing in the winter. This has made agriculture important in the region.

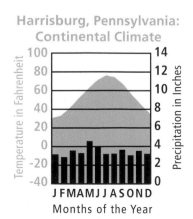

Harrisburg, Pennsylvania: Continental Climate

Months of the Year

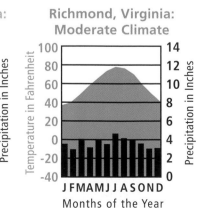

Richmond, Virginia: Moderate Climate

Months of the Year

The rolling hills of the Mid-Atlantic Region are dotted with farms. This scene is in the countryside of Maryland.

Working in the Mid-Atlantic Region

Work in this region is related to the physical geography. On the map below, notice the red band that runs from the center of the region to its northeast corner. This manufacturing area follows the fall line, which is discussed on page 73.

Coal mining is an important industry in the Appalachian Mountains. Coal is used to fuel many of the United States' industries, such as steel making. Steel production in this region allowed the United States to build and prosper in the 20th century.

The indented coastline and deep, protected harbors of the Mid-Atlantic make it an important shipping region. Ships are built in this area, and the United States Navy has several bases here.

Tobacco plant

This coal mine in West Virginia is one of many found in the Mid-Atlantic Region.

Many varieties of apples are grown in Virginia, including Granny Smith.

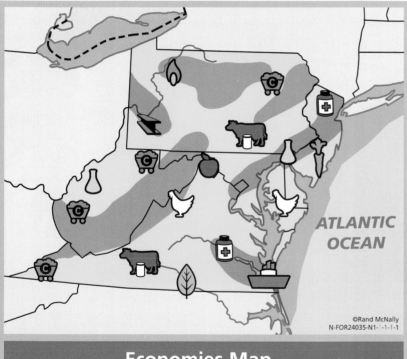

ATLANTIC OCEAN

©Rand McNally
N-FOR24035-N1- -1-1-1

Economies Map

Land Use

- ▢ Agriculture
- ▢ Fishing
- ▢ Forestry
- ▢ Manufacturing

Economic Activity

- 🍎 Apples
- ⚗ Chemicals
- Ⓒ Coal
- 🐄 Dairy cows
- 🔥 Natural gas
- 💊 Pharmaceuticals

- 🐔 Poultry
- 🚢 Shipbuilding
- Steel
- 🌿 Tobacco
- Vegetables

Boats sail through the waters of Chesapeake Bay.

Land

The physical geography of the Mid-Atlantic Region is similar to that of the Northeast. The Appalachian Mountains form the "backbone" of the Mid-Atlantic Region. On the east side of the mountains, the land slopes downhill through a hilly region called the **piedmont**. The green area on the map tells you that the land flattens into a low plain as it nears the ocean.

The White Pine tree is found along the Appalachian Mountains.

Much of the coast in the Mid-Atlantic Region is protected by barrier islands—long ridges of sand covered in grasses and laced with saltwater marshes.

New River Gorge National River, West Virginia

The Appalachians are old mountains that have been worn down by wind and rain. The photo above shows the weathered Seneca Rocks in West Virginia.

The Fall Line

The boundary between the hilly Piedmont and the flat coastal plain is called the **fall line**. It is where the land suddenly drops in elevation. Along this line, rivers flowing downhill from the Appalachian Mountains tumble over waterfalls.

Many factory towns were built along the fall line long ago. The force of the falls turned huge paddle wheels. That generated electricity. Electricity powered the machines in some of the country's first factories.

Ships could travel up rivers such as the Potomac and the Delaware as far as the fall line. Loaded there, they would carry goods downstream to the Atlantic Ocean and then on to other places around the world.

Great Falls on the Potomac River is one of the many waterfalls along the fall line.

Red Mill, located on the fall line in New Jersey, was built in 1810. Notice the paddle wheel. The force of the falls turned the wheel and powered machines that made woolen fabric.

Diagram of the Fall Line

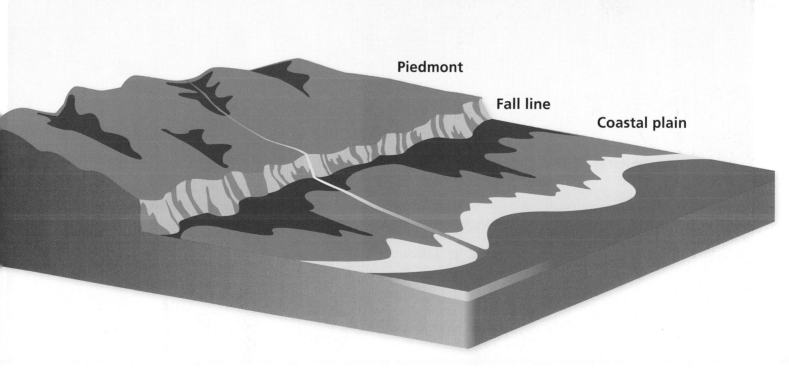

Piedmont

Fall line

Coastal plain

Looking at the Southeast Region

The Southeast Region stretches from the Mississippi River in the west to the Atlantic Ocean in the east. A warm climate helps to make the Southeast a distinct region. With abundant rainfall, much of the region stays green through most of the year. In winter, the peaks of the Appalachian Mountains might be covered in snow, but the rest of the region tends to be mild.

The Southeast is also known for its history. Throughout this region, you can see hints of the country's past. Homes and buildings in some cities—such as Savannah, Georgia, and Charleston, South Carolina—date back to the United States' early history.

The space shuttle is launched at Cape Canaveral, Florida.

The Great Smoky Mountains in Tennessee and North Carolina are part of the Appalachian Mountains. Their name comes from the haze that often surrounds them.

Astronaut suit

States of the Southeast Region

State	Land Area (square miles)	Population	Capital
Alabama	50,645	4,779,736	Montgomery
Florida	53,625	18,801,310	Tallahassee
Georgia	57,513	9,687,653	Atlanta
Mississippi	46,923	2,967,297	Jackson
North Carolina	48,618	9,535,483	Raleigh
South Carolina	30,061	4,625,364	Columbia
Tennessee	41,235	6,346,105	Nashville

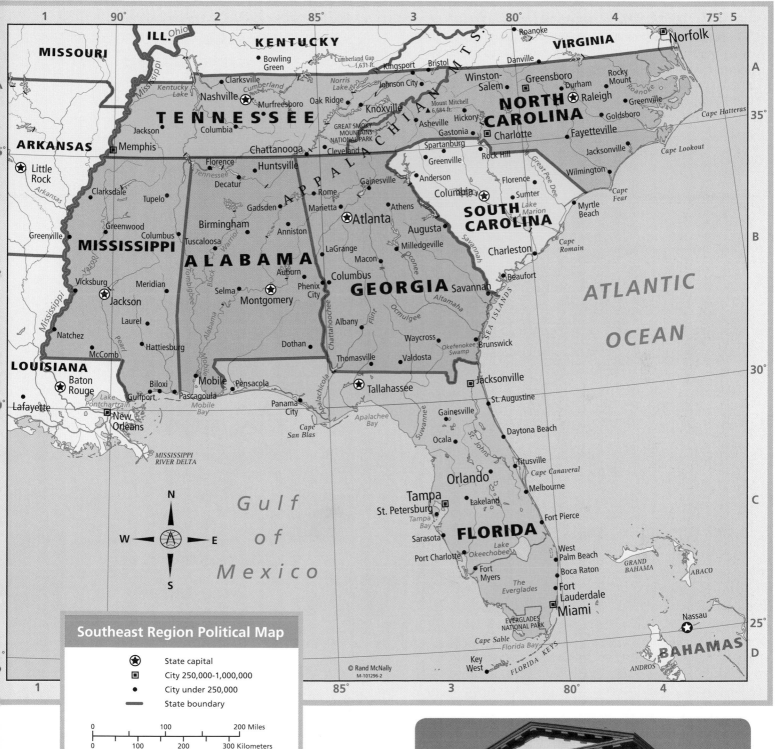

Southeast Region Political Map

⊛ State capital
▣ City 250,000–1,000,000
• City under 250,000
— State boundary

0   100   200 Miles
0   100   200   300 Kilometers

© Rand McNally
M-101296-2

Located near the southern tip of Florida, Miami Beach is a popular vacation spot.

Charleston, South Carolina, is noted for its historic homes and buildings.

Market Hall, built in 1841, is one of many historic buildings in Charleston, South Carolina.

The People of the Southeast

The Southeast is growing in population. Many people move to this region for jobs or when they retire. This movement of people is called the "Sunbelt Shift." Look at the population graph comparing the seven states in the region. Florida is the most popular choice.

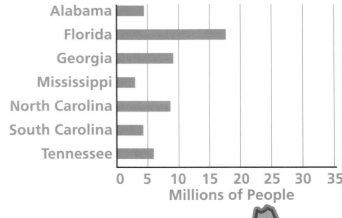

Comparing State Populations

Alabama
Florida
Georgia
Mississippi
North Carolina
South Carolina
Tennessee

0   5   10   15   20   25   30   35
Millions of People

Climate Map

- ■ Tropical - hot and rainy
- □ Dry - very little rain
- ■ Moderate - warm summer and mild rainy winter
- ■ Continental - mild summer and snowy winter
- ■ Highlands - varies with altitude
- — Region boundary

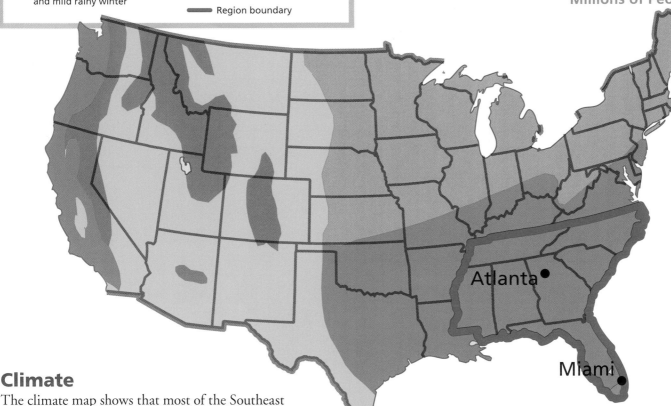

Atlanta●

Miami●

Climate

The climate map shows that most of the Southeast has a moderate climate. The climate graph for Atlanta shows that temperatures are mild even in winter. The southern tip of Florida has a tropical climate, because it is closer to the Equator. The climate graph for Miami shows that this city has warm temperatures throughout the year and heavy rainfall in the hottest months.

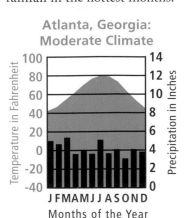

Atlanta, Georgia: Moderate Climate

Temperature in Fahrenheit
100
80
60
40
20
0
-20
-40

Precipitation in Inches
14
12
10
8
6
4
2
0

J F M A M J J A S O N D
Months of the Year

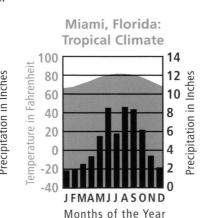

Miami, Florida: Tropical Climate

Temperature in Fahrenheit
100
80
60
40
20
0
-20
-40

Precipitation in Inches
14
12
10
8
6
4
2
0

J F M A M J J A S O N D
Months of the Year

Bald cypress trees thrive in the warm, moist climate of the Southeast Region. These trees, which like to keep their roots wet, are found mostly in low, swampy areas.

Working in the Southeast Region

Because of the region's warm, wet climate and expanse of low, flat plains, farmers in the Southeast grow a variety of crops—cotton, sugar cane, and oranges—that cannot be grown in colder regions. For this reason, many people in the Southeast live in **rural** areas and make their living in agriculture. Manufacturing and tourism are also important to the region's economy.

Ask any tourist what the Southeast is known for. The answer would probably be "sun." Beaches and warm, sunny weather draw tourists from all over the world.

Nashville, the capital of Tennessee, is known as Music City, U.S.A.

The Mississippi River is one of the nation's most important waterways.

A cotton farmer harvests his crop. Cotton grows well in the Southeast Region, because it needs a warm, humid climate.

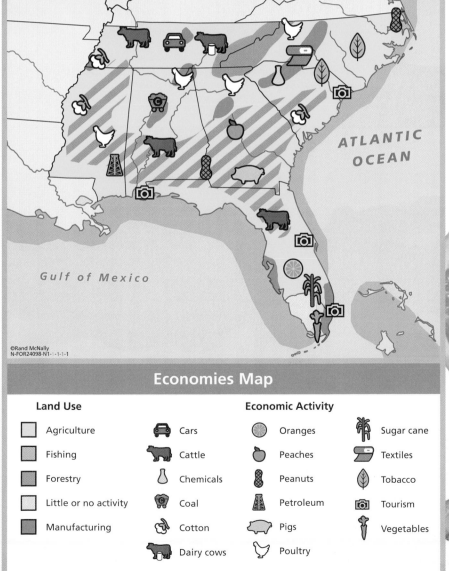

ATLANTIC OCEAN

Gulf of Mexico

©Rand McNally
N-FOR24098-N1-1-1-1-1

Economies Map

Land Use

- ⬜ Agriculture
- ⬜ Fishing
- 🟦 Forestry
- ⬜ Little or no activity
- 🟦 Manufacturing

Economic Activity

- 🚗 Cars
- 🐄 Cattle
- ⚗️ Chemicals
- Ⓒ Coal
- 🌿 Cotton
- 🐄 Dairy cows

- 🍊 Oranges
- 🍑 Peaches
- Peanuts
- Petroleum
- 🐷 Pigs
- 🐔 Poultry

- 🌴 Sugar cane
- Textiles
- 🍃 Tobacco
- 📷 Tourism
- Vegetables

Cotton, oranges, and sugar cane are grown in the warm climate of the Southeast.

Land

The Appalachian Mountains form an unbroken "wall" from the Northeast Region through the Mid-Atlantic Region. But in the Southeast Region, the mountains come to an end, and flat land takes their place. The physical map (page 44) shows the broad, low plains found along the coasts of the Atlantic Ocean and the Gulf of Mexico. Much of Florida is flat, swampy land that lies less than 50 feet above sea level.

The Everglades are a huge swamp in southern Florida. A swamp is land that is permanently wet. The waters of the Everglades are actually a vast river that spreads out over a flat plain.

Wide, sandy beaches outline much of the coastline in the Southeast Region. This beach is in Miami, Florida.

Spring in the North Carolina Appalachian Mountains.

In the Path of Hurricanes

Hurricanes form over oceans, usually in late summer when the temperature of the water is at its warmest. The warm water acts like a furnace, heating the air above it. When the winds are just right, rising heat may cause an ordinary storm to become a powerful hurricane.

The map of hurricane paths below shows how hurricanes seem to aim for the Southeast. Because of global wind currents, hurricanes tend to form off the coast of Africa and head across the Atlantic Ocean toward the United States. They die out when they hit land or cooler water. This is because they are no longer fueled by the heat energy of the warm water.

When hurricanes hit, people on the coastal plains often head for higher ground, away from the surging ocean and the powerful force of the wind and rain.

Hurricane Ike made landfall in September 2008.

This image of a hurricane approaching Florida was taken from a satellite high above the earth.

Diagram of the Common Paths of Hurricanes

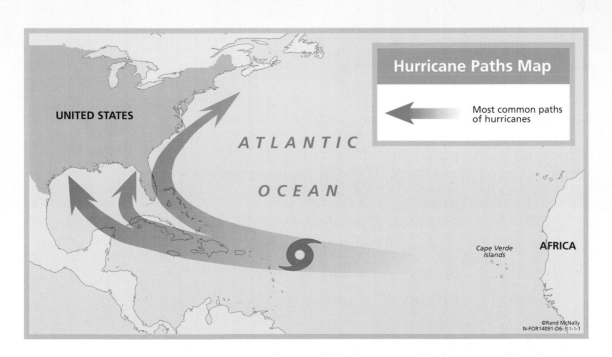

UNITED STATES

ATLANTIC

OCEAN

Hurricane Paths Map

Most common paths of hurricanes

Cape Verde Islands

AFRICA

©Rand McNally
N-FOR14091-D6- 1-1-1

Looking at the Midwest Region

The Midwest is often called "the Heartland" because of its location in the center of the country. Many of the region's cities are located on rivers and lakes and grew up as trade centers. Farm products were hauled to Chicago, for example, and shipped to other parts of the country on a network of waterways.

Later, cities such as Chicago, Detroit, and Cleveland became important manufacturing centers, and their populations soared. A growing network of transportation systems—highways, waterways, and rail lines—connected these cities to surrounding areas and other regions.

Away from the cities, the Midwest has some of the most fertile farmland in the United States. Farmers grow bountiful crops on land that was once covered by prairie and forests.

The Ohio River is a major transportation artery. Tugboats push barges filled with goods like grain and coal to distant places.

Chicago, Illinois, is the most populous city in the Midwest Region and the third most populous in the United States.

Cherries are grown in the Midwest.

States of the Midwest Region

State	Land Area (square miles)	Population	Capital
Illinois	55,519	12,830,632	Springfield
Indiana	35,826	6,483,802	Indianapolis
Kentucky	39,486	4,339,367	Frankfort
Michigan	56,539	9,883,640	Lansing
Ohio	40,861	11,536,504	Columbus
Wisconsin	54,158	5,686,986	Madison

CANADA

MINNESOTA

Lake Superior

ISLE ROYALE NATIONAL PARK

KEWEENAW PENINSULA

Duluth
Superior
Ashland

Marquette

Sault Ste. Marie
Sault Ste. Marie

Sudbury

Rhinelander
Iron Mountain

Escanaba
BEAVER ISLAND

DOOR PENINSULA

Alpena

Lake Huron

Georgian Bay

Minneapolis
St. Paul

WISCONSIN

Wausau
Marinette

Traverse City

45°

Mille Lacs Lake

Eau Claire
Stevens Point

Green Bay
Appleton

Ludington

Saginaw Bay

Rochester

La Crosse

Oshkosh
Manitowoc
Lake Winnebago
Fond du Lac
Sheboygan

Muskegon

MICHIGAN

Midland
Saginaw
Bay City

Toronto

Lake Ontario

Hamilton

IOWA

Madison

Milwaukee

Janesville
Beloit

Racine
Kenosha

Holland

Muskegon

Grand Rapids
Lansing

Flint

Pontiac
Port Huron

Sarnia

London

N.Y.

Dubuque

Rockford

Waukegan
Evanston

Kalamazoo

Battle Creek
Jackson

Detroit
Ann Arbor
Windsor

Lake St. Clair

Lake Erie

Erie

Cedar Rapids

Elgin
Aurora

Chicago

Benton Harbor

Monroe

Ashtabula

Des Moines

Davenport
Moline
Rock Island

Ottawa

Joliet
Gary

South Bend

Toledo

Sandusky

Lorain

Cleveland

Akron

Youngstown

PA.

Galesburg

Kankakee

Fort Wayne

Maumee

Findlay

Mansfield

Canton

Pittsburgh

Pekin
Peoria
Bloomington

Lafayette

INDIANA

Kokomo
Marion

Lima

Marion

OHIO

Steubenville

ILLINOIS

Danville

Anderson
Muncie

Columbus

Newark

Wheeling

40°

Champaign

Decatur

Indianapolis

Richmond

Springfield
Dayton

Lancaster
Zanesville

Ohio

Quincy

Springfield

Mattoon

Terre Haute
Bloomington

Columbus

Hamilton

Cincinnati

Chillicothe

Parkersburg

WEST VIRGINIA

Columbia

St. Charles
Alton
East St. Louis

Vincennes

New Albany

Portsmouth

Ashland

Huntington

Charleston

Jefferson City

St. Louis
Belleville

Centralia

Evansville
Louisville

Frankfort
Lexington

MISSOURI

Carbondale

Owensboro

Richmond

Springfield

Cairo

Paducah

Lake Barkley

Bowling Green
Hopkinsville

MAMMOTH CAVE NATIONAL PARK

Kentucky Lake

KENTUCKY

Cumberland Gap 1,631 ft.

Lake Cumberland

VIRGINIA

ARKANSAS

Nashville

TENNESSEE

NORTH CAROLINA

© Rand McNally
M-101319-2

Midwest Region Political Map

- ⬟ State capital
- ■ City over 1,000,000
- ▣ City 250,000–1,000,000
- • City under 250,000
- ── State boundary
- ━━ Country boundary

0   100   200 Miles
0   100   200   300 Kilometers

Corn is abundant in the Midwest.

The People of the Midwest

As you can see on the political map on the previous page, people live in towns and cities all over the Midwest. However, the states in this region are not densely populated.

Comparing State Populations

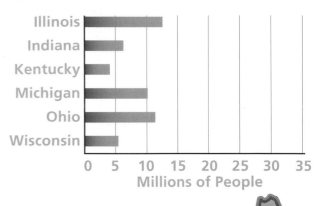

Climate Map

- ▪ Tropical - hot and rainy
- ▫ Dry - very little rain
- ▪ Moderate - warm summer and mild rainy winter
- ▪ Continental - mild summer and snowy winter
- ▪ Highlands - varies with altitude
- ▬ Region boundary

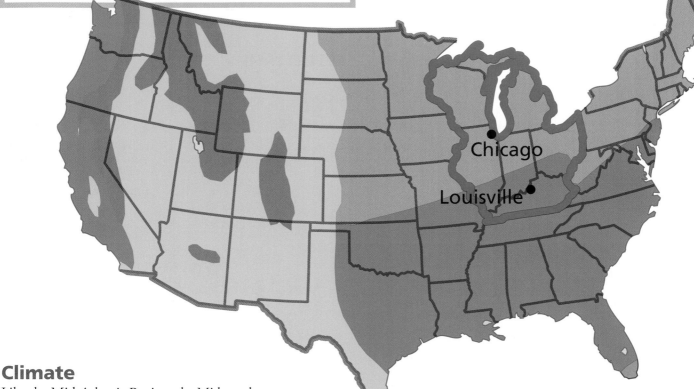

Chicago

Louisville

Climate

Like the Mid-Atlantic Region, the Midwest has a continental climate in the north and a moderate climate in the south. The areas that have a continental climate have longer, colder winters and shorter, milder summers than the areas that have a moderate climate.

The Midwest Region is home to many animals that can live in cold winters, such as foxes, raccoons, skunks, and deer. This photo shows a red fox.

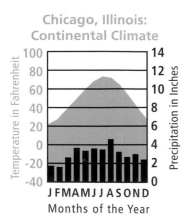

Chicago, Illinois: Continental Climate

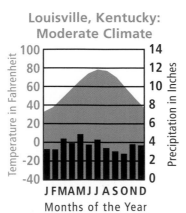

Louisville, Kentucky: Moderate Climate

Working in the Midwest Region

Manufacturing plays a big role in the region's economy. Large cities such as Chicago, Milwaukee, and Cleveland grew up as manufacturing centers along the shores of the Great Lakes. The largest of these areas stretches like a belt across the center of the region, connecting all the major cities that are located on the waterways. Manufactured goods are then carried to ports all over the world.

With some of the best farmland in the world, the Midwest is an important agricultural region. Outside the cities, farmers use the expanse of flat, fertile land for growing the nation's crops. Crops differ from north to south, depending on the length of the summer growing season.

Forestry is important in the northernmost part of the region. That's because it's too cold for farming, but perfect for some types of trees.

Soybeans and corn are two of the most important crops grown in the Midwest Region. This soybean field is in northern Indiana.

Wisconsin is a leading producer of dairy products such as cheese and milk.

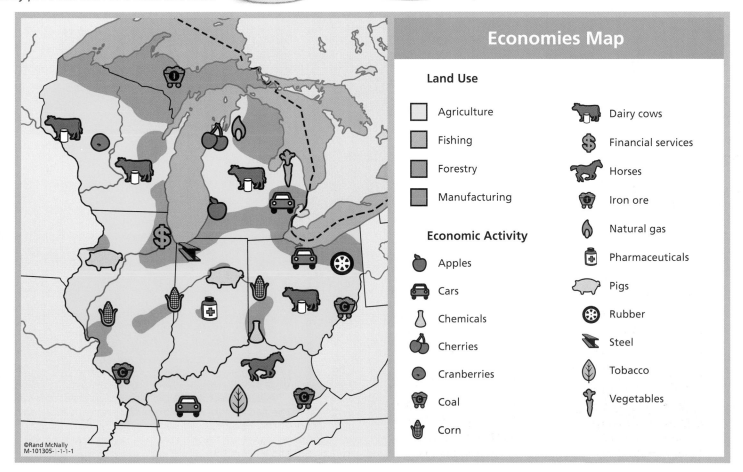

Economies Map

Land Use

- Agriculture
- Fishing
- Forestry
- Manufacturing
- Dairy cows
- Financial services
- Horses
- Iron ore
- Natural gas
- Pharmaceuticals
- Pigs
- Rubber
- Steel
- Tobacco
- Vegetables

Economic Activity

- Apples
- Cars
- Chemicals
- Cherries
- Cranberries
- Coal
- Corn

©Rand McNally
M-101305- -1-1-1

Land

Plains cover most of the Midwest Region. Flat or gently rolling land stretches in all directions as far as the eye can see. Why is the region so flat? Millions of years ago, the land was covered by a shallow sea. When the water drained away, the land left behind was generally flat. Over time, hills and valleys were sculpted by erosion. But later, huge glaciers plowed across the land and smoothed its surface.

Water frames the region. To the north are four of the five Great Lakes. They form part of the border with Canada. The Ohio River flows through the southern part of the region and forms part of its eastern boundary. The Mississippi River forms the region's western boundary. These huge lakes and rivers give the Midwest important outlets to the Gulf of Mexico and the Atlantic Ocean.

The northernmost part of this region is blanketed by forest and dotted with lakes. This photo shows Lake of the Clouds in northwestern Michigan.

The Great Blue Heron can be found on the shores of the Great Lakes.

Lake Superior is one of the Great Lakes north of the Midwest.

The Ohio river forms part of the eastern boundary of the Midwest.

The Mississippi river forms the western boundary of the Midwest.

Land Shaped by Glaciers

Thousands of years ago, vast sheets of ice, or glaciers, spread across much of this region. As they moved, the glaciers were like giant bulldozers. They picked up huge amounts of rock and soil and dragged it across the land. They scraped the tops off hills and filled in valleys. Land that was hilly became flat.

In other places, the glaciers created low hills. Some of these hills were formed when the glaciers melted and deposited rocks and soil along their edges. Others were created as rivers of meltwater beneath the glaciers deposited rocks and soil along their courses.

The glaciers scoured out enormous basins. When the glaciers melted, the basins filled with water. This is how the Great Lakes were created.

Glaciation Map

☐ Maximum extent of glaciation

In some places, the ice sheets were a mile high. That's about four times the height of Chicago's tallest building, the Willis Tower!

Willis Tower

Glaciers like this sculpted the Midwest.

Looking at the North Central Region

The land in the North Central Region is mostly flat or gently rolling, but it rises steadily from east to west. Like the Midwest, the region is a center of our country's farming industry. Flat land and fertile soil make this the perfect place for growing crops and raising cattle on a large scale. Much of the country's wheat is grown on the Great Plains in the western part of the region.

Many of the people in the North Central Region live in small towns in farming areas. Cities in this region are smaller than those in other regions. Still, the region does have a few large cities, such as St. Louis, Missouri, and Minneapolis, Minnesota.

The Gateway Arch in St. Louis, Missouri, symbolizes the city's role as Gateway to the West.

Herds of buffalo roam the plains in parts of South Dakota.

DID YOU KNOW?

In the drier western half of this region, farmers make use of center-pivot irrigation systems, which tap into underground water.

Cattle are important to the economy of the North Central region.

States of the North Central Region

State	Land Area (square miles)	Population	Capital
Iowa	55,857	3,046,355	Des Moines
Kansas	81,759	2,853,118	Topeka
Minnesota	79,627	5,303,925	St. Paul
Missouri	68,741	5,998,927	Jefferson City
Nebraska	76,824	1,826,341	Lincoln
North Dakota	69,000	672,591	Bismarck
South Dakota	75,811	814,180	Pierre

North Central Region Political Map

★	State capital
▣	City 250,000–1,000,000
•	City under 250,000
—	State boundary
▬	Country boundary

0   100   200 Miles
0   100   200   300 Kilometers

CANADA

NORTH DAKOTA
Williston
Minot
Devils Lake
Devils Lake
Grand Forks
Dickinson
Bismarck ★
Jamestown
Moorhead
Fargo
Lake Sakakawea
Lake Oahe
Missouri
Souris
Red
Little Missouri
Yellowstone

MONT.
GREAT

SOUTH DAKOTA
Spearfish
BLACK HILLS
Rapid City
Harney Peak 7,242 ft.
Pierre ★
Aberdeen
Watertown
Huron
Brookings
Mitchell
Sioux Falls
Lake Sharpe
Lake Francis Case
Moreau
White
Cheyenne
James
Big Sioux
Lewis and Clark Lake

WYO.

NEBRASKA
Valentine
Scottsbluff
SAND HILLS
North Platte
Kearney
Grand Island
Hastings
Fremont
Omaha
Council Bluffs
Lincoln
Norfolk
McCook
Beatrice
Lake McConaughy
North Platte
South Platte
Niobrara
Middle Loup
Platte
Republican

GREAT PLAINS

COLORADO
Goodland

KANSAS
Hays
Salina
Junction City
Manhattan
Abilene
Topeka ★
Lawrence
Kansas City
Leavenworth
Atchison
Garden City
Dodge City
Liberal
Great Bend
Hutchinson
Wichita ▣
Winfield
Emporia
Parsons
Pittsburg
Arkansas
Kansas
Neosho
FLINT HILLS

N
W E
S

MINNESOTA
Thunder Bay
International Falls
Upper Red Lake
Lower Red Lake
Bemidji
Lake Winnibigoshish
Leech Lake
Virginia
Hibbing
MESABI RA.
Duluth
Fergus Falls
Brainerd
Mille Lacs Lake
St. Cloud
Willmar
St. Paul ▣ ★
Minneapolis ▣
Mankato
Rochester
Albert Lea
Austin
Winona
Lake of the Woods
Rainy Lake
Lake Superior
Minnesota
St. Croix
Mississippi

MICHIGAN

WISCONSIN
Madison ★
Milwaukee ▣
Rockford
Wisconsin
Lake Winnebago

IOWA
Mason City
Fort Dodge
Waterloo
Dubuque
Cedar Rapids
Clinton
Ames
Marshalltown
Iowa City
Des Moines ★
Davenport
Moline
Rock Island
Ottumwa
Burlington
Fort Madison
Keokuk
Iowa
Cedar
Des Moines
Illinois
Peoria

ILLINOIS
Springfield ★

MISSOURI
Kirksville
St. Joseph
Kansas City ▣
Hannibal
Mark Twain Lake
Moberly
Columbia
Jefferson City ★
Sedalia
St. Charles
St. Louis ▣
Rolla
Springfield
Joplin
Cape Girardeau
Sikeston
Poplar Bluff
Harry S. Truman Reservoir
Lake of the Ozarks
Table Rock Lake
Bull Shoals Lake
Missouri
Osage
Chariton
Black
Ohio
Mississippi

OKLAHOMA
Tulsa ▣
Oklahoma City ★
Cimarron

ARKANSAS

KY.
TENN.

© Rand McNally
M-101318-1

The People of the North Central

Fewer people live in this region. Cities tend to be smaller in population. The states that have the fewest people are in the western part of the region. North Dakota and South Dakota, for example, both rank among our country's five smallest states in population.

Comparing State Populations

State	Millions of People
Iowa	
Kansas	
Minnesota	
Missouri	
Nebraska	
North Dakota	
South Dakota	

0 5 10 15 20 25 30 35
Millions of People

Climate Map

■ Tropical - hot and rainy
□ Dry - very little rain
■ Moderate - warm summer and mild rainy winter
■ Continental - mild summer and snowy winter
■ Highlands - varies with altitude
── Region boundary

Rapid City

Des Moines

Springfield

Climate

Much of the North Central Region has a continental climate. As you move from north to south, the climate gradually becomes more moderate. For example, winters in North Dakota and northern Minnesota are much longer and colder than they are in southern Kansas and Missouri.

The climate changes across the region, too. It gradually becomes drier from east to west. Look at the climate graphs and compare the amounts of precipitation in Rapid City, Des Moines, and Springfield. As you can see, the climate gradually becomes drier.

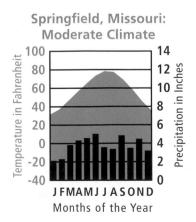

Springfield, Missouri:
Moderate Climate

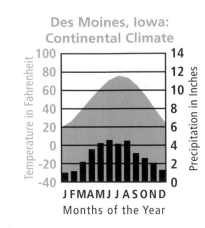

Des Moines, Iowa:
Continental Climate

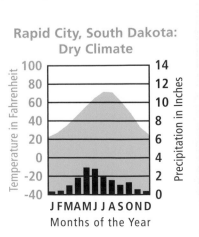

Rapid City, South Dakota:
Dry Climate

Working in the North Central Region

With such good soil and wide-open spaces, it's no wonder that the North Central Region is called our country's "breadbasket." Wheat is grown in the higher plains where the climate is cooler and drier. Corn tends to be grown at lower elevations where summers are hot and humid. The crops of the region feed our entire country and much of the world.

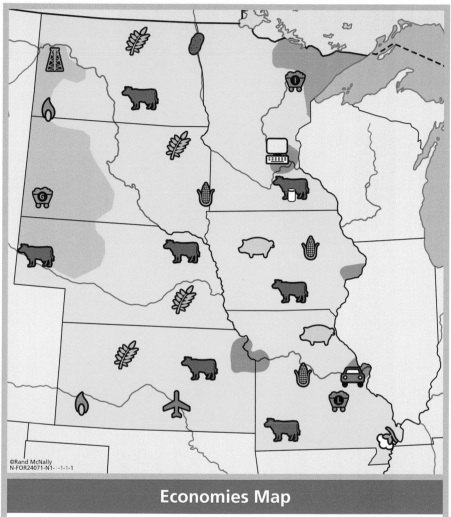

©Rand McNally
N-FOR24071-N1-·-1-1-1

Economies Map

Land Use

- ☐ Agriculture
- ☐ Fishing
- ☐ Forestry
- ☐ Manufacturing
- ☐ Stock raising

Economic Activity

- ✈ Aircraft
- 🚗 Cars
- 🐄 Cattle
- 🌽 Corn
- 🌿 Cotton
- 🐄 Dairy cows
- ⌨ Electronics
- Ⓖ Gold
- Ⓘ Iron ore
- Ⓛ Lead
- 🔥 Natural gas
- 🛢 Petroleum
- 🐖 Pigs
- 🥔 Potatoes
- 🌾 Wheat

The flat farmland of the North Central Region seems to go on forever, as in this scene in southern Minnesota.

Kansas City is located in two states—Kansas and Missouri. It grew up as a place where cattle were brought to be shipped to other parts of the country. Today, it is an important manufacturing city.

Land

Most of the land in the North Central Region is flat or gently rolling. The Great Plains at the region's western edge are about 2,000 feet higher than the plains at the eastern edge.

The highest mountains in the North Central Region are the Black Hills, which rise near the western edge of South Dakota.

Two of our country's greatest rivers are found in this region. The Mississippi River begins in Minnesota and forms most of the region's eastern boundary. The Missouri River begins its journey as melting snow in the Rocky Mountains. It flows eastward through the North Central Region and eventually joins the Mississippi.

The sculpted faces of four U.S. Presidents stare out from Mount Rushmore in the Black Hills of South Dakota.

Sunflowers grow on fertile prairie land in southeastern Minnesota.

Sylvan Lake in the Black Hills of South Dakota.

Roughly nine-tenths of the land in Iowa is used for farming.

Abandoned farms are a common sight in the western half of this region. Some areas have been losing population for decades.

In the Badlands of South Dakota, wind and water have sculpted the land into fantastic shapes.

Tornado Alley

The area known as "Tornado Alley" is hit by more twisters than any other part of the United States. Every year, hundreds of tornadoes tear through the North Central Region.

An invisible war between air masses takes place here. In the spring and early summer, air temperatures change as the seasons change. Hot, humid air flows north from the Gulf of Mexico. When it smashes into cool, dry air moving eastward from the Rocky Mountains, severe thunderstorms occur. Sometimes the air begins to rotate during a storm. When this happens, a spinning funnel cloud forms. White at first, tornadoes get blacker and blacker as they pick up soil and other objects from the ground.

This tornado struck a small town near Wichita, Kansas, on June 12, 2004. That year, 124 tornadoes hit Kansas alone!

Map of Tornado Alley

Tornado Alley Map

Tornado Alley

Looking at the South Central Region

The South Central Region is similar to the North Central Region in many ways. From east to west, the land rises and the climate becomes drier. Farmers in this region grow crops such as wheat, cotton, and rice, and they raise cattle and sheep. Oil production is an important part of the economy.

Dallas and Houston, in Texas, are some of the biggest cities in the region—and in the country. Other cities in the region are smaller by comparison, but just as rich in history and culture. For example, New Orleans, Louisiana, is one of the country's oldest cities. It was founded almost three hundred years ago as a port city on the Mississippi River.

Suffolk Sheep

The Dallas-Fort Worth area is the fourth-largest metropolitan area in the United States.

New Orleans is home to many historic buildings in the French Quarter.

States of the South Central Region

State	Land Area (square miles)	Population	Capital
Arkansas	52,035	2,915,918	Little Rock
Louisiana	43,204	4,533,372	Baton Rouge
Oklahoma	68,595	3,751,351	Oklahoma City
Texas	261,231	25,145,561	Austin

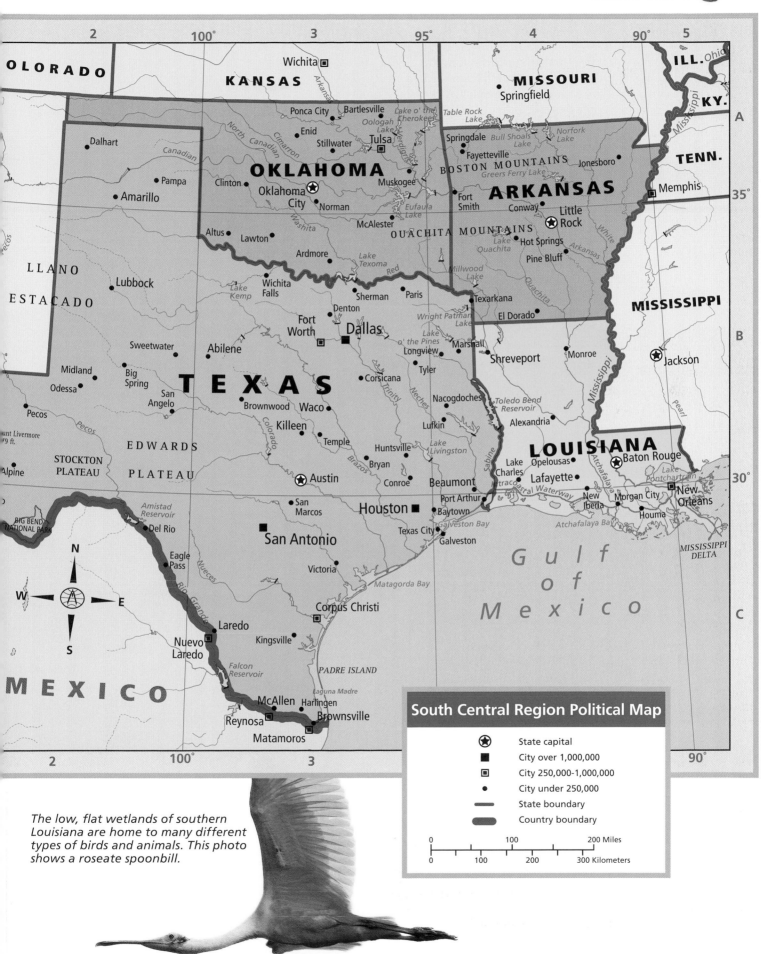

2 100° **3** 95° **4** 90° **5**

COLORADO

KANSAS

Wichita

MISSOURI
Springfield

ILL. Ohio
KY.

Dalhart

Ponca City · Bartlesville
Enid
Stillwater

Lake o' the
Cherokees
Oologah
Lake

Table Rock
Lake

Springdale
Fayetteville

Bull Shoals
Lake

Norfork
Lake

TENN.

A

Pampa

Tulsa

Jonesboro

Amarillo

Clinton

OKLAHOMA

Muskogee

BOSTON MOUNTAINS
Greers Ferry Lake

ARKANSAS

Memphis

35°

Oklahoma
City
Norman

Fort
Smith

Conway

Little
Rock

Altus · Lawton

McAlester

OUACHITA MOUNTAINS

Hot Springs

LLANO
ESTACADO

Lubbock

Ardmore

Lake
Texoma

Red

Lake
Quachita

Pine Bluff

Sweetwater

Wichita
Falls

Lake
Kemp

Sherman
Denton

Paris

Texarkana

Millwood
Lake

Wright Patman
Lake

El Dorado

Arkansas

MISSISSIPPI

B

Abilene

Fort
Worth

Dallas

Lake
o' the Pines
Longview · Marshall

Shreveport

Monroe

Jackson

Midland
Odessa

Big
Spring

San
Angelo

TEXAS

Brownwood · Waco

Corsicana

Tyler

Nacogdoches

Toledo Bend
Reservoir

Pecos

Pecos

Killeen

Colorado

Lufkin

Alexandria

Mount Livermore
79 ft.

EDWARDS

Temple

Trinity

Neches

LOUISIANA

Baton Rouge

STOCKTON
PLATEAU

PLATEAU

Huntsville

Brazos

Bryan

Lake
Livingston

Sabine

Lake
Charles

Opelousas
Lafayette

Atchafalaya

Lake
Pontchartrain

30°

Alpine

Austin

Conroe

Beaumont

New
Iberia

Morgan City

New
Orleans

BIG BEND
NATIONAL PARK

Amistad
Reservoir

San
Marcos

Houston

Port Arthur
Baytown

Intracoastal Waterway

Atchafalaya Bay

Houma

Del Rio

Texas City
Galveston

Galveston Bay

MISSISSIPPI
DELTA

Eagle
Pass

Rio Grande

San Antonio

Victoria

Matagorda Bay

Gulf

N

Nueces

W   E

of

S

Laredo

Kingsville

Mexico

C

Nuevo
Laredo

Falcon
Reservoir

PADRE ISLAND

MEXICO

Laguna Madre

McAllen

Harlingen

Reynosa

Brownsville

South Central Region Political Map

Matamoros

⊛ State capital

■ City over 1,000,000

▣ City 250,000–1,000,000

• City under 250,000

—— State boundary

━━ Country boundary

0   100   200 Miles

0   100   200   300 Kilometers

2 100° **3** 90°

The low, flat wetlands of southern Louisiana are home to many different types of birds and animals. This photo shows a roseate spoonbill.

The People of the South Central

Most of the people in the South Central Region live in the eastern and central parts. The population thins out in the west, where the climate is drier. As you can tell from the bar graph, Texas is by far the largest state in the region in population. It has more people than the other three states combined. In fact, Texas has more people than any other state in the country except California.

Comparing State Populations

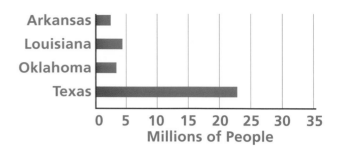

Climate Map

- ⬛ Tropical - hot and rainy
- ⬜ Dry - very little rain
- ⬛ Moderate - warm summer and mild rainy winter
- ⬛ Continental - mild summer and snowy winter
- ⬛ Highlands - varies with altitude
- ▬ Region boundary

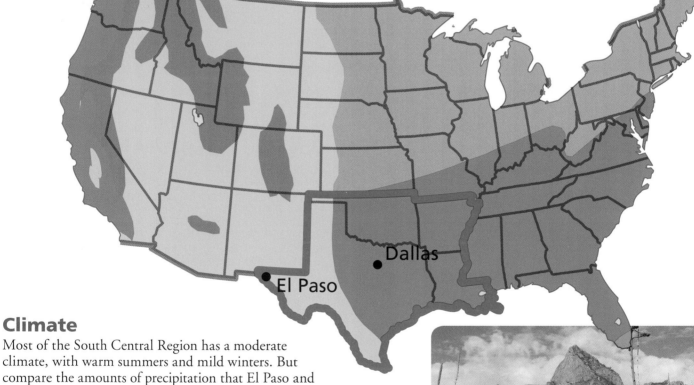

Dallas

El Paso

Climate

Most of the South Central Region has a moderate climate, with warm summers and mild winters. But compare the amounts of precipitation that El Paso and Dallas receive. As you can see, the western part of the region has a much drier climate. This affects how the land is used.

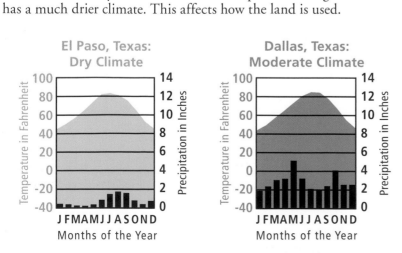

El Paso, Texas: Dry Climate

Dallas, Texas: Moderate Climate

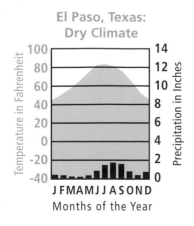

Only desert plants grow in this dry landscape in western Texas.

Working in the South Central Region

A few types of economic activity are especially important in this region. Can you tell what they are by looking at the economies map? Many of the people work in agriculture, stock raising, or businesses related to petroleum or natural gas.

Much of the region's land is used for agriculture. In the drier parts of the region, instead of farming, the land is used for raising livestock, such as cattle and sheep. That is because grazing animals don't need as much water as crops do.

On a rice farm in eastern Arkansas, huge grain silos tower above flooded fields. Arkansas leads the United States in rice production.

©Rand McNally
N-FOR24072-N1-·-1-1-1

Economies Map

Land Use

- Agriculture
- Fishing
- Forestry
- Manufacturing
- Stock raising

Economic Activity

- Cattle
- Chemicals
- Cotton
- Electronics
- Natural gas
- Petroleum
- Poultry
- Rice
- Sheep
- Sugar cane
- Vegetables
- Wheat

Gulf of Mexico

Raising livestock is an important economic activity in Texas and Oklahoma.

Land

As you move west through the South Central Region, the land rises in a series of steps. The Great Plains in western Texas and Oklahoma are several thousand feet higher than the land near the Mississippi River and the Gulf of Mexico.

Alligators and crawfish live in the bayous of Louisiana.

Swamps and bayous cover much of southern Louisiana.

Canoeing, hiking, and other types of outdoor recreation are popular in the mountains of northwestern Arkansas.

The western half of this region is far more rugged than the eastern half. This photo is from Big Bend National Park in western Texas.

Riches of the Earth

Deposits of oil, or petroleum, are found across the South Central Region. From these deposits, oil companies produce about one-quarter of the oil the country uses.

Petroleum formed from ancient plants and animals that lived in the sea millions of years ago. When these living things died, they settled into the mud and sand on the seafloor. Over time, the ooze pressed into rock, and the living matter became petroleum. The word petroleum means "rock oil."

Today, petroleum is often found within layers of sandstone on coastal plains and along coasts. However, it is also found in areas once covered by seas but now located far inland, such as central Texas and central Oklahoma.

Looking like giant grasshoppers, oil pumps are found everywhere you look in the South Central Region, even in some urban areas.

Map of the South Central Oil Fields

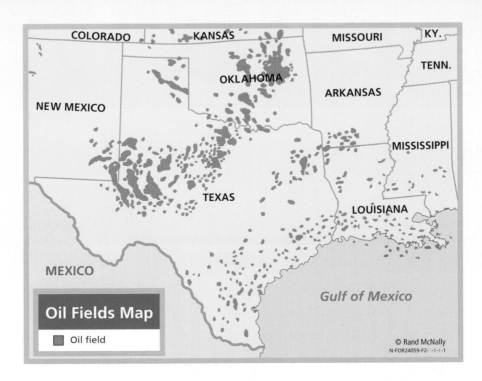

Oil Fields Map
- Oil field

© Rand McNally
N-FOR24059-F2-·-1-1-1

Looking at the Southwest Region

The Southwest Region is the largest region in both land area and population. This region stretches from the Great Plains in the east to the Pacific Ocean in the west. In between are high mountains, rugged canyonlands, barren deserts, and areas of rich farmland. In recent decades, the population has boomed in many parts of the region. It is home to 53 million people. That means that one out of every six people in the United States lives in the Southwest! Some of the cities in this region are very large. As you can see on the map, most of these cities are located in the coastal areas of California.

Much of this region has a Spanish flavor, which dates back to the colonial days when Spain controlled the area. If you study the map, you can see that many towns and cities have Spanish names, like Santa Fe, Los Angeles, and Las Vegas.

Los Angeles is the largest city in the Southwest Region.

The California poppy flourishes in dry climates. It is the state flower of California.

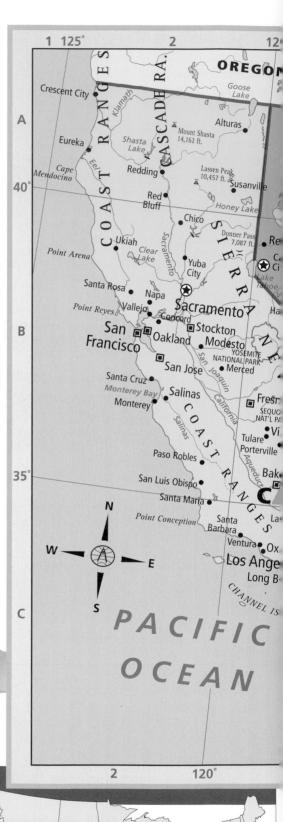

States of the Southwest Region

State	Land Area (square miles)	Population	Capital
Arizona	113,594	6,392,017	Phoenix
California	155,799	37,253,956	Sacramento
Colorado	103,642	5,029,196	Denver
Nevada	109,781	2,700,551	Carson City
New Mexico	121,298	2,059,179	Santa Fe
Utah	82,169	2,763,885	Salt Lake City

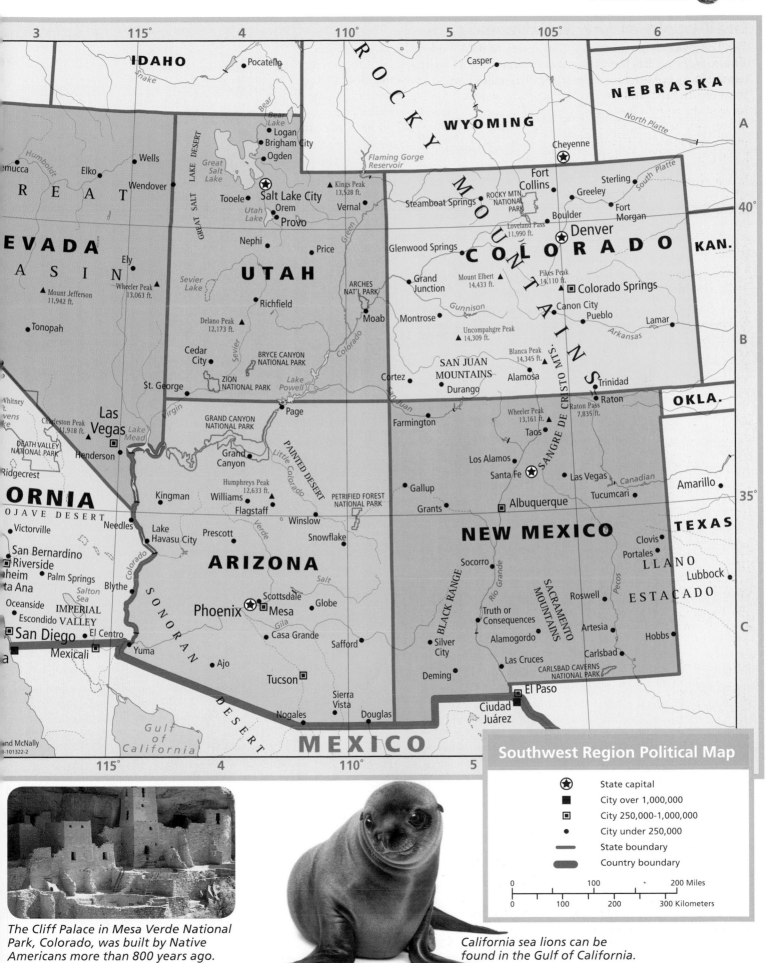

3 115° 4 110° 5 105° 6

IDAHO
• Pocatello

ROCKY

WYOMING
Casper •

NEBRASKA

North Platte

A

Snake

Bear

Bear
Lake

Flaming Gorge
Reservoir

Cheyenne ☆

Fort
Collins

Sterling •

South Platte

mucca
Elko •

Wells •

• Logan
• Brigham City
• Ogden

Great Salt
Lake

Steamboat
Springs

ROCKY MTN.
NATIONAL
PARK

Greeley •
Boulder •

• Fort
Morgan

40°

Humboldt

Wendover •

Kings Peak
13,528 ft. ▲

Glenwood Springs

Loveland Pass
11,990 ft.

• Denver

EVADA

Tooele •
☆ Salt Lake City
• Orem
• Provo

Great Salt Lake Desert

Utah
Lake

Vernal •

COLORADO

KAN.

Ely •

Nephi •

• Price

Green

MOUNTAINS

Grand
Junction

Mount Elbert
14,433 ft.

Pikes Peak
14,110 ft.

ASIN

Wheeler Peak
13,063 ft. ▲

UTAH

Sevier
Lake

ARCHES
NAT'L PARK

Gunnison

• Canon City

Pueblo •

■ Colorado Springs

▲ Mount Jefferson
11,942 ft.

Delano Peak
12,173 ft. ▲

Richfield •

Moab •

Montrose •

Uncompahgre Peak
▲ 14,309 ft.

Lamar •

Arkansas

• Tonopah

Cedar
City •

Sevier

BRYCE CANYON
NATIONAL PARK

Colorado

Cortez •

SAN JUAN
MOUNTAINS

Blanca Peak
14,345 ft. ▲

Alamosa •

SANGRE DE CRISTO MTS.

B

St. George •

ZION
NATIONAL PARK

Lake
Powell

• Durango

• Trinidad

Whitney
t.

Charleston Peak
11,918 ft. ▲

Page •

San Juan

Farmington •

Wheeler Peak
13,161 ft. ▲

Raton Pass
7,835 ft.

OKLA.

vens
ke

Las
Vegas

Virgin

GRAND CANYON
NATIONAL PARK

Little Colorado

• Raton

DEATH VALLEY
NATIONAL PARK

Lake
Mead

Taos •

PAINTED DESERT

Los Alamos •

☆

Ridgecrest

Henderson •

Grand
Canyon

Humphreys Peak
12,633 ft. ▲

PETRIFIED FOREST
NATIONAL PARK

• Gallup

Santa Fe ☆

• Las Vegas

Canadian

Amarillo •

35°

ORNIA

OJAVE DESERT

Kingman •

Williams •

Grants •

■ Albuquerque

Tucumcari •

Flagstaff •

Winslow •

NEW MEXICO

TEXAS

• Victorville

Needles •

Lake
Havasu City

Prescott •

Verde

Snowflake •

Clovis •

Portales •

LLANO

• Lubbock

San Bernardino ■
■ Riverside

Blythe •

ARIZONA

Socorro •

Roswell •

ESTACADO

heim
ta Ana

• Palm Springs

Salton
Sea

Salt

Rio Grande

SACRAMENTO
MOUNTAINS

Pecos

• Oceanside

IMPERIAL
VALLEY
Escondido •

Phoenix ☆
Scottsdale
■ Mesa

Globe •

BLACK RANGE

Truth or
Consequences •

Artesia •

Hobbs •

C

■ San Diego

• El Centro

Gila

Casa Grande •

Safford •

• Silver
City

Alamogordo •

Carlsbad •

a

• Mexicali

Yuma •

SONORAN

• Ajo

Tucson ■

Deming •

Las Cruces •

CARLSBAD CAVERNS
NATIONAL PARK

DESERT

Sierra
Vista

■ El Paso

Nogales •

Douglas •

■ Ciudad
Juárez

nd McNally
-101322-2

Gulf
of
California

MEXICO

115° 4 110° 5

The Cliff Palace in Mesa Verde National Park, Colorado, was built by Native Americans more than 800 years ago.

California sea lions can be found in the Gulf of California.

The People of the Southwest

California has by far the largest population of all the states in the Southwest Region. In fact, with more than 35 million people, California has the largest population of all the 50 states.

The five other states in the region have relatively small populations. All five rank among the least densely populated states in the nation. Population tends to be concentrated in urban centers, many of which are separated by large stretches of open space.

Comparing State Populations

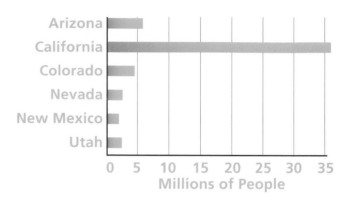

Climate Map

- Tropical - hot and rainy
- Dry - very little rain
- Moderate - warm summer and mild rainy winter
- Continental - mild summer and snowy winter
- Highlands - varies with altitude
- Region boundary

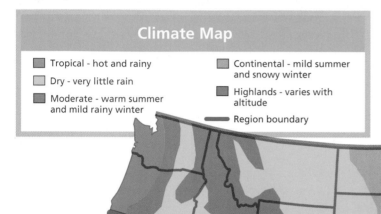

Climate

Hot sun and dry conditions give the Southwest a distinct character. Most of the region gets less than 10 inches of rain per year. But look at the climate graphs for Los Angeles and Boulder. As you can see, their climates are milder. Look at their locations. California is located on the Pacific Ocean, where moist, cool air blows in to air condition the land. Boulder is located in a mountainous area. There, temperatures get cooler as the elevation gets higher.

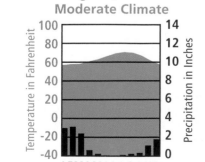

DID YOU KNOW?

Because of the dry climate, lack of water is a growing problem.

Los Angeles, California: Moderate Climate

Las Vegas, Nevada: Dry Climate

Boulder, Colorado: Highlands Climate

Working in the Southwest Region

The work that people do in the Southwest Region is related to the land and climate patterns. You can see that forestry occurs in the mountainous areas. Now look at the climate map and the economies map. Stock raising takes place in the driest areas. Crops are grown only where farmers can irrigate in this dry region. Where that is not possible, the land can only be used for grazing.

Peaches are grown in central California.

Las Vegas is Nevada's economic center and largest city.

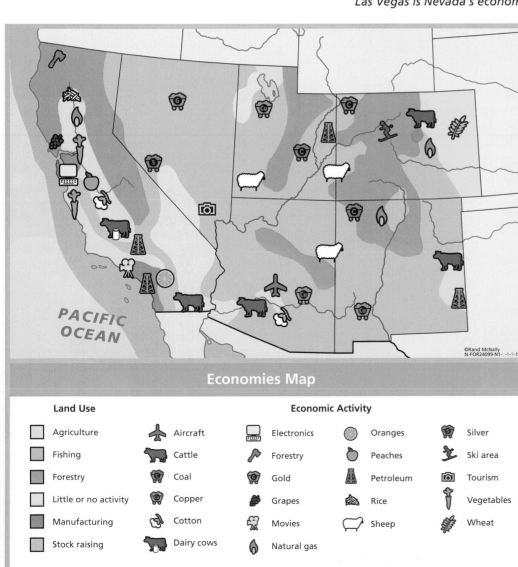

©Rand McNally
N-FOR24099-N1-|-1-1-1

Economies Map

Land Use

☐	Agriculture
☐	Fishing
☐	Forestry
☐	Little or no activity
☐	Manufacturing
☐	Stock raising

Economic Activity

✈ Aircraft	💻 Electronics	🍊 Oranges	Ⓢ Silver
🐂 Cattle	🍄 Forestry	🍑 Peaches	⛷ Ski area
Ⓒ Coal	Ⓖ Gold	🛢 Petroleum	📷 Tourism
Ⓠ Copper	🍇 Grapes	🌾 Rice	🥕 Vegetables
🐏 Cotton	🎬 Movies	🐑 Sheep	🌿 Wheat
🐄 Dairy cows	🔥 Natural gas		

In the San Joaquin Valley in central California, irrigation canals make it possible to grow vegetables of all kinds in a dry area.

Land

Physical features make the Southwest different from other regions. Most of the region lies between two great mountain ranges: the Rocky Mountains in the east and the Sierra Nevada in the west. In between them lie the Great Basin and the Colorado Plateau. The Colorado Plateau has been eroded by wind and water into strange shapes. Deep canyons, like the Grand Canyon, were carved out by racing rivers.

Snowy peaks of the Rocky Mountains soar above a colorful valley in Colorado.

Rock formations called "hoodoos" rise majestically in Utah's Bryce Canyon National Park.

The Grand Canyon in Arizona was carved by the Colorado River over the course of millions of years.

San Francisco, California, is located on one of the world's finest natural harbors.

Lifeline of a Dry Region

From its source high in the Rocky Mountains, the Colorado River flows southwest for 1,450 miles. It is the major source of water in this desert land. Cities in the Southwest are growing rapidly, so all along the river's length, people tap this precious resource.

They have built canals to carry the water to distant places. The water is used for drinking as well as for making electricity and for irrigation. Irrigation allows farmers to grow crops in areas that otherwise would be too dry for farming.

The Colorado River once flowed into the Gulf of California. However, because people now use so much of its water, the river dries to a trickle in the desert miles from the Gulf.

The Colorado River snakes through Horseshoe Bend in Arizona.

Map of the Colorado River

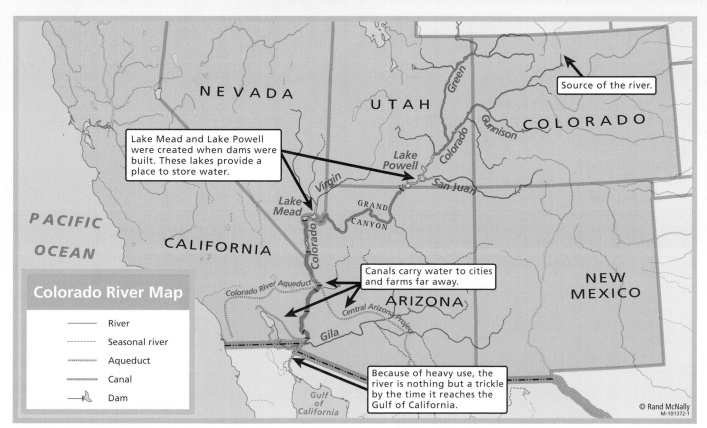

Source of the river.

Lake Mead and Lake Powell were created when dams were built. These lakes provide a place to store water.

Canals carry water to cities and farms far away.

Because of heavy use, the river is nothing but a trickle by the time it reaches the Gulf of California.

Colorado River Map

— River
----- Seasonal river
········· Aqueduct
▬▬▬ Canal
⊣ Dam

© Rand McNally
M-101372-1

Looking at the Northwest Region

The Northwest Region, like the Southwest Region, extends from the Great Plains in the east to the Pacific Ocean in the west. Much of the land is mountainous and thinly populated. Many of the region's people live near its western edge, between the Pacific Ocean and the Cascade Mountain Range.

The population of the entire Northwest Region—close to 14 million people—is less than the urban area population of Los Angeles, California. The region's largest city is Seattle, Washington. With a location on the Pacific Ocean, Seattle is an important port city. Over the last 50 years, trade across the Pacific Rim has increased. Goods move in and out of Seattle's busy harbor every day.

The Grand Teton Mountains were sculpted by glaciers and rise up like jagged peaks in western Wyoming.

DID YOU KNOW?

The city of Seattle, Washington, sits in the shadow of Mount Rainier, a volcano that last erupted in the 1840s.

Evergreen trees are abundant in the Northwest.

States of the Northwest Region

State	Land Area (square miles)	Population	Capital
Idaho	82,643	1,567,582	Boise
Montana	145,546	989,415	Helena
Oregon	95,988	3,831,074	Salem
Washington	66,455	6,724,540	Olympia
Wyoming	97,093	563,626	Cheyenne

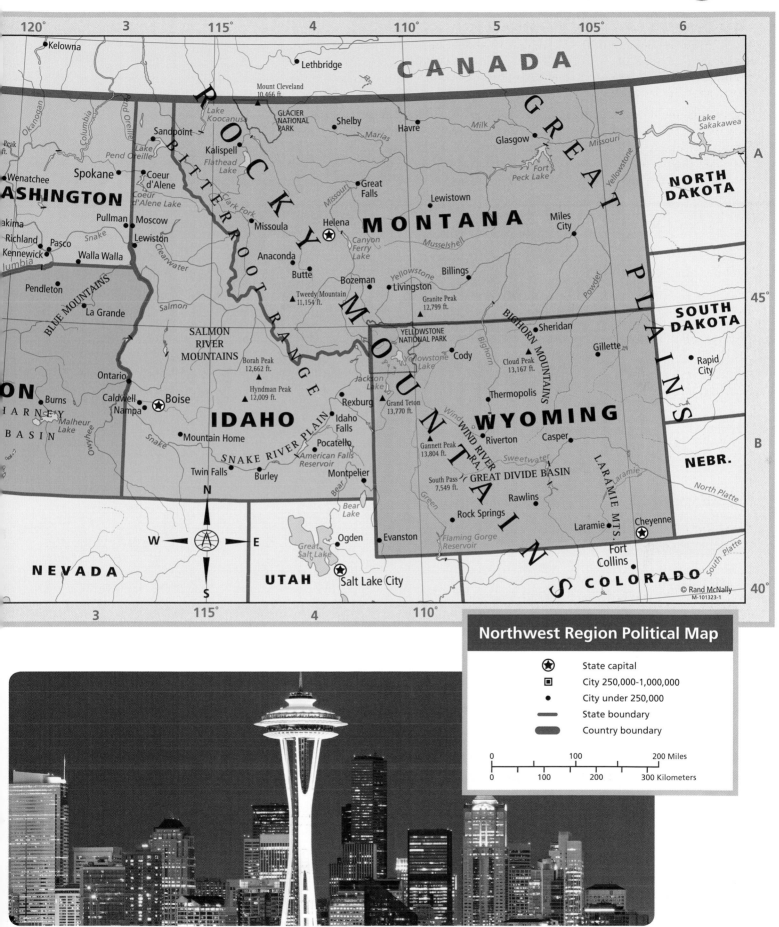

120° 3 115° 4 110° 5 105° 6

Kelowna

CANADA

Lethbridge

Mount Cleveland
10,466 ft.

GLACIER
NATIONAL
PARK

Lake
Koocanusa

Shelby

Havre

Milk

Glasgow

Fort
Peck Lake

Missouri

Lake
Sakakawea

NORTH
DAKOTA

A

Peak
ft.

Okanogan

Columbia

Pend Oreille

Sandpoint

ROCKY

BITTERROOT

Kalispell

Flathead
Lake

Great
Falls

Missouri

Marias

Lewistown

Miles
City

Yellowstone

WENATCHEE

Spokane

Coeur
d'Alene

Coeur
d'Alene Lake

Clark Fork

Missoula

Helena

MONTANA

Canyon
Ferry
Lake

Musselshell

ASHINGTON

akima

Richland

Kennewick

lumbia

Pullman

Moscow

Lewiston

Snake

Clearwater

Walla Walla

Anaconda

Butte

Tweedy Mountain
11,154 ft.

Bozeman

Livingston

Yellowstone

Billings

Granite Peak
12,799 ft.

RANGE

Powder

45°

SOUTH
DAKOTA

Pendleton

BLUE MOUNTAINS

La Grande

Salmon

SALMON
RIVER
MOUNTAINS

MOUNTAINS

YELLOWSTONE
NATIONAL PARK

Yellowstone
Lake

Cody

Bighorn

BIGHORN

MOUNTAINS

Sheridan

Cloud Peak
13,167 ft.

Gillette

Rapid
City

ON

Burns

ARNEY

BASIN

Malheur
Lake

Ontario

Owyhee

Borah Peak
12,662 ft.

Hyndman Peak
12,009 ft.

Caldwell

Nampa

Boise

Snake

IDAHO

Mountain Home

Jackson
Lake

Rexburg

Idaho
Falls

Grand Teton
13,770 ft.

Thermopolis

WYOMING

Gannett Peak
13,804 ft.

Riverton

Casper

WIND RIVER

RA.

Windriver

LARAMIE MTS.

Laramie

B

NEBR.

North Platte

SNAKE RIVER PLAIN

American Falls
Reservoir

Pocatello

Montpelier

South Pass
7,549 ft.

GREAT DIVIDE BASIN

Sweetwater

Green

Rawlins

Laramie

Cheyenne

Twin Falls

Burley

Bear

N

W E

S

Bear
Lake

Rock Springs

Flaming Gorge
Reservoir

Fort
Collins

South Platte

NEVADA

Great
Salt Lake

UTAH

Ogden

Salt Lake City

Evanston

COLORADO

© Rand McNally
M-101323-1

40°

3 115° 4 110°

Northwest Region Political Map

- ⊛ State capital
- ▣ City 250,000–1,000,000
- • City under 250,000
- ▬ State boundary
- ▬ Country boundary

0 100 200 Miles
0 100 200 300 Kilometers

Seattle, Washington, is a technology center and an important trading partner with nations across the Pacific Ocean.

The People of the Northwest

The region's two largest cities—Seattle and Portland—are located near the western edge of the Northwest Region. Most of the area east of the Cascades if more thinly populated. For example, Montana and Wyoming both rank among the 10 largest states in our country in land area, but they rank among the 10 smallest in population.

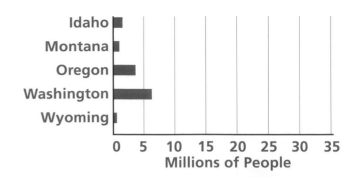

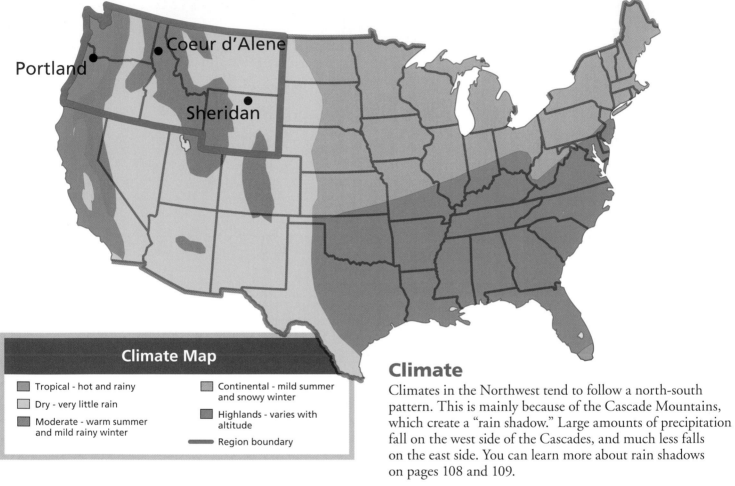

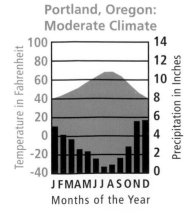

Climate Map

- Tropical - hot and rainy
- Dry - very little rain
- Moderate - warm summer and mild rainy winter
- Continental - mild summer and snowy winter
- Highlands - varies with altitude
- Region boundary

Climate

Climates in the Northwest tend to follow a north-south pattern. This is mainly because of the Cascade Mountains, which create a "rain shadow." Large amounts of precipitation fall on the west side of the Cascades, and much less falls on the east side. You can learn more about rain shadows on pages 108 and 109.

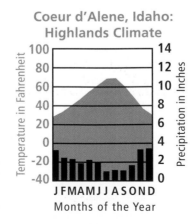

Portland, Oregon:
Moderate Climate

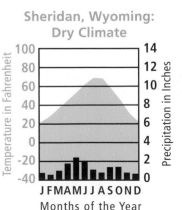

Coeur d'Alene, Idaho:
Highlands Climate

Sheridan, Wyoming:
Dry Climate

Working in the Northwest Region

Compare the economies map below to the climate map on page 106. As you can see, stock raising takes place in the Northwest Region's driest areas, and forestry is important in its mountainous areas.

On the rolling land of eastern Washington, farms produce large amounts of wheat, barley, lentils, and peas.

Loggers use large equipment to move conifer trees in a log yard in Oregon.

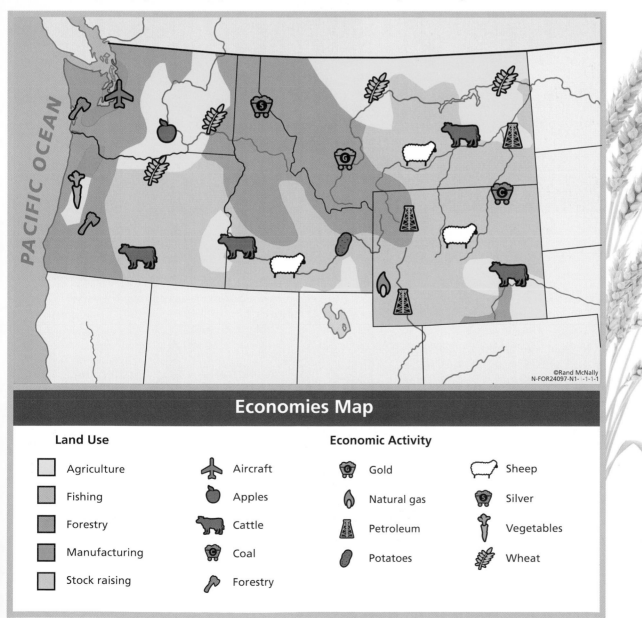

Economies Map

Land Use

- Agriculture
- Fishing
- Forestry
- Manufacturing
- Stock raising

- ✈ Aircraft
- 🍎 Apples
- 🐄 Cattle
- Ⓒ Coal
- 🪓 Forestry

Economic Activity

- Ⓖ Gold
- 🔥 Natural gas
- Petroleum
- Potatoes

- 🐑 Sheep
- Ⓢ Silver
- Vegetables
- 🌾 Wheat

©Rand McNally
N-FOR24097-N1- -1-1-1

Land

Mountains are a major land feature in the Northwest Region. The Rocky Mountains cross the center of the region and the Cascade Range rises in the west. Between them lies the Columbia Plateau, where the land is lower, flatter, and drier. East of the Rockies, the land opens up into the Great Plains. This is known as Big Sky Country, where the whole expanse of the sky can be seen in any direction.

Oregon's Crater Lake lies in the crater of a dormant volcano.

Ice-chiseled peaks soar skyward in Montana's Glacier National Park.

Some of the richest agricultural land in the United States is found along the Snake River in Idaho. This photo shows rows of potato plants.

The Rain Shadow Effect

Mountains play a big part in shaping rainfall patterns in the Northwest Region. The mountains of the Cascade Range, the Coast Ranges, and the Olympic Mountains act like huge walls. Moist air blowing off the Pacific Ocean hits the "walls" and is forced upward. When air rises, it cools. Cool air cannot hold as much moisture as warmer air, so all that moisture falls to earth on the western side of the mountains as rain or snow. That leaves the other side of the mountains in a rain shadow, a region that gets very little rain.

South of this region, the Sierra Nevada and Coast Ranges of California also create a rain shadow. This explains why much of the western United States has a dry climate.

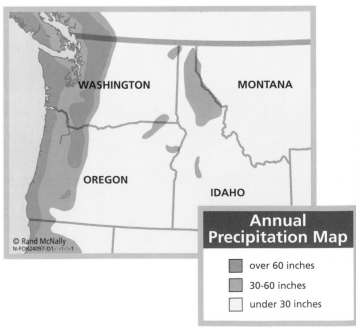

WASHINGTON

MONTANA

OREGON

IDAHO

© Rand McNally
N-FOR24097-D1- -1-1-1

Annual Precipitation Map

over 60 inches

30-60 inches

under 30 inches

A lush rain forest grows in Olympic National Park, Washington, on the western side of the Olympic Mountains.

This arid landscape in eastern Oregon shows the effect of the rain shadow.

Diagram of the Rain Shadow Effect

Direction of prevailing winds

Moist air

Dry air

Jagged mountains rise above a glacier and a valley filled with wildflowers in southeastern Alaska. Much of Alaska is pristine wilderness.

Alaska

Alaska lies hundreds of miles northwest of the lower 48 states. It is by far the largest of the 50 states. From its easternmost point to its westernmost point, in the Aleutian Islands, Alaska stretches about 2,400 miles. That is about the same as the distance between New York City and San Francisco.

Look at Alaska's location on the map. You can see that it is closer to Russia than it is to the rest of the United States. Flying from its capital city, Juneau, to Seattle, Washington, the nearest city in the lower 48 states, would take about four hours!

Because of its cold climate, it has a smaller population than all but three other states. Most Alaskans live in the southern part of the state. Alaska's landforms include broad plains, vast plateaus, and long mountain ranges.

Fireweed

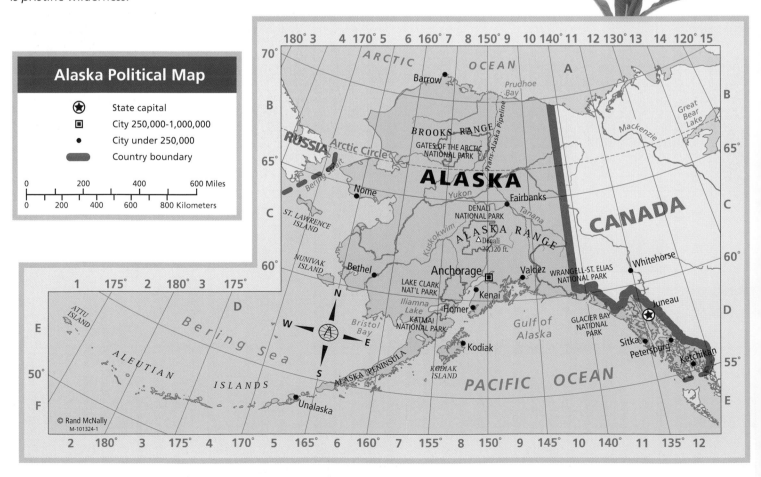

Alaska Political Map

- ⭐ State capital
- ▣ City 250,000–1,000,000
- • City under 250,000
- ▬ Country boundary

0 200 400 600 Miles
0 200 400 600 800 Kilometers

© Rand McNally
M-101324-1

Anchorage is Alaska's most populous city with more than one-third of Alaska's people.

The People of Alaska

With about 700,000 people, Alaska is the fourth smallest state in population. Comparing its population and area, Alaska has a population density of less than two people per square mile! Most Alaskans live near Anchorage, the largest city, located in the southern part of the state. Study the climate graphs below to find out why. As you can see, Anchorage has much milder temperatures than Barrow and is far less rainy than Juneau.

Climate Map

- Moderate - warm summer and mild rainy winter
- Polar - cold and dry
- Continental - mild summer and snowy winter

Climate

Three different climates are found in Alaska. The northern third of the state has a polar climate, with cold temperatures and little precipitation. Most of the rest of the state has a continental climate and is not as cold or dry. Southern Alaska is warmer because of its latitude and the warming effect of the ocean. The "panhandle," where Juneau is located, has a moderate climate but much greater rainfall than the rest of the state.

Barrow, Alaska: Polar Climate

Anchorage, Alaska: Continental Climate

Juneau, Alaska: Moderate Climate

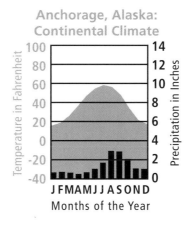

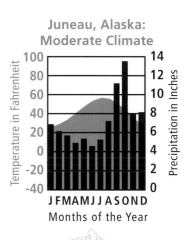

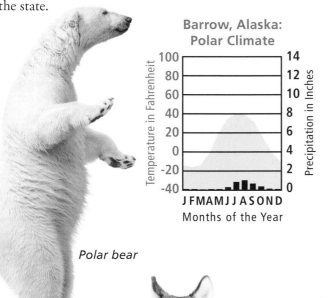

Polar bear

The Alaskan Malamute is a popular sledding dog in Alaska.

CANADA

Alaska

State	Land Area (square miles)	Population	Capital
Alaska	570,641	710,231	Juneau

Working in Alaska

Because of its location on the Pacific Rim, Anchorage has become a transportation hub. Ships and planes from all over the world stop in Anchorage to refuel. As you can see on the economies map, hunting and fishing are the main economic activities over much of the state. Many Native Americans make their homes in Alaska. Their lifestyles fit their environment. They hunt seals and whales for food, depending on the season. Petroleum and natural gas production are important economic activities in the northernmost part of the state.

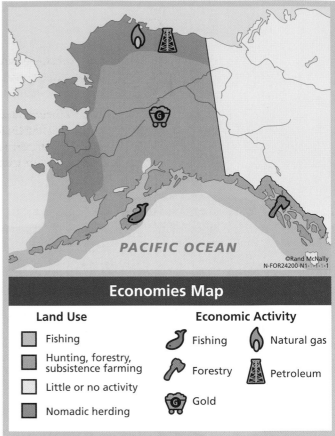

Soaring to 20,320 feet, Alaska's Denali is the highest peak in North America.

Land

Several mountain ranges tower over the Alaskan landscape. The highest mountains are found in the Alaska Range. This range was created over millions of years as two of the earth's tectonic plates crashed together in a slow-motion collision and forced the crust upward. Denali, rising nearly four miles into the sky, is the highest peak in North America.

Between Alaska's mountain ranges are vast plains and plateaus. North of the Brooks Range is a coastal lowland that is home to huge herds of caribou.

The mountainous Aleutian Islands extend in a long arc from the southwestern tip of the mainland.

DID YOU KNOW?

Alaska has more than 40 active volcanoes.

Economies Map

Land Use
- Fishing
- Hunting, forestry, subsistence farming
- Little or no activity
- Nomadic herding

Economic Activity
- Fishing
- Forestry
- Gold
- Natural gas
- Petroleum

PACIFIC OCEAN

©Rand McNally
N-FOR24200-N1-1-1-1

North of the Brooks Range lies a coastal lowland that is home to enormous herds of caribou.

Volcanic Islands

Like fireworks from the earth, volcanoes sometimes erupt in Alaska's Aleutian Islands. Earthquakes frequently shake the ground. This is because the islands are located along the tectonically active Ring of Fire.

Compare the physical map of Alaska on page 54 to the plate tectonics map on page 39. As you can see, the Aleutians line up along the boundary where the Pacific Plate rams under the North American Plate.

The diagram below shows how the edge of the Pacific Plate is forced downward. When that happens, pressure and friction cause magma to rise to the surface. Over time, eruptions of magma formed many of the islands in the Aleutian chain. These islands are really volcanoes that rise from the ocean floor. More than a dozen of the volcanoes have erupted in the past 100 years.

Flying over the Aleutian Islands is like looking down the "throats" of live volcanoes. Shishaldin Volcano is one of many in a long line of volcanic islands.

Map of the Volcanic Islands of Alaska

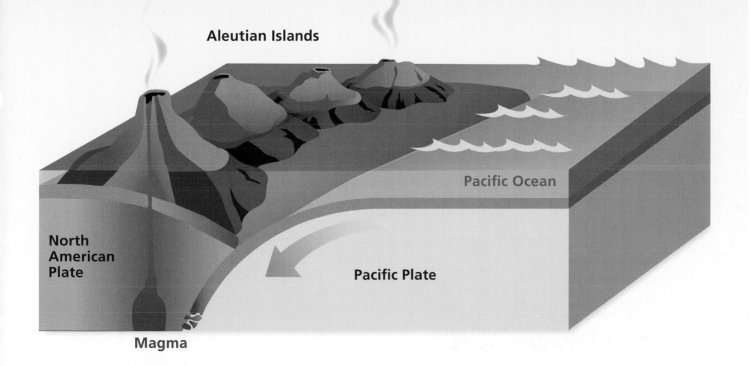

Aleutian Islands

Pacific Ocean

North American Plate

Pacific Plate

Magma

Some people call the island of Kaua'i the most beautiful of all the Hawai'ian Islands.

Hawaii

The island chain that makes up the state of Hawaii is located in the middle of the Pacific Ocean. It is made up of eight main islands, which are shown on the map below, and many smaller ones. The islands are actually the tops of volcanic mountains that rise from the ocean floor. Some of the volcanoes are still active.

Most of the islands have steep, forested mountains and lush, green valleys. On some islands there are brownish-black lava fields that look like huge rivers of spilled chocolate. Beaches ring the islands. Some are long expanses of white sand. Some are black sand made of ground-up lava. Because of Hawaii's warm, sunny climate, its beaches, and its spectacular scenery, the state is a popular destination for tourists from other states and from all over the world.

DID YOU KNOW?

Hawaii is the southernmost of the 50 states, and it is also the newest state. It did not become a state until 1959.

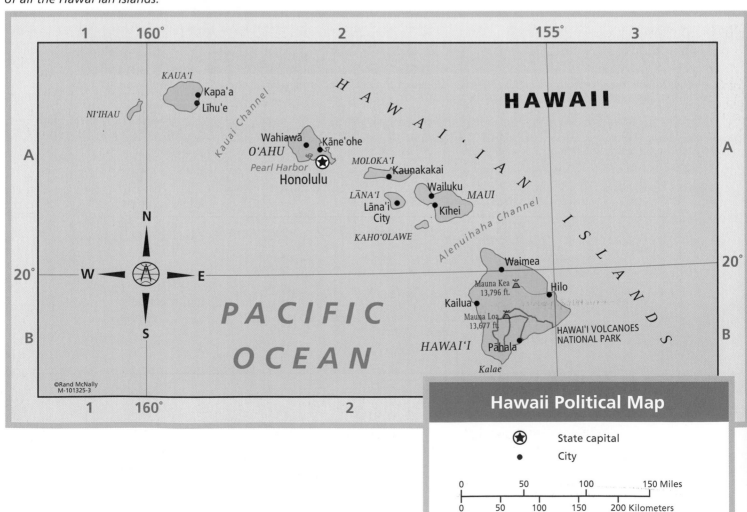

Hawaii Political Map

⭐ State capital

• City

0 50 100 150 Miles

0 50 100 150 200 Kilometers

Honolulu is Hawaii's capital and main port. It is the most populous city, with more than 400,000 people! It stretches for about 10 miles along the coast of O'ahu.

The People of Hawaii

Hawaii is like a stepping stone in the middle of a big sea. For this reason, people have come to Hawaii from places all around the Pacific Ocean—from Japan, China, and Polynesia, to name a few. Many school children in Hawaii today still learn the languages and practice the traditions of their ancestors who came to the islands from far away.

Honolulu, on the island of O'ahu, is the only large city in Hawaii. Population thins out on the other islands, where most people live in small towns.

Climate

Hawaii is located at a latitude where the climate is always warm. The climate is also very rainy. Look at the climate graph for Hilo. This city's monthly rainfall ranges from about 7 inches to more than 14 inches. Mount Waialeale on the island of Kaua'i is the rainiest place in the world. Each year it receives about 460 inches of rainfall—that's more than 38 feet!

Climate Map

◼ Tropical - hot and rainy

Hawaii's pleasant climate is a result of its location in the tropics, the fact that it is surrounded by ocean, and the moderating effect of trade winds.

Thanks to abundant rainfall and mild temperatures, lush vegetation covers much of Hawaii. This rain forest is on the island of Hawai'i.

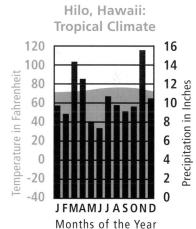

Hilo, Hawaii: Tropical Climate

The tropical yellow hibiscus is the state flower of Hawaii.

State	Land Area (square miles)	Population	Capital
Hawaii	6,423	1,360,301	Honolulu

Hawaii

Working in Hawaii

Hawaii draws tourists by the millions, so many Hawaiians work in the tourism industry. Because rain keeps the islands well-watered, Hawaii is also an important agricultural state. Tropical foods like pineapples and sugar cane are grown in its fertile, volcanic soil.

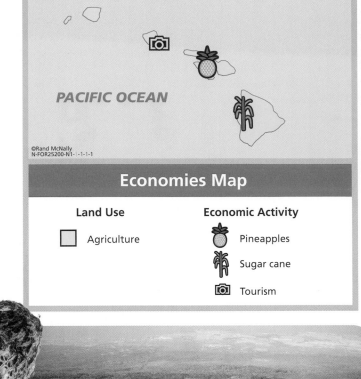

PACIFIC OCEAN

©Rand McNally
N-FOR25200-N1-|-1-1-1

Economies Map

Land Use

☐ Agriculture

Economic Activity

🍍 Pineapples

🎋 Sugar cane

📷 Tourism

Taro fields are a common sight in Hawaii. A staple food for many Hawaiians, taro grows well in areas that receive abundant rainfall.

Land

When you study Hawaii's physical map on page 54, you will notice that the Hawai'ian Islands are very mountainous. Most of the volcanoes are no longer active, but the island of Hawai'i has two volcanoes that continue to erupt: Mauna Loa and Kilauea.

Lava once poured from the craters of Hualalai, a volcano on the island of Hawai'i.

Rugged cliffs rise thousands of feet above the Pacific Ocean along the Na Pali Coast on the island of Kaua'i.

On the island of Hawai'i, lava flowing from Kilauea can close roads forever.

The Hawaiian Hot Spot

The Hawai'ian Islands formed over a hot spot, a vent where magma from the earth's mantle shoots up and melts the crust above it. As the crust of the Pacific Plate slowly moved across the hot spot, volcanoes grew into islands, one at a time. We know this because the islands are in order by age. The oldest island is at the northwest end of the chain, so it formed first.

The youngest is Hawai'i, "the Big Island." It formed last and is the only island that still has active volcanoes. Having moved off the hot spot, the volcanoes on the older islands are now extinct.

Located right over the hot spot, the volcanic Kilauea crater on the island of Hawai'i continues to be one of the most active volcanoes in the world.

Diagram of the Hot Spot

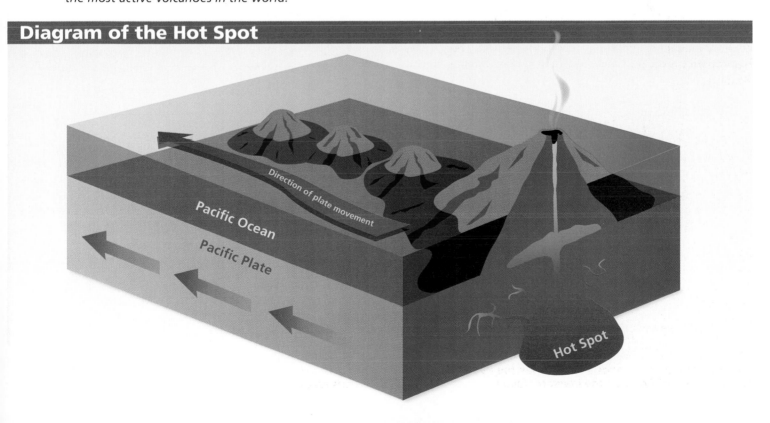

SETTLEMENT OF THE UNITED STATES

Introduction

From its beginning, the United States has grown steadily larger—in both population and land area. The graph below shows the growth of the country's population. Compare it to events on the timeline to see when new lands were acquired.

The maps in this section show some important changes from early in our history to later times. As you look at these maps, you will see that our population is mixed. Native Americans were the first Americans, then came Europeans and Africans, then people from all over the world. But no matter where people came from, their lives were affected by geography. They settled where it was possible to survive and make a living. Landforms, climates, water bodies, and resources affected their choices.

Population Growth of the United States

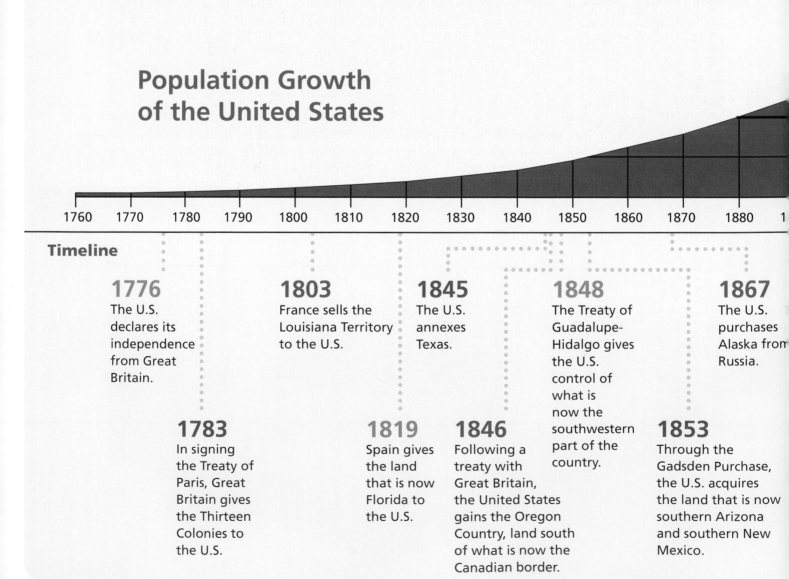

1760 1770 1780 1790 1800 1810 1820 1830 1840 1850 1860 1870 1880 1

Timeline

1776
The U.S. declares its independence from Great Britain.

1783
In signing the Treaty of Paris, Great Britain gives the Thirteen Colonies to the U.S.

1803
France sells the Louisiana Territory to the U.S.

1819
Spain gives the land that is now Florida to the U.S.

1845
The U.S. annexes Texas.

1846
Following a treaty with Great Britain, the United States gains the Oregon Country, land south of what is now the Canadian border.

1848
The Treaty of Guadalupe-Hidalgo gives the U.S. control of what is now the southwestern part of the country.

1853
Through the Gadsden Purchase, the U.S. acquires the land that is now southern Arizona and southern New Mexico.

1867
The U.S. purchases Alaska from Russia.

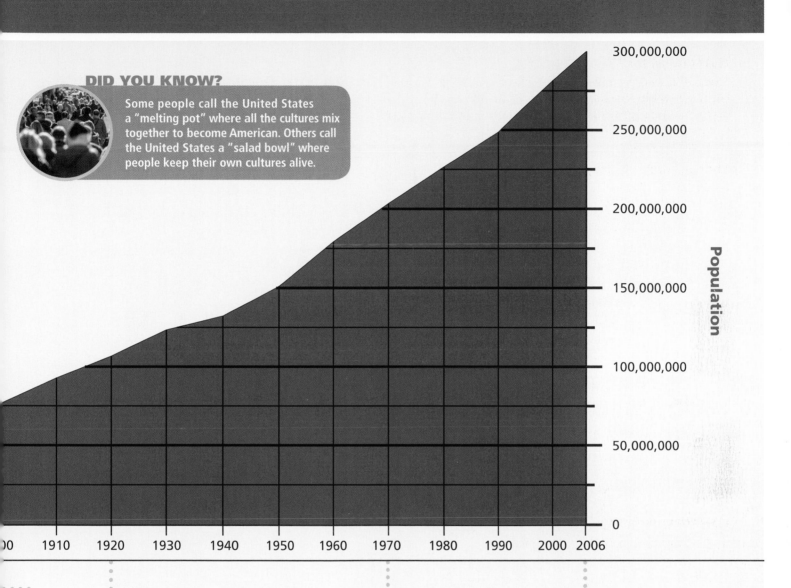

DID YOU KNOW?

Some people call the United States a "melting pot" where all the cultures mix together to become American. Others call the United States a "salad bowl" where people keep their own cultures alive.

Population

300,000,000

250,000,000

200,000,000

150,000,000

100,000,000

50,000,000

0

1910 1920 1930 1940 1950 1960 1970 1980 1990 2000 2006

1898
The U.S. annexes Hawaii.

1920
The population of the U.S. exceeds 100 million.

1970
The population of the U.S. exceeds 200 million.

2006
The population of the U.S. reaches 300 million.

THE FIRST PEOPLE

Native Americans

Native Americans were the first Americans. For thousands of years, they had made their homes in North America. They belonged to many different groups and spoke many different languages. They used the land in different ways, depending on the climate.

Some, like the Apache, spent their lives hunting and making camp in new places in the Southwestern desert. Others, like the Iroquois, who lived in the wooded Northeast, settled in one place for generations.

Native American Homelands

OASIS — Culture area

Blackfoot — Major tribe

Each culture area is shown in a different color.

© Rand McNally
N-FOR20000-V3- -1-1-1

Newcomers Arrive

By 1600, explorers from England, Spain, and France had journeyed to North America. Others followed and formed colonies. Over time, their settlements grew into towns and cities. With a warm, moist climate, the colonies in the southeast became farming regions. Many workers were needed. Africans were brought to the Americas as slaves to work in the fields. They did not come because they wanted to, but because they were forced to.

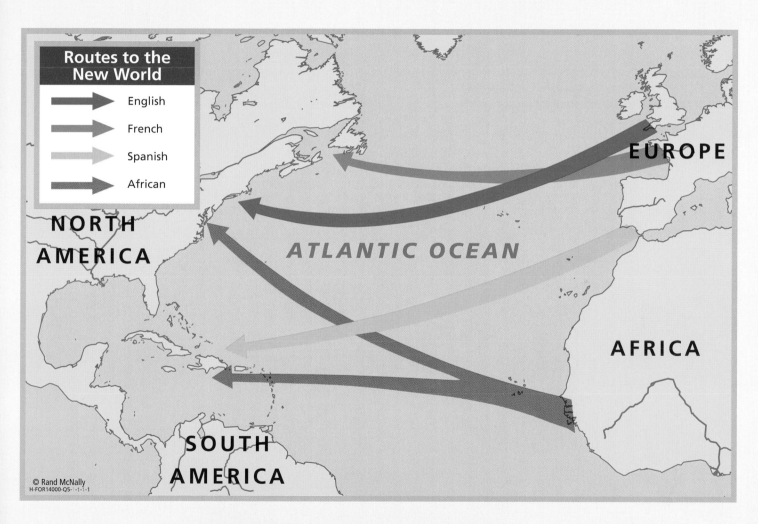

Routes to the New World

English
French
Spanish
African

NORTH AMERICA

ATLANTIC OCEAN

EUROPE

AFRICA

SOUTH AMERICA

© Rand McNally
H-FOR14000-Q5- -1-1-1

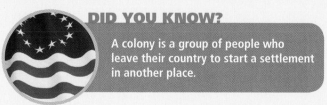

DID YOU KNOW?

A colony is a group of people who leave their country to start a settlement in another place.

THE COUNTRY GROWS

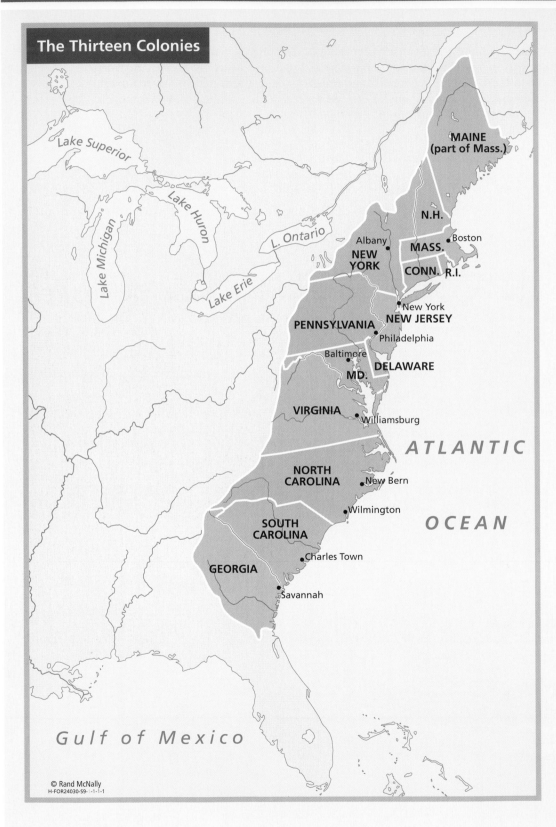

The Thirteen Colonies

The Thirteen Colonies

MAINE
(part of Mass.)

N.H.

Albany
MASS.
Boston

NEW
YORK

CONN. R.I.

New York

PENNSYLVANIA
NEW JERSEY

Philadelphia

Baltimore

DELAWARE

MD.

VIRGINIA

Williamsburg

ATLANTIC

NORTH
CAROLINA
New Bern

Wilmington

OCEAN

SOUTH
CAROLINA

GEORGIA
Charles Town

Savannah

Lake Superior

Lake Michigan

Lake Huron

L. Ontario

Lake Erie

Gulf of Mexico

© Rand McNally
H-FOR24030-S9- -1-1-1

The Thirteen Colonies

The Thirteen Colonies were established in the period from 1607 to 1733. They were ruled by Great Britain, and the first people were British citizens. But the years passed. Three generations of people were born and raised on American soil. The people of these generations had never even seen Britain. They felt more American than they did British. With that strong feeling of patriotism for America, the colonists declared and fought for their own independence. They finally won it in 1783.

The United States Gains Land

In the 1700s and 1800s, the United States grew in land area as well as in population. Some of the territory, like the land between the original Thirteen Colonies and the Mississippi River, was added by treaty with Great Britain. Land in the Southwest was won after fighting a war with Mexico. Some land, like the vast Louisiana Territory, was purchased from France. When that happened, the United States gained full control of the Mississippi River. That meant that Americans could float their crops to the Gulf of Mexico and sell them around the world.

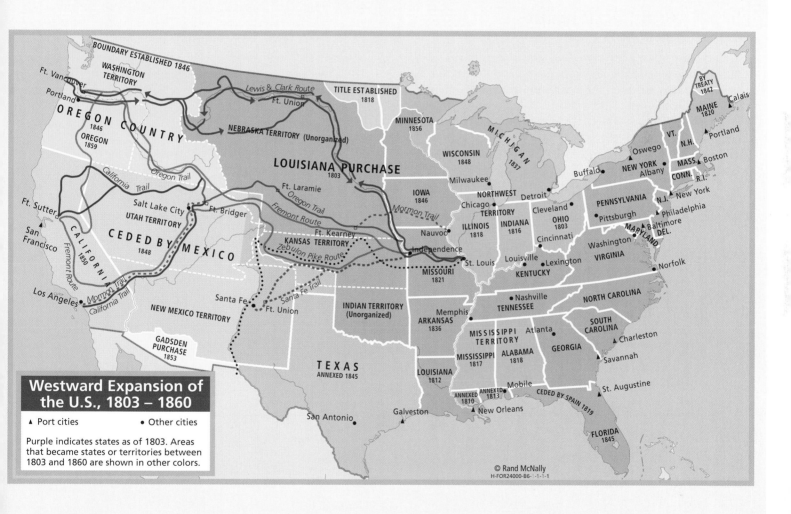

Westward Expansion of the U.S., 1803 – 1860

▲ Port cities   • Other cities

Purple indicates states as of 1803. Areas that became states or territories between 1803 and 1860 are shown in other colors.

© Rand McNally
H-FOR24000-B6- -1-1-1

SETTLEMENT PATTERNS

Early Settlement and Roads

Map A shows settlement at the beginning of the 1800s. Most of the settled area lay between the Atlantic Ocean and the Appalachian Mountains. Roads connecting cities and towns were mud ruts. Traveling the length of what had been the Thirteen Colonies took nearly three months. Most east-west roads ended at the mountains.

Expanding Settlement and New Roads

Map B shows how settlement had spread west of the Appalachians by 1850. The U.S. government ordered roads built. The new roads connected farms to the towns along rivers, so businesses could grow. Canals were built to link the Ohio River and the Great Lakes with the Atlantic Ocean. That opened up a whole new direction of trade and made New York City boom.

Railroads and the Growth of the West

By 1890, railroads stretched across the country, as Map C shows. In the West, "cow towns" formed along the tracks. These were towns where cowboys would drive their herds to be loaded onto trains. People settled in the West in larger numbers. Businesses grew, and that drew even more people.

Map A

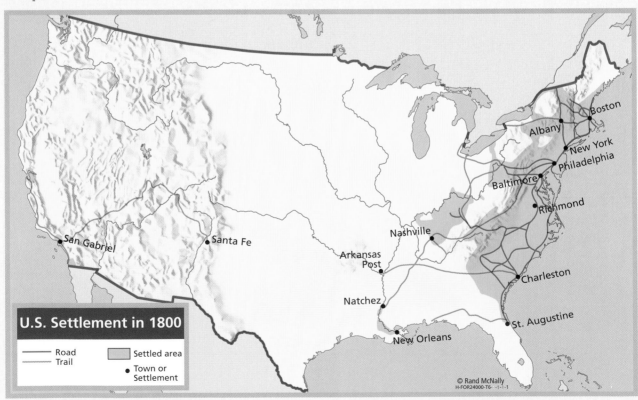

U.S. Settlement in 1800

— Road
— Trail
Settled area
• Town or Settlement

© Rand McNally
H-FOR24000-T6- -1-1-1

Map B

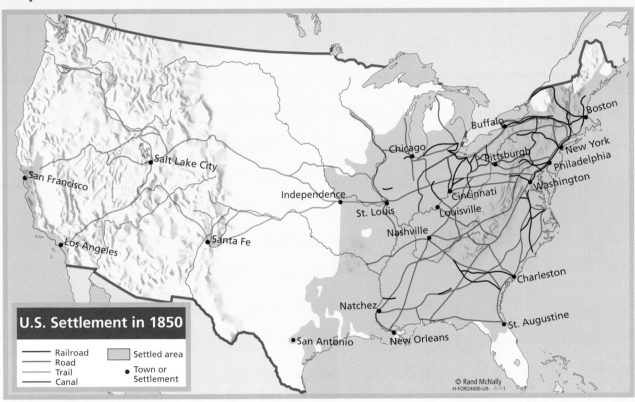

U.S. Settlement in 1850

- Railroad
- Road
- Trail
- Canal
- Settled area
- • Town or Settlement

© Rand McNally
H-FOR24000-U9- -1-1-1

Map C

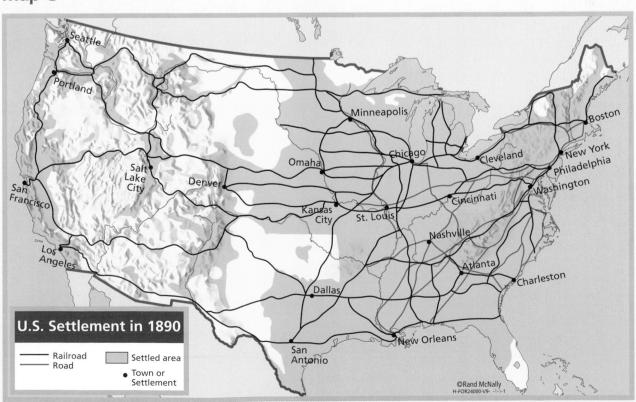

U.S. Settlement in 1890

- Railroad
- Road
- Settled area
- • Town or Settlement

©Rand McNally
H-FOR24000-V9- -1-1-1

WAVES OF IMMIGRATION

A Nation of Immigrants

The United States has always been a nation of immigrants. As Map A shows, a wave of immigration between 1820 and 1870 brought nearly 7 million people from northwestern and central Europe. In the period from 1880 to 1920, more than 20 million new immigrants came from these areas as well as from eastern and southern Europe, as shown on Map B.

Map C shows another large wave of immigrants that arrived in the United States between the 1960s and the 1990s. This time, most of the immigrants were from Asia, South America, Central America, and Mexico. Many of the people from Southeast Asia came to America to escape conflict. For all of these newcomers, America meant freedom and a chance to build better lives.

DID YOU KNOW?

Immigrants are people who move from one country to another to live.

Map A

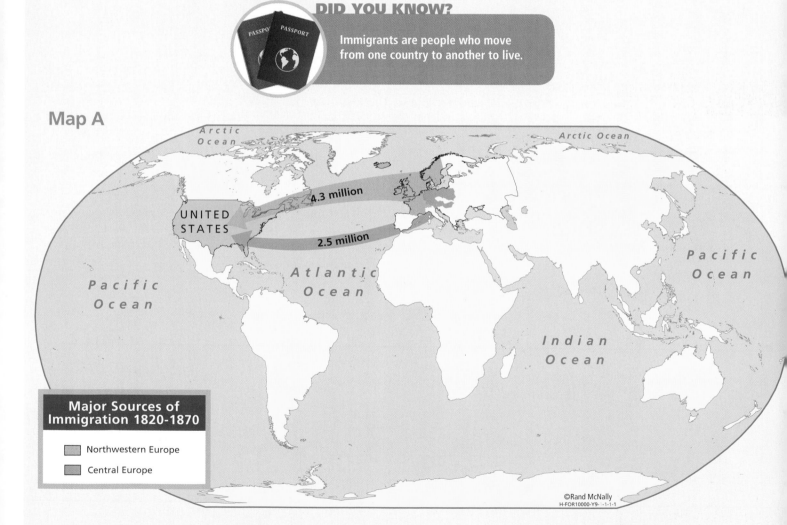

Arctic Ocean

Arctic Ocean

4.3 million

2.5 million

UNITED STATES

Pacific Ocean

Atlantic Ocean

Pacific Ocean

Indian Ocean

Major Sources of Immigration 1820-1870

- Northwestern Europe
- Central Europe

©Rand McNally
H-FOR10000-Y9- -1-1-1

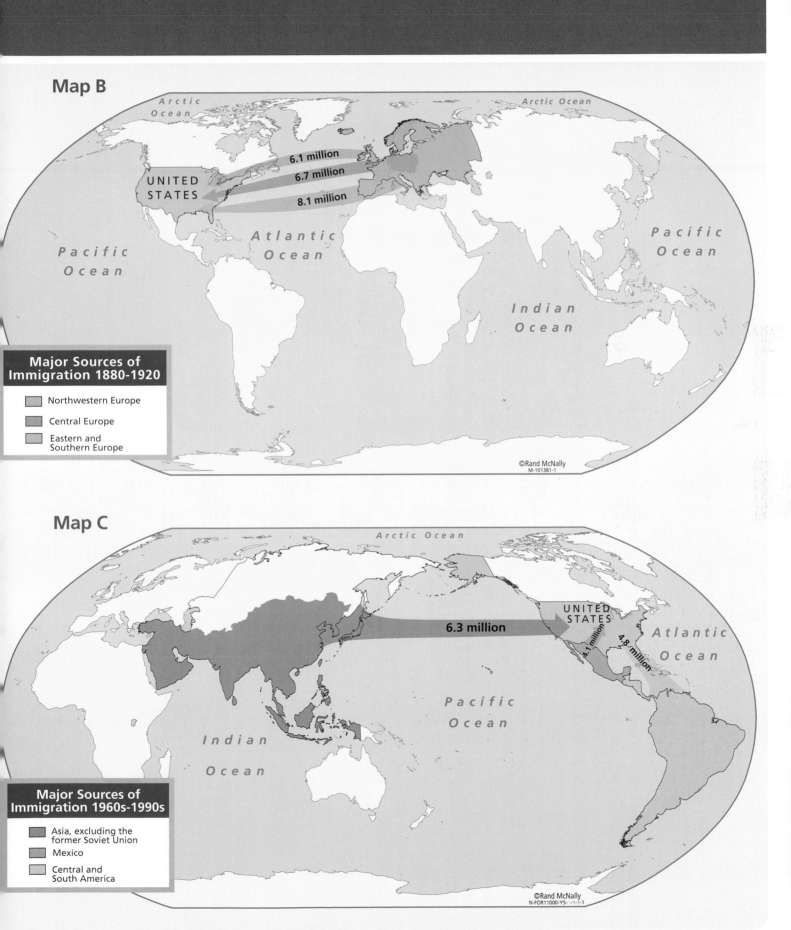

Map B

6.1 million

6.7 million

8.1 million

UNITED STATES

Arctic Ocean

Arctic Ocean

Pacific Ocean

Atlantic Ocean

Pacific Ocean

Indian Ocean

Major Sources of Immigration 1880-1920

- Northwestern Europe
- Central Europe
- Eastern and Southern Europe

©Rand McNally
M-101381-1

Map C

Arctic Ocean

6.3 million

UNITED STATES

4.1 million

4.8 million

Atlantic Ocean

Pacific Ocean

Indian Ocean

Major Sources of Immigration 1960s-1990s

- Asia, excluding the former Soviet Union
- Mexico
- Central and South America

©Rand McNally
N-FOR11000-Y5- -1-1-1

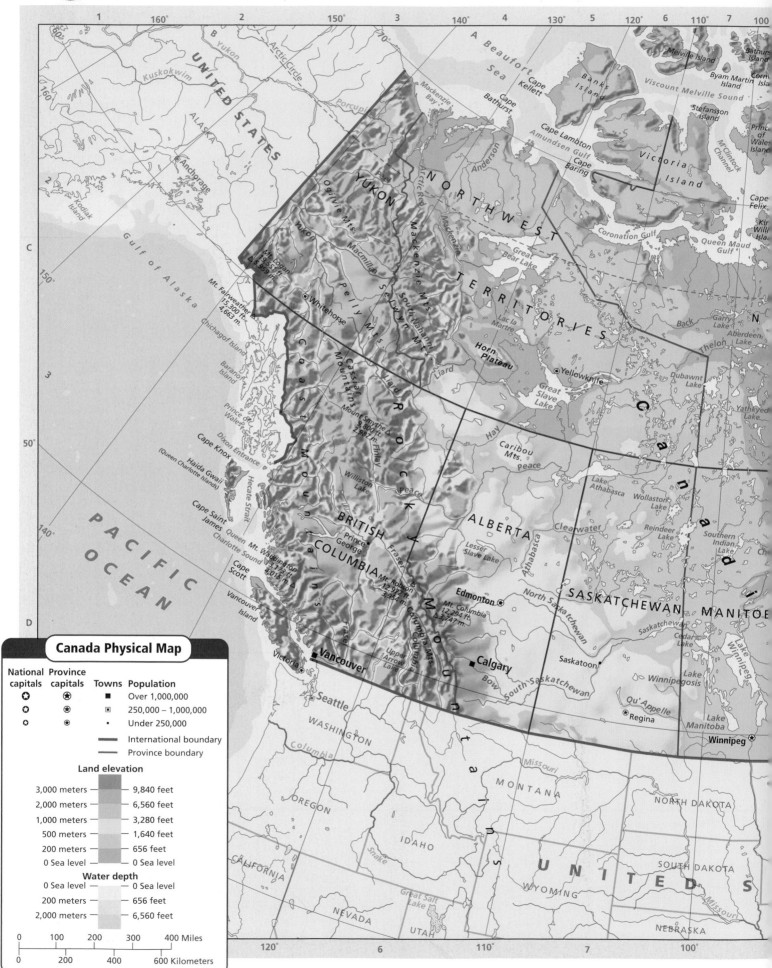

Canada Physical Map

National capitals	Province capitals	Towns	Population
✪	✪	■	Over 1,000,000
✪	✪	◰	250,000 – 1,000,000
✪	✪	•	Under 250,000

International boundary

Province boundary

Land elevation

3,000 meters	9,840 feet
2,000 meters	6,560 feet
1,000 meters	3,280 feet
500 meters	1,640 feet
200 meters	656 feet
0 Sea level	0 Sea level

Water depth

0 Sea level	0 Sea level
200 meters	656 feet
2,000 meters	6,560 feet

0 100 200 300 400 Miles

0 200 400 600 Kilometers

Ellesmere Island
Jones Sound
Devon Island
Cape Parker
Lancaster Sound
Cape Liverpool
Bylot Island
Cape Adair
Baffin Bay
Baffin Island
Gulf of Boothia
Melville Peninsula
Prince Charles Island
Cumberland Sound
Cape Dyer
Cape Mercy
Davis Strait
GREENLAND (Denmark)
Arctic Circle
ATLANTIC OCEAN
Labrador Sea
Cape Wilson
Foxe Basin
NUNAVUT
Cape Dorchester
Foxe Peninsula
Amadjuak Lake
Iqaluit
Frobisher Bay
Resolution Island
Hudson Strait
Cap Hopes Advance
Akpatok Island
Killiniq Island
Seahorse Point
Salisbury Island
Fair Ness
Nottingham Island
Southampton Island
Cape Kendall
Coats Island
Mansel Island
Péninsule d'Ungava
Ungava Bay
Cape Southampton
Mt. d'Iberville 2,420 ft. 4,652 m.
George
NEWFOUNDLAND AND LABRADOR
Hudson Bay
N E S
Feuilles
Belcher Islands
Smallwood Reservoir
Cape Bauld
Cape Tatnam
Cape Henrietta Maria
Pointe Louis-XIV
Cape Churchill
Akimiski Island
Lac Sakami
Rés. Eastmain-Opinaca
Monts Otish
Réservoir Manicouagan
Bonavista Bay
Newfoundland
St. John's
James Bay
Severn
Albany
Missinaibi
Lac Mistassini
QUÉBEC
Réservoir Gouin
Les Laurentides
Île d'Anticosti
Gulf of St. Lawrence
Cap Gaspé
Cape Ray
Cape Race
ST. PIERRE AND MIQUELON (Fr.)
Lac Seul
ONTARIO
Shield
Réservoir Cabonga
Monts Notre-Dame
St. Lawrence
Îles de la Madeleine
PRINCE EDWARD ISLAND
Charlottetown
Cape Breton Island
Lake Nipigon
NEW BRUNSWICK
Fredericton
NOVA SCOTIA
Halifax
of Woods
Lake Superior
Ottawa
Québec
Montréal
MAINE
Bay of Fundy
Cape Sable
MINNESOTA
Manitoulin Island
Georgian Bay
Ottawa
VT.
N.H.
Gulf of Maine
ATLANTIC OCEAN
Lake Michigan
Lake Huron
Toronto
Lake Ontario
NEW YORK
MASS.
CONN. R.I.
WISCONSIN
Niagara Falls
Lake Erie
Minneapolis
UNITED STATES
MICHIGAN
Detroit
PENNSYLVANIA
New York
N.J.
Mississippi

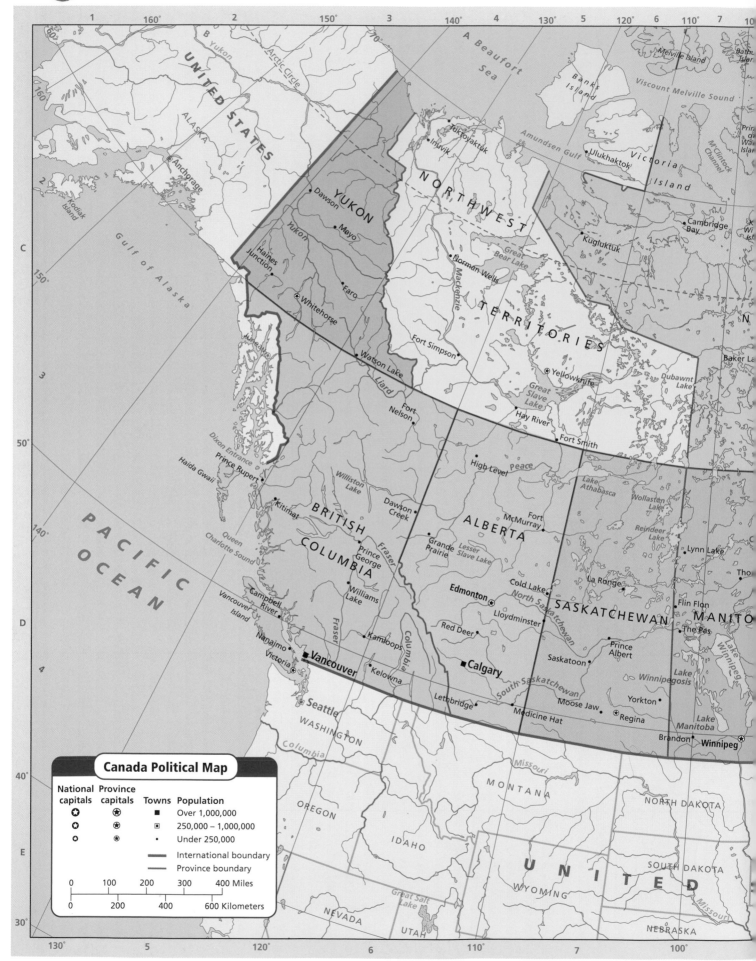

Canada Political Map

National capitals	Province capitals	Towns	Population
✪	✪	■	Over 1,000,000
✪	✪	▣	250,000 – 1,000,000
✪	✪	•	Under 250,000

International boundary

Province boundary

0   100   200   300   400 Miles

0   200   400   600 Kilometers

UNITED STATES

ALASKA

PACIFIC OCEAN

Gulf of Alaska

Kodiak Island

Anchorage

Arctic Circle

Beaufort Sea

Banks Island

Viscount Melville Sound

Melville Island

Amundsen Gulf

Victoria Island

Ulukhaktok

Cambridge Bay

McClintock Channel

YUKON

Dawson

Mayo

Faro

Haines Junction

Whitehorse

Yukon

Juneau

Watson Lake

Liard

NORTHWEST TERRITORIES

Tuktoyaktuk

Inuvik

Norman Wells

Mackenzie

Great Bear Lake

Fort Simpson

Yellowknife

Great Slave Lake

Hay River

Fort Smith

Kugluktuk

Dubawnt Lake

Baker Lake

NUNAVUT

Dixon Entrance

Prince Rupert

Haida Gwaii

Kitimat

Queen Charlotte Sound

BRITISH COLUMBIA

Williston Lake

Dawson Creek

Fort Nelson

Prince George

Fraser

Campbell River

Vancouver Island

Williams Lake

Nanaimo

Victoria

Vancouver

Kamloops

Columbia

Kelowna

Fraser

Seattle

WASHINGTON

Columbia

High Level

Peace

ALBERTA

McMurray

Fort McMurray

Grande Prairie

Lesser Slave Lake

Edmonton

Red Deer

Calgary

Lloydminster

North Saskatchewan

Cold Lake

Lethbridge

Medicine Hat

South Saskatchewan

Lake Athabasca

Wollaston Lake

Reindeer Lake

La Ronge

SASKATCHEWAN

Saskatoon

Prince Albert

Moose Jaw

Regina

Yorkton

Lynn Lake

Flin Flon

The Pas

MANITOBA

Lake Winnipegosis

Lake Winnipeg

Lake Manitoba

Brandon

Winnipeg

Thompson

OREGON

IDAHO

MONTANA

Missouri

WYOMING

Great Salt Lake

NEVADA

UTAH

UNITED STATES

NORTH DAKOTA

SOUTH DAKOTA

NEBRASKA

Missouri

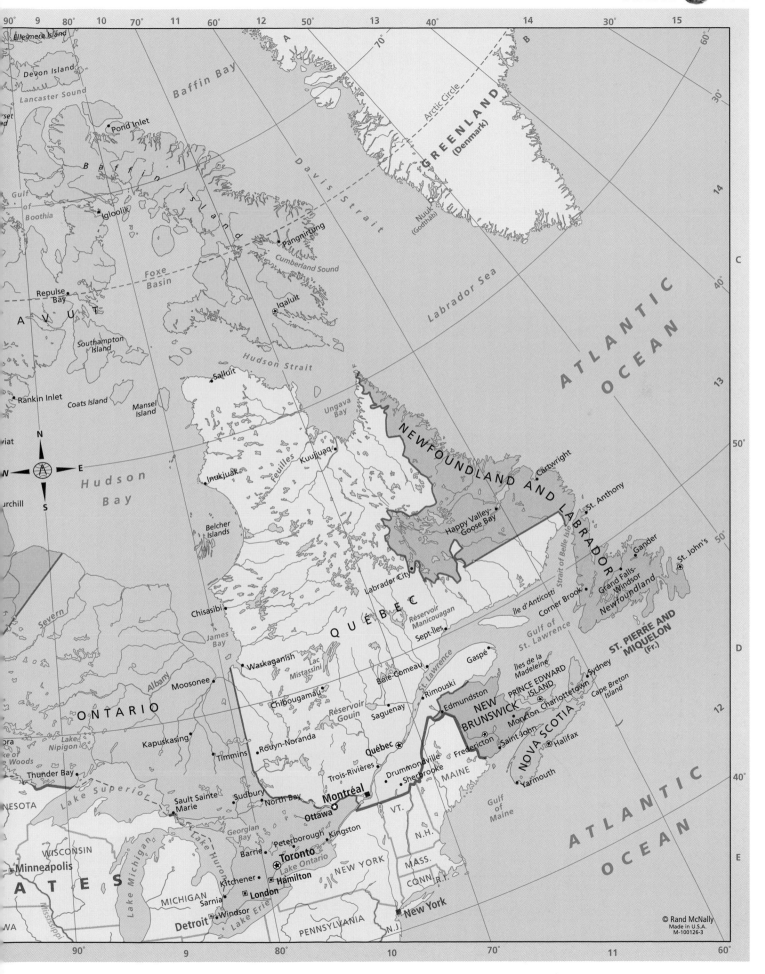

Population

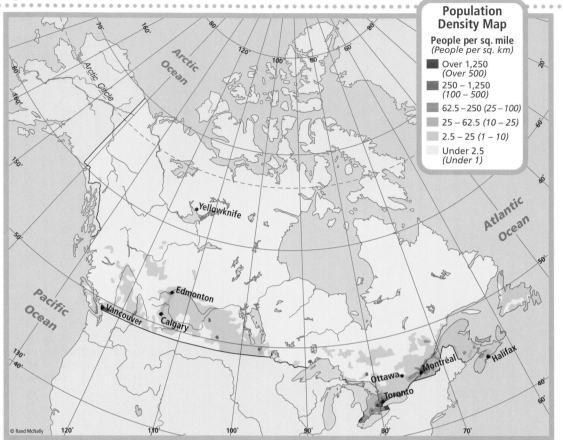

Population Density Map

People per sq. mile
(People per sq. km)

- ■ Over 1,250 *(Over 500)*
- ■ 250 – 1,250 *(100 – 500)*
- ■ 62.5 – 250 *(25 – 100)*
- ■ 25 – 62.5 *(10 – 25)*
- ■ 2.5 – 25 *(1 – 10)*
- □ Under 2.5 *(Under 1)*

Approximately 90% of Canada's population lives within 100 miles of the United States border.

Canada's Population Growth since 1851

Canada's population grew rapidly in the twentieth century when many immigrants arrived from other countries.

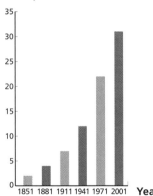

Population in millions

(bar chart showing years 1851, 1881, 1911, 1941, 1971, 2001 on the horizontal axis and values from 0 to 35 on the vertical axis)

Environments

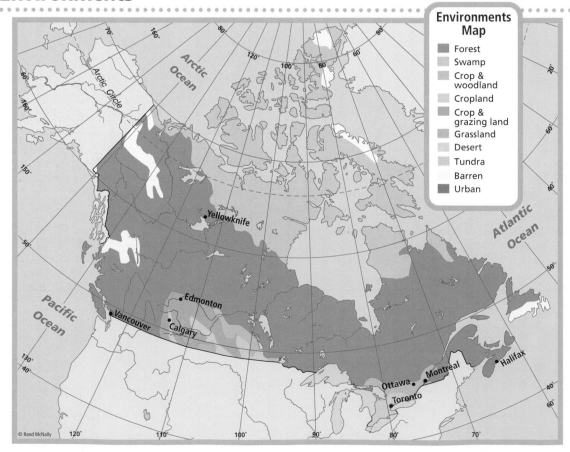

Environments Map

- ■ Forest
- ■ Swamp
- ■ Crop & woodland
- □ Cropland
- ■ Crop & grazing land
- ■ Grassland
- □ Desert
- □ Tundra
- □ Barren
- ■ Urban

The Canadian Rocky Mountains extend through Alberta, British Columbia, and the Yukon territory.

The rocky plateau known as the Canadian Shield ends as headlands at the water's edge. Lighthouses help to guide ships away from the danger.

Transportation

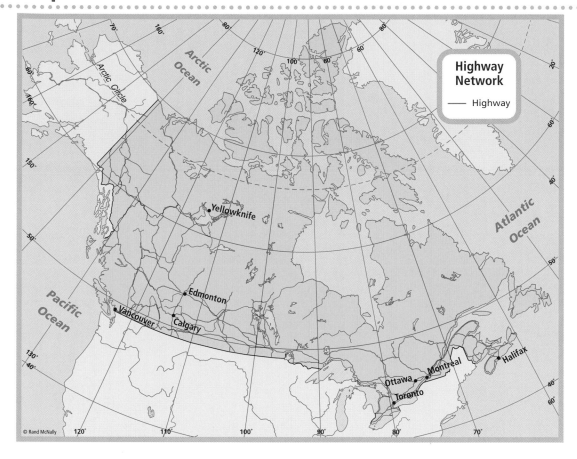

Highway Network
— Highway

Scenic roads wind along the coasts of Canada's Maritime Provinces.

Canada's highways help to connect widely separated clusters of people across the country's vast expanse.

Economic Activities

Most of Canada's grain is grown in the "prairie provinces" of Alberta, Saskatchewan, and Manitoba.

Atlantic coast fishing is important to Canada's economy.

Toronto is Canada's financial center and the headquarters for many of the country's largest companies.

World Export of Oats

Oats are grains that are eaten by people and used for animal feed. On a global scale, Canada is a major oat producer. If Canadian weather interrupts oat growth, this can affect supply of oats across the world.

Canada's Economy

Services—such as banking, transportation, and government—account for more than two-thirds of Canada's economic output.

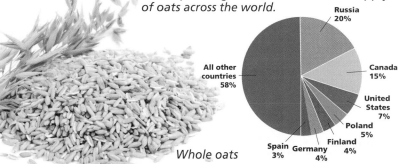

Agriculture 2%
Services 69%
Industry 29%

Whole oats

Russia 20%
All other countries 58%
Canada 15%
United States 7%
Poland 5%
Finland 4%
Germany 4%
Spain 3%

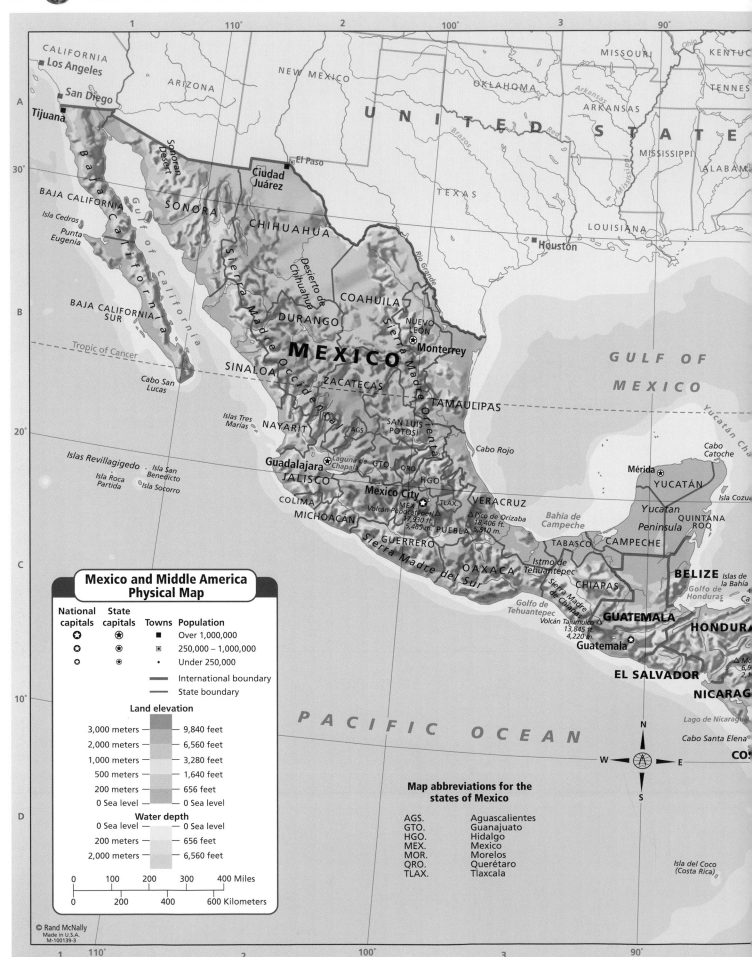

Mexico and Middle America Physical Map

National capitals	State capitals	Towns	Population
✪	✪	■	Over 1,000,000
✪	✪	◫	250,000 – 1,000,000
✪	✪	•	Under 250,000

International boundary
State boundary

Land elevation

3,000 meters —	— 9,840 feet
2,000 meters —	— 6,560 feet
1,000 meters —	— 3,280 feet
500 meters —	— 1,640 feet
200 meters —	— 656 feet
0 Sea level —	— 0 Sea level

Water depth

0 Sea level —	— 0 Sea level
200 meters —	— 656 feet
2,000 meters —	— 6,560 feet

0   100   200   300   400 Miles
0   200   400   600 Kilometers

Map abbreviations for the states of Mexico

AGS.	Aguascalientes
GTO.	Guanajuato
HGO.	Hidalgo
MEX.	Mexico
MOR.	Morelos
QRO.	Querétaro
TLAX.	Tlaxcala

© Rand McNally
Made in U.S.A.
M-100139-3

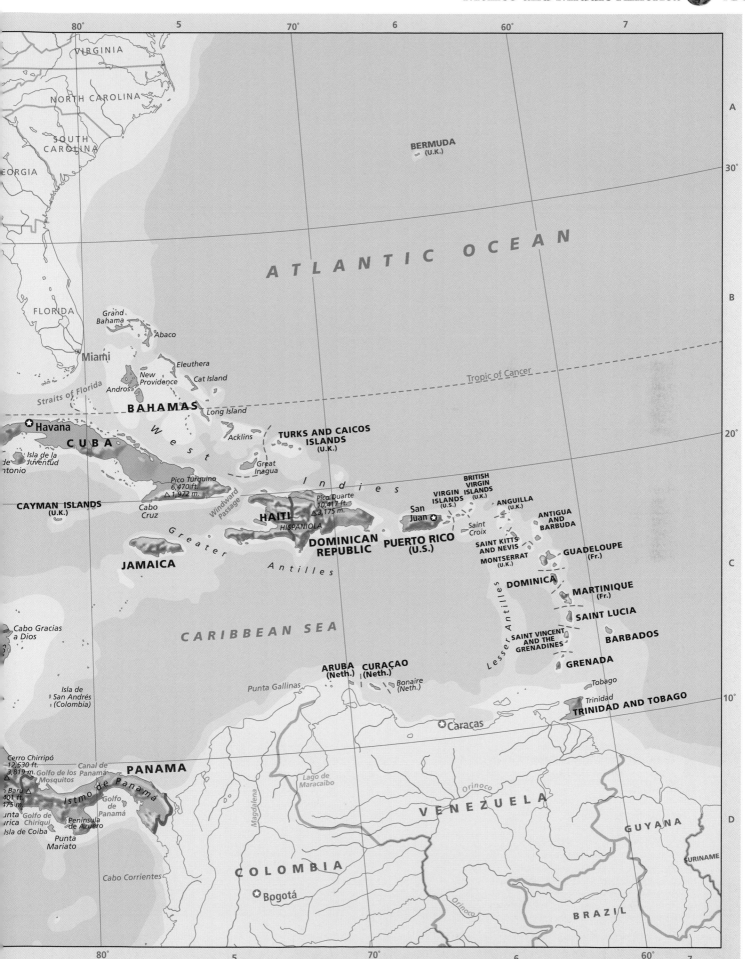

A

30°

ATLANTIC OCEAN

BERMUDA
(U.K.)

VIRGINIA

NORTH CAROLINA

SOUTH CAROLINA

GEORGIA

B

FLORIDA

Miami

Grand
Bahama
Abaco

Eleuthera
Cat Island

Straits of Florida

New
Providence
Andros

BAHAMAS

Long Island

Tropic of Cancer

20°

Havana

CUBA

West

Acklins

Turks and Caicos
Islands
(U.K.)

Isla de la
Juventud

Antonio

Pico Turquino
6,470 ft.
△1,972 m.

Great
Inagua

I n d i e s

BRITISH
VIRGIN
ISLANDS
(U.K.)

CAYMAN ISLANDS
(U.K.)

Cabo
Cruz

Windward
Passage

Pico Duarte
10,417 ft.
△3,175 m.

San
Juan

VIRGIN
ISLANDS
(U.S.)

ANGUILLA
(U.K.)

ANTIGUA
AND
BARBUDA

HAITI

HISPANIOLA

Saint
Croix

Greater

JAMAICA

DOMINICAN
REPUBLIC

PUERTO RICO
(U.S.)

SAINT KITTS
AND NEVIS

GUADELOUPE
(Fr.)

MONTSERRAT
(U.K.)

Antilles

DOMINICA

C

Lesser Antilles

MARTINIQUE
(Fr.)

SAINT LUCIA

Cabo Gracias
a Dios

CARIBBEAN SEA

SAINT VINCENT
AND THE
GRENADINES

BARBADOS

GRENADA

Isla de
San Andrés
(Colombia)

ARUBA
(Neth.)

CURAÇAO
(Neth.)

Bonaire
(Neth.)

Punta Gallinas

Tobago

Trinidad

TRINIDAD AND TOBAGO

10°

Caracas

Cerro Chirripó
12,530 ft.
△3,819 m.

Canal de
Panamá

Golfo de los
Mosquitos

PANAMA

Lago de
Maracaibo

Orinoco

n Barú △
,401 ft.
,175 m.

Istmo de Panamá

Golfo
de
Panamá

Magdalena

VENEZUELA

GUYANA

D

unta
rica

Golfo de
Chiriquí

Isla de Coiba

Peninsula
de Azuero

Punta
Mariato

COLOMBIA

Cabo Corrientes

Bogotá

Orinoco

SURINAME

BRAZIL

80°

5

70°

6

60°

7

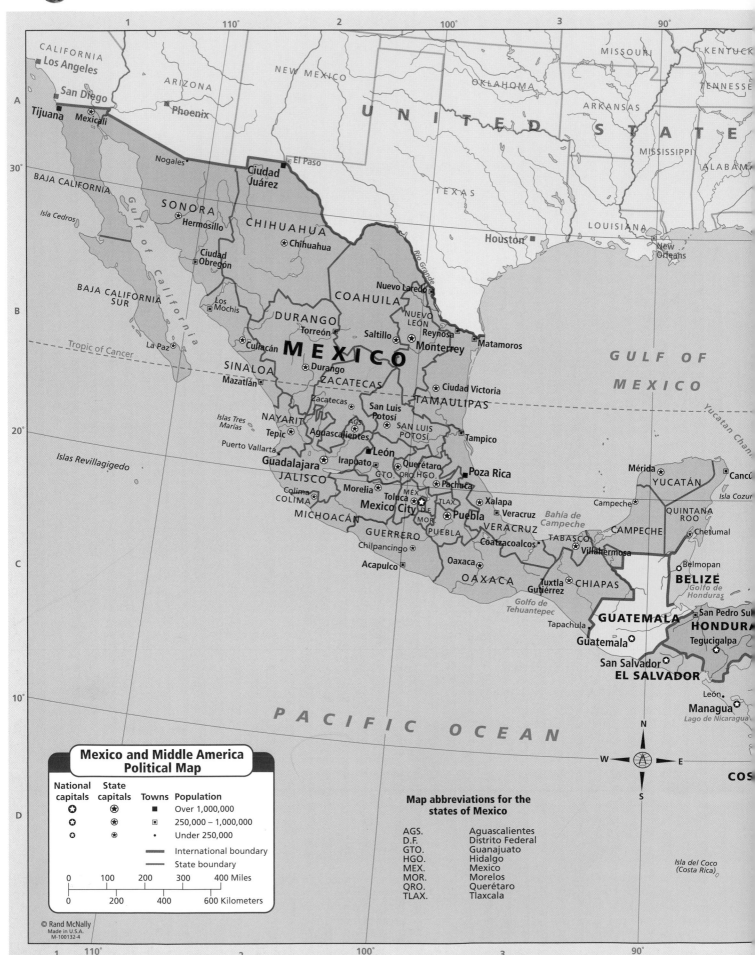

Mexico and Middle America Political Map

National capitals	State capitals	Towns	Population
⊛	⊛	■	Over 1,000,000
⊛	⊛	▣	250,000 – 1,000,000
⊛	⊛	•	Under 250,000

International boundary
State boundary

0   100   200   300   400 Miles
0   200   400   600 Kilometers

© Rand McNally
Made in U.S.A.
M-100132-4

Map abbreviations for the states of Mexico

AGS.	Aguascalientes
D.F.	Distrito Federal
GTO.	Guanajuato
HGO.	Hidalgo
MEX.	Mexico
MOR.	Morelos
QRO.	Querétaro
TLAX.	Tlaxcala

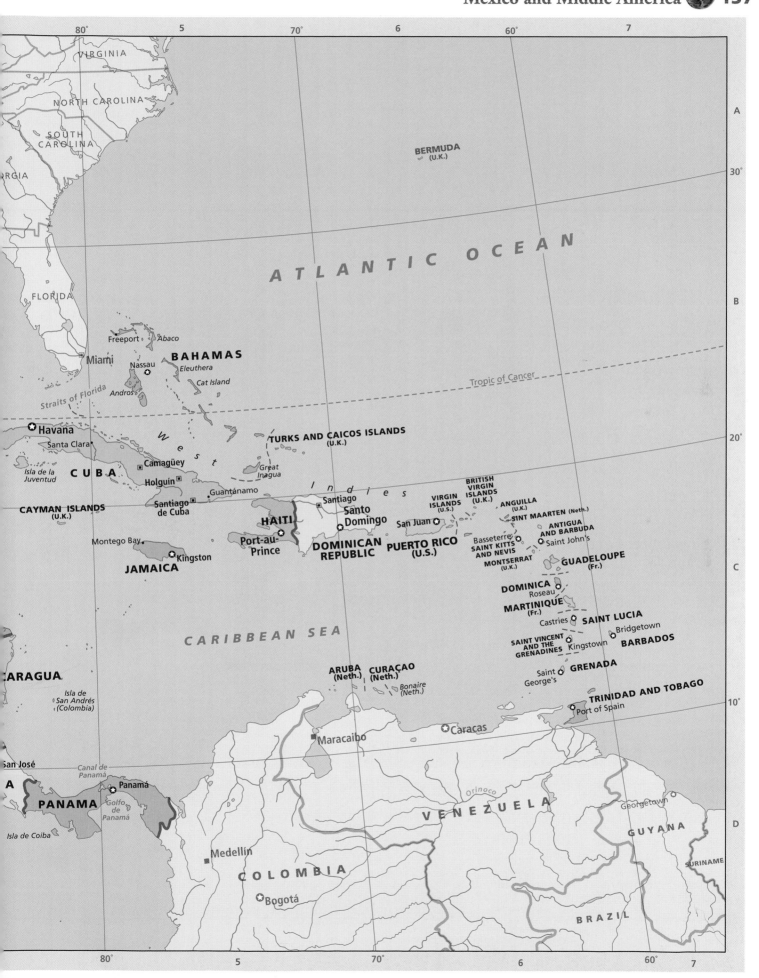

VIRGINIA

NORTH CAROLINA

SOUTH CAROLINA

RGIA

FLORIDA

A T L A N T I C   O C E A N

BERMUDA
(U.K.)

Freeport • Abaco

Miami

Nassau ⊛

Andros

Straits of Florida

BAHAMAS

Eleuthera

Cat Island

⊛ Havana

Santa Clara

C U B A

Isla de la Juventud

Camagüey ▪

Holguín ▪

Santiago de Cuba ▪

Guantánamo ▪

CAYMAN ISLANDS
(U.K.)

Montego Bay •

JAMAICA

⊛ Kingston

W e s t

Great Inagua

TURKS AND CAICOS ISLANDS
(U.K.)

I n d i e s

Santiago ▪

Santo
Domingo ⊛

San Juan ⊛

HAITI

Port-au-
Prince ⊛

**DOMINICAN
REPUBLIC**

PUERTO RICO
(U.S.)

**VIRGIN
ISLANDS**
(U.S.)

**BRITISH
VIRGIN
ISLANDS**
(U.K.)

ANGUILLA
(U.K.)

SINT MAARTEN (Neth.)

Basseterre ⊛
**SAINT KITTS
AND NEVIS**

**ANTIGUA
AND BARBUDA**

⊛ Saint John's

MONTSERRAT
(U.K.)

GUADELOUPE
(Fr.)

DOMINICA
Roseau ⊛

MARTINIQUE
(Fr.)

Castries ⊛ **SAINT LUCIA**

Bridgetown ⊛

**SAINT VINCENT
AND THE
GRENADINES** Kingstown ⊛

BARBADOS

Tropic of Cancer

C A R I B B E A N   S E A

Saint
George's ⊛ **GRENADA**

ARAGUA

*Isla de
San Andrés
(Colombia)*

ARUBA
(Neth.)

CURAÇAO
(Neth.)

Bonaire
(Neth.)

⊛ **TRINIDAD AND TOBAGO**
Port of Spain ⊛

San José

*Canal de
Panamá*

⊛ Panamá

PANAMA

*Golfo
de
Panamá*

Isla de Coiba

▪ Maracaibo

⊛ Caracas

Orinoco

V E N E Z U E L A

Georgetown ⊛

G U Y A N A

SURINAME

Medellín ▪

C O L O M B I A

⊛ Bogotá

B R A Z I L

80° 5 70° 6 60° 7

30°

20°

10°

A

B

C

D

Population

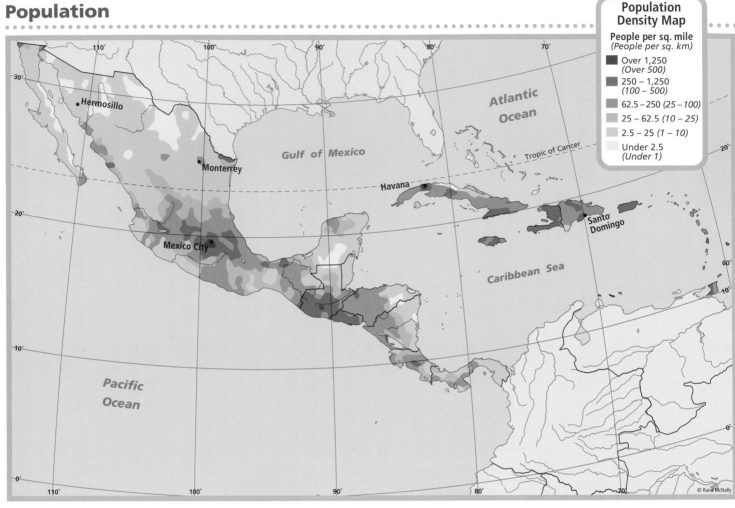

Population Density Map

People per sq. mile
(People per sq. km)

- Over 1,250 *(Over 500)*
- 250 – 1,250 *(100 – 500)*
- 62.5 – 250 *(25 – 100)*
- 25 – 62.5 *(10 – 25)*
- 2.5 – 25 *(1 – 10)*
- Under 2.5 *(Under 1)*

Hermosillo

Monterrey

Mexico City

Atlantic Ocean

Gulf of Mexico

Tropic of Cancer

Havana

Santo Domingo

Caribbean Sea

Pacific Ocean

© Rand McNally

Comparing Urban and Rural Population

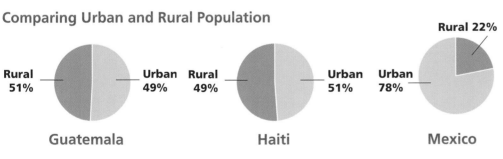

Rural 51%   **Urban 49%**
Guatemala

Rural 49%   **Urban 51%**
Haiti

Urban 78%   **Rural 22%**
Mexico

Mexico City is home to nearly one-fifth of Mexico's people.

A Timeline of Mexico City, Mexico

1500 B.C.E.
Native Americans settle in farm villages along the shores of Lake Texcoco.

1325 C.E.
Aztecs build the city of Tenochtitlán on an island in Lake Texcoco.

1521
Spaniards capture and destroy Tenochtitlán. They drain the lake, fill it with land, and build a new city they call Mexico City.

1960
Mexico City's population reaches 7 million.

1985
An earthquake does extensive damage, partly because Mexico City is built on soft, spongy soil.

2000
Mexico City's population reaches 18 million.

2010
Mexico City becomes the eighth richest metropolitan area in the world. The rating is based on the value of goods and services provided by the city in one year.

Economies

Per capita income is one way of measuring the relative wealth of countries. This graph compares the per capita income of six countries in Middle America. It shows how greatly wealth varies across the region, from relatively rich countries like Aruba to poor countries like Haiti.

Annual per capita income (in U.S. dollars)

Country	Income
Puerto Rico	$26,000
Aruba	$23,000
Mexico	$9,000
Cuba	$5,700
Jamaica	$4,900
Haiti	$600

Cactuses grow in the hot, dry climate of Baja California, Mexico.

Tropical rain forest covers much of Central America.

Palm trees flourish in the warm climate of the Caribbean Sea.

Transportation

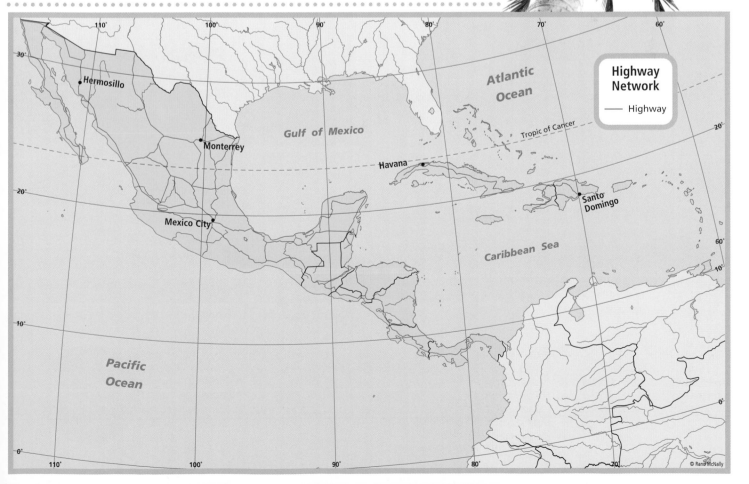

SOUTH AMERICA

South America is a continent of extremes. The Andes Mountains stretch 4,500 miles (7,200 kilometers) from north to south. They form the longest mountain chain in the world. Lake Titicaca, on the Peru-Bolivia border, is the highest lake in the world used for transportation. Arica, Chile, experienced the longest dry period ever recorded: No rain fell there for more than 14 years!

The Amazon River has the greatest volume of water of any river in the world. The Amazon discharges so much water into the Atlantic that it changes the color of the ocean's water for more than 100 miles (160 kilometers) off the shore.

Most South Americans live in cities that are major ports or are near major ports. São Paulo and Rio de Janeiro, Brazil, and Buenos Aires, Argentina, are among the world's largest cities. Altogether, almost 367 million people live in South America.

Iguassu Falls on the Brazil-Argentina border is among the most spectacular sights in South America.

Colorful buildings in Buenos Aires, Argentina

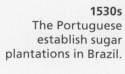

Giant tortoises on Ecuador's Galapagos Islands

A Historical Look At South America

Circa C.E. 600
Tiahuanaco civilization prospers along the shore of Lake Titicaca.

1498
Christopher Columbus reaches the Orinoco River.

1438-1535
The Inca Empire controls the Andes and the Pacific Coast.

1530s
The Portuguese establish sugar plantations in Brazil.

Rain Forests

A rain forest is a dense forest that receives at least 100 inches (250 centimeters) of rain a year. The Amazon rain forest is rich in plant and animal life, and new species are discovered almost daily. Scientists have learned that many of the plants can be used to produce life-saving drugs.

However, the rain forest is becoming smaller. Mining, logging, and industrial developments such as hydroelectric factories, are attracting people to the rain forest. From 2000 to 2010, the Amazon population has grown 23%. These people are looking for a place to work, and they also need a place to live. As a result, land is cleared of trees and other plants. Clearing and settling the land lead to deforestation. Nearly 20% of rain forest has been lost to deforestation.

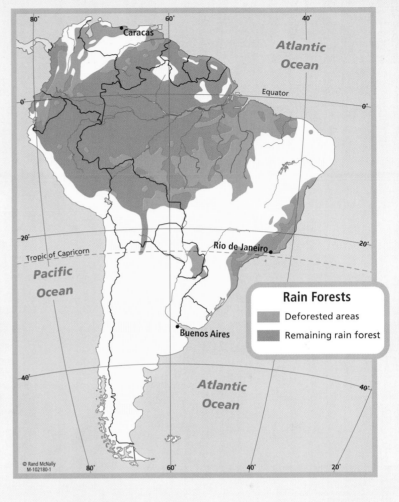

Rain Forests
- Deforested areas
- Remaining rain forest

DID YOU KNOW?

The Amazon River is the world's largest river by volume. Some scientists believe that this river is the longest river in the world, too. But other scientists believe that the Nile River is the longest.

Sights of the Andes Mountains

More than 40 peaks in the Andes rise 20,000 feet (6,000 meters) or higher. Mining is important in the Andes, and tourism is a growing industry.

The ancient Incan city of Machu Picchu, Peru

Lake Titicaca on the Peru-Bolivia border

A jagged peak along the Argentina-Chile border

The South American llama, a relative of the camel

1580
Spaniards found the city of Buenos Aires in Argentina.

1726
The first coffee plantation is established in Brazil.

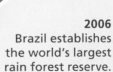

2004
South America's population reaches 365 million.

2006
Brazil establishes the world's largest rain forest reserve.

South America Physical Map

National capitals
- ✪ Over 1,000,000
- ✪ 250,000 – 1,000,000
- ✪ Under 250,000

Towns
- ■ Over 1,000,000
- ◨ 250,000 – 1,000,000
- • Under 250,000

—— International boundary

Population
- Over 1,000,000
- 250,000 – 1,000,000
- Under 250,000

Land elevation

3,000 meters	9,840 feet
2,000 meters	6,560 feet
1,000 meters	3,280 feet
500 meters	1,640 feet
200 meters	656 feet
0 Sea level	0 Sea level

Water depth

0 Sea level	0 Sea level
200 meters	656 feet
2,000 meters	6,560 feet

0 200 400 600 800 1000 Miles
0 300 600 900 1200 1500 Kilometers

GULF OF MEXICO
NORTH AMERICA
MEXICO
GUATEMALA
BELIZE
HONDURAS
EL SALVADOR
NICARAGUA
COSTA RICA
PANAMA
Yucatan Channel
CUBA
Greater Antilles
JAMAICA
HAITI
DOMINICAN REPUBLIC
PUERTO RICO (U.S.)
CARIBBEAN SEA
Lesser Antilles
TRINIDAD AND TOBAGO
Boca Grande

ATLANTIC OCEAN

Punta Gallinas
Pico Cristóbal Colón 18,947 ft. 5,775 m.
✪ Caracas
Lago de Maracaibo
Orinoco
Llanos
VENEZUELA
Angel Falls
Pakaraima Mts.
GUYANA
SURINAME
FRENCH GUIANA (FR.)
Cabo Orange

✪ Bogotá
COLOMBIA
Golfo de Panamá
Nev. del Huila 18,865 ft. 5,750 m.
Punta Galera
Galapagos Islands (Ec.)
Equator
ECUADOR
Chimborazo 20,702 ft. 6,310 m.
Putumayo
Japurá
Negro
Amazon
Manaus
Tapajós
Xingu
Tocantins
Ilha de Marajó
Equator

Punta Pariñas
Amazon Basin
Selvas
Juruá
Madeira
BRAZIL
Cabo de São Roque

Andes
PERU
Nev. Huascarán 22,133 ft. 6,746 m.
Ucayali
Recife
Planalto do Mato Grosso
São Francisco
Serra do Espinhaço

Lima
Punta Carreta
Lago Titicaca
Nev. Illampu 21,066 ft. 6,421 m.
La Paz
Cordillera Real
BOLIVIA
Brasília
Represa de Sobradinho

PACIFIC OCEAN
Nev. Sajama 21,463 ft. 6,542 m.
Gran Chaco
PARAGUAY
Paraná
Cabo de São Tomé
São Paulo
Rio de Janeiro
Tropic of Capricorn

Isla San Ambrosio (Chile)
Isla San Felix (Chile)
Nev. Ojos del Salado 22,615 ft. 6,893 m.
Atacama Desert
Andes
Paraná
Iguassu Falls
Uruguay
Lagoa dos Patos

Archipiélago Juan Fernández (Chile)
Cerro Aconcagua 22,831 ft. 6,959 m.
CHILE
ARGENTINA
URUGUAY
Lagoa Mirim

Santiago
Buenos Aires
Río de la Plata
Pampas

Punta Lavapié
Isla Grande de Chiloé
Golfo San Matías
Península Valdés
N
W E
S
20°

Archipiélago de los Chonos
Patagonia
Cabo Dos Bahías
Golfo San Jorge
Cabo Tres Puntas

ATLANTIC OCEAN

Isla Wellington
Bahía Grande
FALKLAND ISLANDS (U.K.)
West Falkland
East Falkland
South Georgia (U.K.)

Isla Santa Inés
Tierra del Fuego
Strait of Magellan
Cape Horn
Drake Passage
South Shetland Islands (U.K.)
South Orkney Islands (U.K.)
South Sandwich Islands (U.K.)

© Rand McNally
Made in U.S.A.
M-100306-2

Tropic of Cancer
Tropic of Capricorn

Tropic of Cancer

GULF OF MEXICO
Havana
CUBA
NORTH AMERICA
MEXICO
BELIZE
GUATEMALA
EL SALVADOR
HONDURAS
NICARAGUA
COSTA RICA
PANAMA

CARIBBEAN SEA
JAMAICA
HAITI
DOMINICAN REPUBLIC
PUERTO RICO (U.S.)

ATLANTIC OCEAN

Barranquilla
Cartagena
Maracaibo
Caracas
Barquisimeto
Valencia
Cúcuta
Ciudad Guayana
Orinoco
VENEZUELA
TRINIDAD AND TOBAGO
Bucaramanga
GUYANA
Georgetown
Paramaribo
SURINAME
Cayenne
FRENCH GUIANA (FR.)
Medellín
Manizales
Bogotá
COLOMBIA
Cali
Boa Vista
Macapá

Equator
Galapagos Islands (Ec.)
Quito
ECUADOR
Guayaquil
Iquitos
Negro
Manaus
Amazon
Santarem
BRAZIL
Belém
São Luis
Imperatriz
Teresina
Fortaleza

Amazon
Chiclayo
Trujillo
PERU
Madeira
Porto Velho
Natal
João Pessoa
Recife
Maceió

Lima
Huancayo
Cusco
Lago Titicaca
BOLIVIA
Cuiabá
Feira de Santana
Aracaju
Salvador

La Paz
Cochabamba
Santa Cruz
Goiânia
Brasília
Montes Claros

PACIFIC OCEAN
Arequipa
Arica
Sucre
Uberlândia
Belo Horizonte

Campo Grande
Paraná
Ribeirão Preto
Campinas
Rio de Janeiro
Tropic of Capricorn
PARAGUAY
São Paulo
Antofagasta
Salta
Curitiba
Isla San Ambrosio (Chile)
San Miguel de Tucumán
Resistencia
Caxias do Sul
Isla San Felix (Chile)
Asunción
Porto Alegre

Córdoba
ARGENTINA
Santa Fe
URUGUAY
Archipiélago Juan Fernández (Chile)
Valparaíso
Mendoza
Rosario
CHILE
Santiago
Buenos Aires
La Plata
Montevideo
Río de la Plata

Concepción
Bahía Blanca
Mar del Plata

N
W E
S

Puerto Montt

Archipiélago de los Chonos
Comodoro Rivadavia

ATLANTIC OCEAN

FALKLAND ISLANDS (ISLAS MALVINAS) (U.K.)
Río Gallegos
Strait of Magellan
Punta Arenas
Tierra del Fuego

South Georgia (U.K.)

Drake Passage
South Shetland Islands (U.K.)
South Orkney Islands (U.K.)
South Sandwich Islands (U.K.)

© Rand McNally
Made in U.S.A.
M-100129-3

South America Political Map

National capitals	Towns	Population
✪	■	Over 1,000,000
✪	▣	250,000 – 1,000,000
✪	•	Under 250,000
	—	International boundary

200 400 600 800 1000 Miles
300 600 900 1200 1500 Kilometers

Natural Hazards

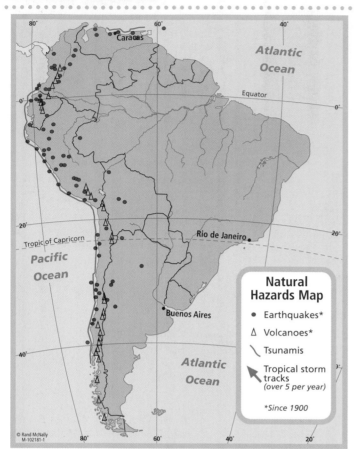

Natural Hazards Map

- ● Earthquakes*
- △ Volcanoes*
- \ Tsunamis
- ↖ Tropical storm tracks (over 5 per year)

*Since 1900

© Rand McNally
M-102181-1

Climate

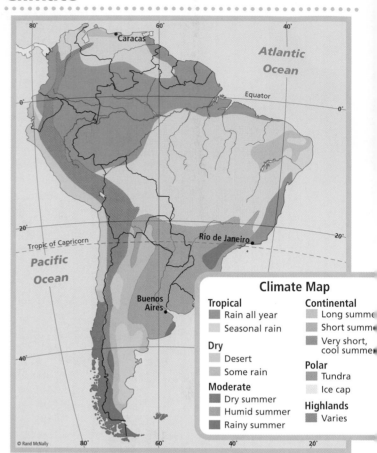

Climate Map

Tropical
- Rain all year
- Seasonal rain

Dry
- Desert
- Some rain

Moderate
- Dry summer
- Humid summer
- Rainy summer

Continental
- Long summer
- Short summer
- Very short, cool summer

Polar
- Tundra
- Ice cap

Highlands
- Varies

© Rand McNally

Environments

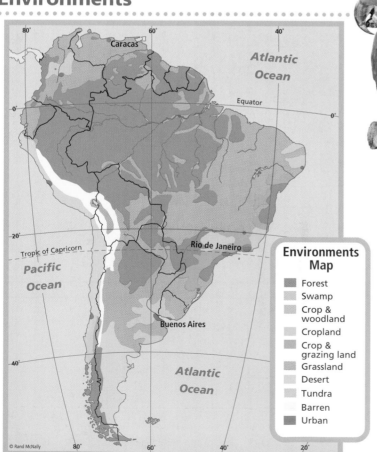

Environments Map

- Forest
- Swamp
- Crop & woodland
- Cropland
- Crop & grazing land
- Grassland
- Desert
- Tundra
- Barren
- Urban

© Rand McNally

The Amazon rain forest supports almost half of Earth's animal and plant species.

WHAT IF?

? What could happen if all of the rain forests in South America are destroyed?

Population

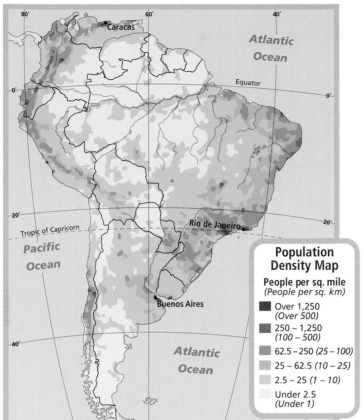

Population Density Map
People per sq. mile
(People per sq. km)

- ■ Over 1,250 (Over 500)
- ■ 250 – 1,250 (100 – 500)
- ■ 62.5 – 250 (25 – 100)
- ■ 25 – 62.5 (10 – 25)
- ■ 2.5 – 25 (1 – 10)
- □ Under 2.5 (Under 1)

© Rand McNally

Most Brazilians live in large cities such as Rio de Janeiro.

Roughly three out of five people living in Brazil are under the age of 29.

DID YOU KNOW?

São Paulo, Brazil, is South America's most populous city.

Cusco, Peru, was once capital of the Incan empire.

The forest in the Amazon River Basin is so thick in parts that sunlight cannot reach the ground.

Economic Activities

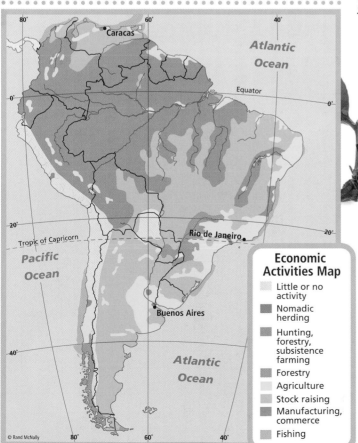

Economic Activities Map

- □ Little or no activity
- ■ Nomadic herding
- ■ Hunting, forestry, subsistence farming
- ■ Forestry
- □ Agriculture
- ■ Stock raising
- ■ Manufacturing, commerce
- ■ Fishing

© Rand McNally

Coffee plants thrive in the tropical climates of South America.

World Coffee Production

Europe and Australia 1%
Africa 12%
North America 14%
South America 46%
Asia 27%

Gross Domestic Product (GDP) in billions of U.S. dollars

Country

Bolivia
Paraguay
Uruguay
Ecuador
Venezuela
Peru
Chile
Colombia
Argentina

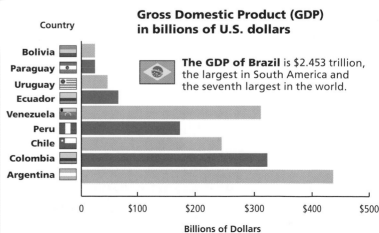

The GDP of Brazil is $2.453 trillion, the largest in South America and the seventh largest in the world.

0    $100 $200 $300 $400 $500

Billions of Dollars

EUROPE

Prague, Czech Republic

Do you know what a *lago* is? A *lac*? A *loch*? These are just some of the words for "lake" in Europe. Europe is the world's second-smallest continent, but it has many countries and many languages.

Only the giant continents of Asia and Africa have more people than Europe. Because more than 729,000,000 live in the small continent of Europe, it is one of the most densely populated regions in the world.

The two smallest countries in the world are in Europe. Vatican City and Monaco are each less than one square mile (2.6 square kilometers) in size.

In recent decades, there have been great changes in Europe. East and West Germany were reunited in 1990 after being separated for 45 years. In 1991, the Soviet Union split up into 15 different countries. The following year, Czechoslovakia peacefully divided into two new countries: the Czech Republic and Slovakia.

Slovenia, Croatia, Macedonia, and Bosnia and Herzegovina broke away from Yugoslavia in 1991-92 to become independent countries. In 2003, Yugoslavia changed its name to Serbia and Montenegro. Then, in 2006, Montenegro split from Serbia to become an independent country. In 2008, a region known as Kosovo declared its independence from Serbia.

Church in the Alps of Austria

Hilltop village in Spain

Donkey and farmhouse, Aran Islands, Ireland

A Historical Look At Europe

Circa 2200 B.C.E.
Erecting of Stonehenge pillars begins in Great Britain.

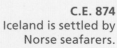

753 B.C.E.
Rome is founded.

776 B.C.E.
The first recorded Olympic Games are held in Greece.

C.E. 874
Iceland is settled by Norse seafarers.

The European Union

Twenty-eight nations have joined the European Union to form a single, powerful market for business and trade.

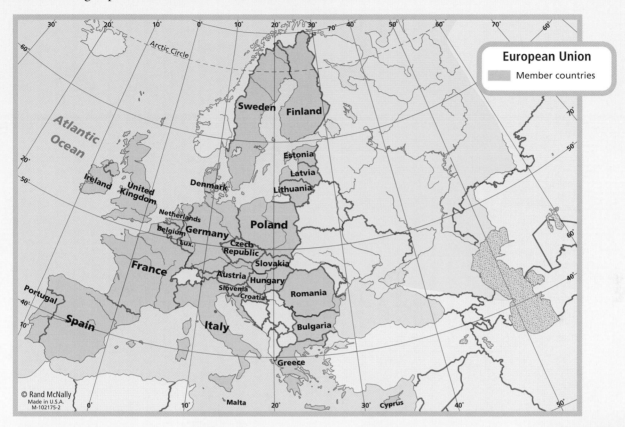

European Union

Member countries

Atlantic Ocean

Arctic Circle

Sweden
Finland
Estonia
Latvia
Lithuania
Denmark
Ireland
United Kingdom
Netherlands
Belgium
Lux.
Germany
Poland
Czech Republic
Slovakia
France
Austria
Hungary
Slovenia
Croatia
Romania
Portugal
Spain
Italy
Bulgaria
Greece
Malta
Cyprus

© Rand McNally
Made in U.S.A.
M-102175-2

The headquarters of the European Union is in Brussels, Belgium.

Some countries of the European Union use the euro as their currency.

ENTRADA ENTRÉE
ENTRANCE ENTRATTA
EINGANG

Because Europe has so many languages, there are 24 official languages of the European Union.

The European Union has its own passports. Citizens of all countries can move freely around the entire area.

1163–1200
The great gothic Notre Dame Cathedral is built in Paris.

1300s–1500s
The period known as the Renaissance marks a rebirth in art and science.

Circa 1750
The Industrial Revolution begins in England.

2007
Romania and Bulgaria join the European Union.

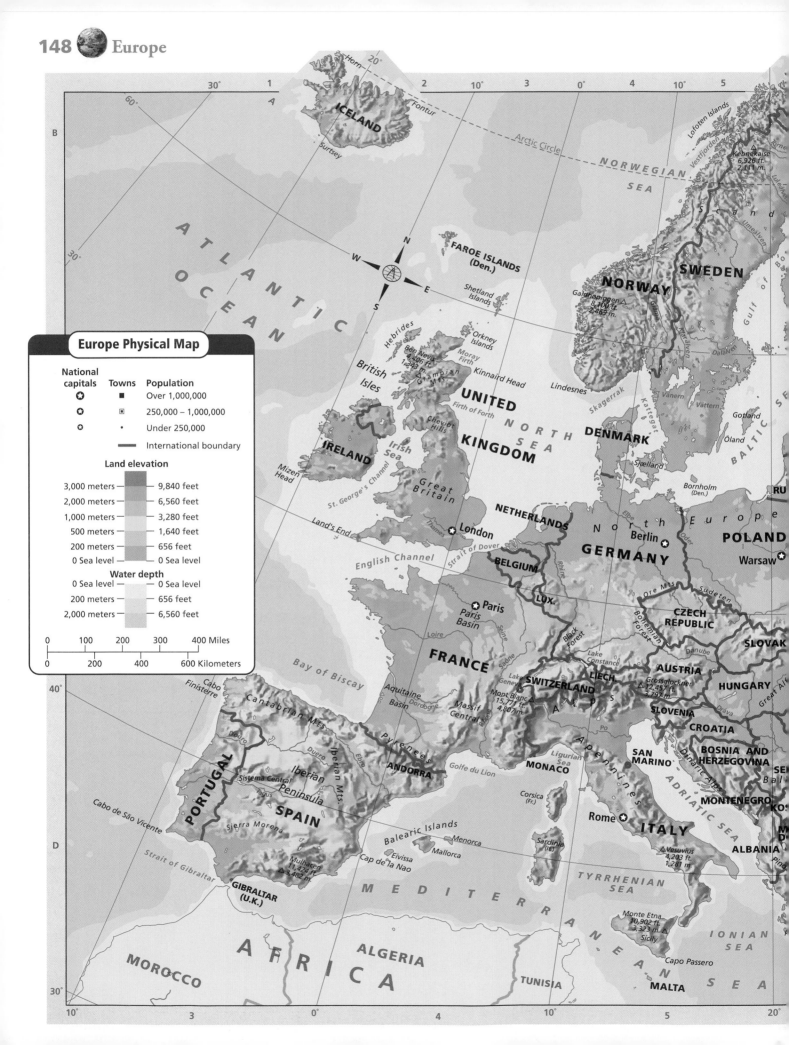

Europe Physical Map

National capitals | **Towns** | **Population**
☆ | ■ | Over 1,000,000
☆ | ▣ | 250,000 – 1,000,000
☆ | · | Under 250,000
— | | International boundary

Land elevation

3,000 meters — 9,840 feet
2,000 meters — 6,560 feet
1,000 meters — 3,280 feet
500 meters — 1,640 feet
200 meters — 656 feet
0 Sea level — 0 Sea level

Water depth

0 Sea level — 0 Sea level
200 meters — 656 feet
2,000 meters — 6,560 feet

0 100 200 300 400 Miles
0 200 400 600 Kilometers

ICELAND
Horn
Surtsey
Fontur

ATLANTIC OCEAN

FAROE ISLANDS (Den.)

Arctic Circle

NORWEGIAN SEA

Lofoten Islands
Vestfjorden
Kebnekaise 6,926 ft. 2,111 m.
Scand

NORWAY
Galdhøpiggen △ 8,100 ft. 2,469 m.
Glåma

SWEDEN
Umeälven
Dalälven
Gulf of Bo

Shetland Islands
Orkney Islands
Moray Firth
Kinnaird Head

Hebrides
Ben Nevis 4,406 ft. 1,343 m.
Grampian Mts.

British Isles

UNITED KINGDOM
Firth of Forth
Cheviot Hills

NORTH SEA

DENMARK
Skagerrak
Kattegat
Sjælland

Lindesnes
Vänern
Vättern
Gotland
Öland

BALTIC SEA
Bornholm (Den.)
RU

IRELAND
Irish Sea
Mizen Head

Great Britain
St. George's Channel
Land's End

NETHERLANDS
London
Thames
Strait of Dover
English Channel

BELGIUM
LUX.

GERMANY
Berlin
Elbe
Oder

North
Europe
POLAND
Warsaw

Paris
Paris Basin
Loire
Seine

FRANCE
Aquitaine Basin
Dordogne
Massif Central
Saône

Bay of Biscay

Cabo Finisterre
Cantabrian Mts.

Black Forest
Rhine
Ore Mts.
Bohemian Forest
Sudeten

CZECH REPUBLIC
Danube
Lake Constance
Lake Geneva

SWITZERLAND
LIECH
Mont Blanc △ 15,771 ft. 4,807 m.

AUSTRIA
Grossglockner △ 12,457 ft. 3,797 m.

SLOVAK
HUNGARY
Drava
Great Al

SLOVENIA
CROATIA

A L P S
Po

Pyrenees
ANDORRA
Golfe du Lion

MONACO
Ligurian Sea
Apennines

SAN MARINO

Adriatic

BOSNIA AND HERZEGOVINA
Dinaric Alps
SE
Bal

MONTENEGRO
KO

PORTUGAL
Sistema Central
Tagus
Iberian Peninsula
SPAIN
Sierra Morena
Mulhacén 11,424 ft. △ 3,482 m.

Douro
Duero
Ebro
Iberian Mts.

Balearic Islands
Menorca
Eivissa
Mallorca
Cap de la Nao

Corsica (Fr.)

Sardinia (It.)

Rome
ITALY
ADRIATIC SEA
Vesuvius △ 4,203 ft. 1,281 m.
ALBANIA
Pind
M
D

Cabo de São Vicente
Strait of Gibraltar

GIBRALTAR (U.K.)

TYRRHENIAN SEA

M E D I T E R R A N E A N
Monte Etna 10,902 ft. 3,323 m. △
Sicily

IONIAN SEA
Capo Passero

MOROCCO

AFRICA

ALGERIA

TUNISIA

MALTA

S E A

60°
30°
40°
30°

20° 10° 0° 10° 20°
1 2 3 4 5
A B C D
30° 0° 10° 20°
3 4 5

70°

7   40°   8   50°   9   60°   10   70°   11   80°

Murmansk

Kola
Peninsula

Ponoy

WHITE SEA

Timan Ridge

Pechora

Gora Narodnaya
6,214 ft.
1,894 m.

Ob'

Irtysh

80°

B

Mezen'

Severnaya Dvina

Onega

Ural Mountains

Kama
Reservoir

50°

FINLAND

Lake
Onega

Sukhona

Severnyye Uvaly
(Hills)

Kama

70°

Lake
Ladoga

Lake
Peipus

Rybinsk
Res.

Volga

Gorki
Res.

RUSSIA

Kuybyshev
Res.

ASIA

f Finland

LATVIA

Valdai
Hills

Moscow

Oka

Volga

C

UANIA

Central
Russian
Upland

Oka-Don Plain

Don

Khopër

Volga
Upland

Volgograd
Res.

Ural

KAZAKHSTAN

Caspian Depression

Aral Sea

Néman

BELARUS

Prypjac'

Dnieper Lowland

Tsymlyansk
Res.

Volga

UZBEKISTAN

Amu Darya

Kiev

Donets Basin

Dnieper

40°

UKRAINE

niester

MOLDOVA

Sea of Azov

60°

TURKMENISTAN

MANIA

vanian Alps

Crimean
Peninsula

C a u c a s u s

Gora El'brus
18,510 ft.
5,642 m.

GEORGIA

CASPIAN SEA

Danube

ninsula

BLACK SEA

ARMENIA

AZERBAIJAN

AZER.

BULGARIA

Rhodope Mts

D

Istanbul

Sea of
Marmara

TURKEY

IRAN

lympus
ft.
m.

AEGEAN SEA

Tigris

IRAQ

GREECE

Sea of Crete

Rhodes

CYPRUS

SYRIA

LEBANON

Euphrates

30°

Crete

© Rand McNally
Made in U.S.A.
M-100138-4

6   30°   7   40°   8   50°   9

Europe Political Map

National capitals	State capitals	Towns	Population
✪	✪	■	Over 1,000,000
✪	✪	▣	250,000 – 1,000,000
✪	✪	•	Under 250,000

International boundary
State boundary

0   100   200   300   400 Miles
0   200   400   600 Kilometers

ICELAND
Reykjavik

FAROE ISLANDS (Den.)

ATLANTIC OCEAN

Arctic Circle

NORWEGIAN SEA

Kiru

Trondheim
Umeå
Tam

SWEDEN

NORWAY

Bergen
Oslo
Stockholm
Göteborg
Vänern
Vättern

Gulf of Bot

Skagerrak
Kattegat

BALTIC SE

SCOTLAND
Aberdeen
Glasgow
Edinburgh

UNITED KINGDOM

NORTHERN IRELAND
Belfast
Dublin
IRELAND
Cork

St. George's Channel

Irish Sea

Liverpool
Manchester
WALES
Birmingham
ENGLAND
Cardiff
Plymouth

Thames
London

English Channel

Strait of Dover

Le Havre

Brest

NORTH SEA

DENMARK
Copenhagen

LITHUA
Kaliningrad
RU
Gdańsk

NETHERLANDS
Amsterdam
The Hague
Antwerp
Brussels
BELGIUM
Luxembourg
LUX.

Hamburg
Szczecin
Berlin
Essen
Cologne
Bonn
Frankfurt
Dresden

GERMANY

POLAND
Warsaw
Łódź
Wrocław
Katowice
Krak

Elbe
Oder
Vistula

Prague
CZECH REPUBLIC
SLOVAK

Rhine

Paris

Nantes

Loire

FRANCE

Bordeaux

Seine
Strasbourg
Stuttgart
Munich

Danube

Zurich
Bern
SWITZERLAND
Genève
Lyon
LIECH.

Vienna
AUSTRIA
Graz
Bratislava
Budapest
HUNGARY

SLOVENIA
Ljubljana
Zagreb
CROATIA

A Coruña
Gijón
Bilbao
Toulouse
Porto

Bay of Biscay

Valladolid

ANDORRA

Marseille
Golfe du Lion

MONACO
Nice

Turin
Milan
Genoa
Bologna
Venice

Ligurian Sea

SAN MARINO
Florence
Split

BOSNIA AND HERZEGOVINA
Sarajevo
MONTENEGRO
Podgorica
Belgr
SER
KOS
Pri

Rhône
Po

LISBON
PORTUGAL
Lisbon
Tagus
Madrid
SPAIN
Zaragoza
Ebro
València
Barcelona
Palma

Córdoba
Seville
Alacant
Málaga
GIBRALTAR (U.K.)
Strait of Gibraltar

Corsica

Sardinia

ITALY
Rome
VATICAN CITY
Naples
Bari

ADRIATIC SEA

ALBANIA
Tiranë
Skop
M
D

GRE

Cagliari

TYRRHENIAN SEA

Palermo
Messina
Sicily
Catania

IONIAN SEA

MEDITERRANEAN SEA

Algiers

AFRICA

MOROCCO

ALGERIA

TUNISIA

MALTA

70°　7　40°　8　50°　9　60°　10　70°　11　80°

Murmansk

WHITE SEA

Ukhta

Arkhangel'sk

Severnaya Dvina

Syktyvkar

R U S S I A

Berezniki

FINLAND

Petrozavodsk
Lake Onega

Kirov

Perm'

Helsinki

Saint Petersburg

Lake Ladoga

Cherepovets
Rybinsk Res.

Izhevsk

Naberezhnye Chelny

Ufa

of Finland

Tallinn

ESTONIA
Lake Peipus

Yaroslavl'

Ivanovo

Gorki Res.

Nizhniy Novgorod

Kazan'

Kuybyshev Res.

A S I A

Tver'

Riga

LATVIA

Moscow ✪

Oka

Ryazan'

Penza

Samara

Volga

Vicebsk

Tula

Bryansk

Saratov

Volgograd Res.

Ural

Vilnius

✪ Minsk

Homel'

Lipetsk

Don

Voronezh

KAZAKHSTAN

Aral Sea

BELARUS

Chornobyl'

✪ Kiev

Kharkiv

Volgograd

Volga

Atyraū

UZBEKISTAN

L'viv

Vinnytsia

UKRAINE

Dnipro-petrovs'k

Dnieper

Luhans'k

Tsymlyansk Res.

Astrakhan'

Dniester

Donets'k

Rostov-na-Donu

Volga

Kryvyi Rih

MOLDOVA

Zaporizhzhia

Mariupol'

TURKMENISTAN

Iaşi

Chişinău

Sea of Azov

Krasnodar

Stavropol'

CASPIAN SEA

Cluj-Napoca

ROMANIA

Odesa

Simferopol'

Vladikavkaz

Galaţi

Sevastopol'

B L A C K   S E A

GEORGIA

Tbilisi

Baku ✪

AZERBAIJAN

Bucharest

Constanţa

Craiova

BULGARIA

Varna

Danube

ARMENIA

AZER.

Sofia

Plovdiv

İstanbul

Yerevan

Sea of Marmara

Tehran ✪

Thessaloníki

Ankara ✪

T U R K E Y

IRAN

AEGEAN SEA

Athens

SYRIA

IRAQ

Baghdad

CYPRUS

LEBANON

Crete

© Rand McNally
Made in U.S.A.
M-100128-4

6　30°　6　7　40°　8　50°　9

B　50°　C　40°　D　30°

Climate

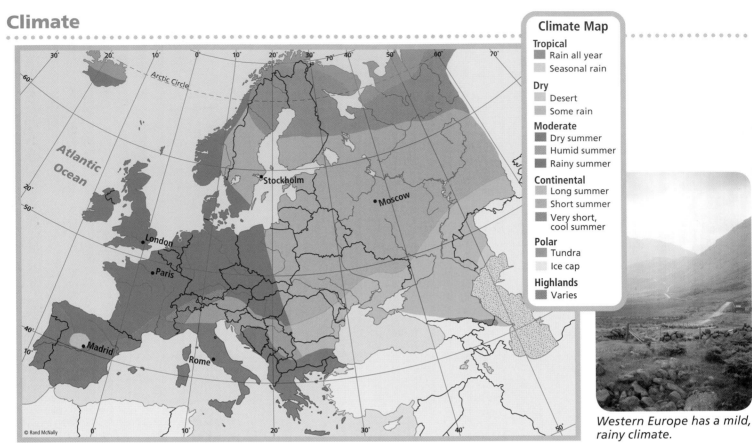

Climate Map

Tropical
- Rain all year
- Seasonal rain

Dry
- Desert
- Some rain

Moderate
- Dry summer
- Humid summer
- Rainy summer

Continental
- Long summer
- Short summer
- Very short, cool summer

Polar
- Tundra
- Ice cap

Highlands
- Varies

Western Europe has a mild, rainy climate.

Population

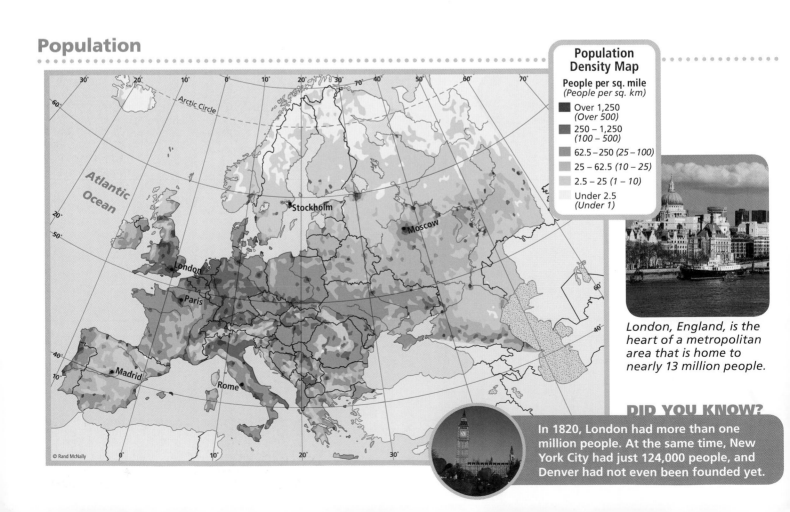

Population Density Map

People per sq. mile
(People per sq. km)

- Over 1,250 *(Over 500)*
- 250 – 1,250 *(100 – 500)*
- 62.5 – 250 *(25 – 100)*
- 25 – 62.5 *(10 – 25)*
- 2.5 – 25 *(1 – 10)*
- Under 2.5 *(Under 1)*

London, England, is the heart of a metropolitan area that is home to nearly 13 million people.

DID YOU KNOW?

In 1820, London had more than one million people. At the same time, New York City had just 124,000 people, and Denver had not even been founded yet.

Environments

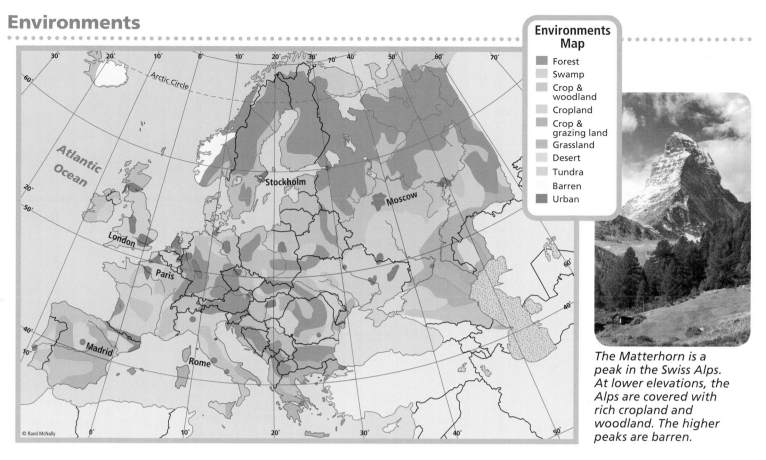

Environments Map

- Forest
- Swamp
- Crop & woodland
- Cropland
- Crop & grazing land
- Grassland
- Desert
- Tundra
- Barren
- Urban

The Matterhorn is a peak in the Swiss Alps. At lower elevations, the Alps are covered with rich cropland and woodland. The higher peaks are barren.

Economic Activities

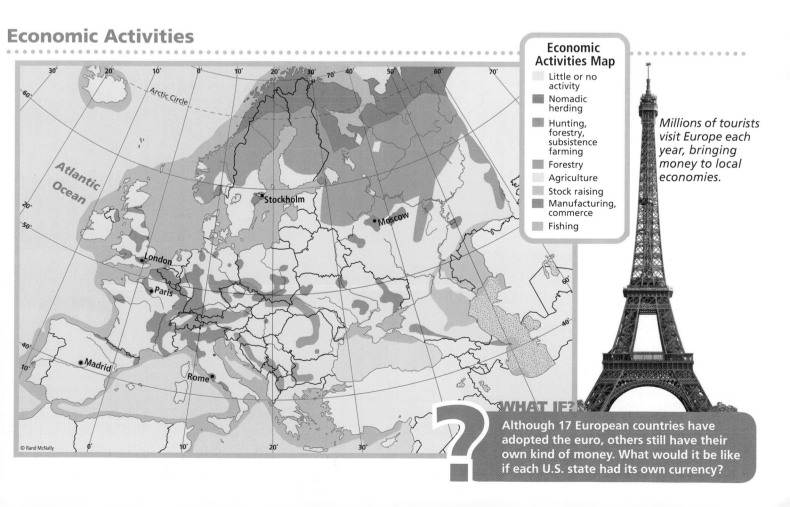

Economic Activities Map

- Little or no activity
- Nomadic herding
- Hunting, forestry, subsistence farming
- Forestry
- Agriculture
- Stock raising
- Manufacturing, commerce
- Fishing

Millions of tourists visit Europe each year, bringing money to local economies.

WHAT IF?

Although 17 European countries have adopted the euro, others still have their own kind of money. What would it be like if each U.S. state had its own currency?

Natural Hazards

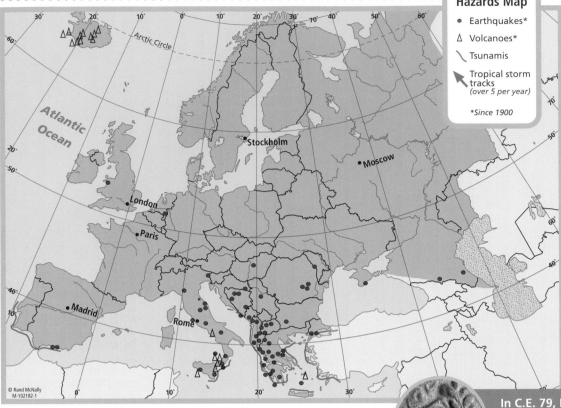

Natural Hazards Map

- • Earthquakes*
- △ Volcanoes*
- ╲ Tsunamis
- ↖ Tropical storm tracks *(over 5 per year)*

*Since 1900

© Rand McNally
M-102182-1

Lisbon, the capital of Portugal, was devastated by an earthquake in 1755.

Volcanic eruptions are a natural hazard in Italy. This photo shows Mt. Etna on the island of Sicily.

DID YOU KNOW?

In C.E. 79, Mt. Vesuvius erupted and buried the ancient city of Pompeii, Italy, under approximately 20 feet (6 meters) of volcanic ash.

Transportation

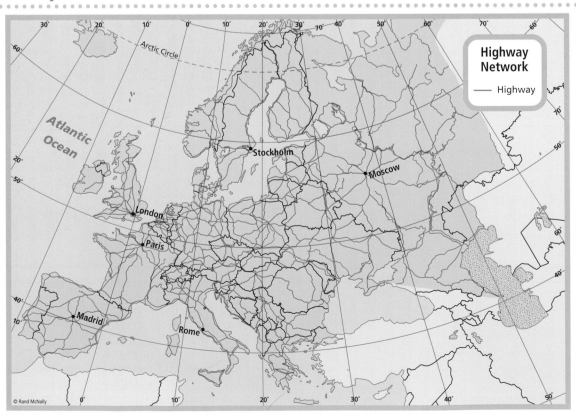

Highway Network

— Highway

© Rand McNally

A canal boat is a modern means of transportation in Amsterdam, the Netherlands.

High-speed rail systems connect many European cities.

Energy

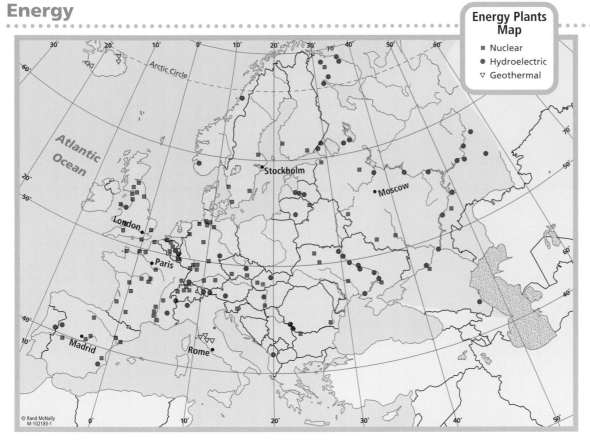

Energy Plants Map
- ■ Nuclear
- ● Hydroelectric
- ▽ Geothermal

© Rand McNally
M-102183-1

In Iceland, water from hot springs heats homes and fuels geothermal plants.

Hydroelectric power is important in some parts of Europe. This dam is in Switzerland.

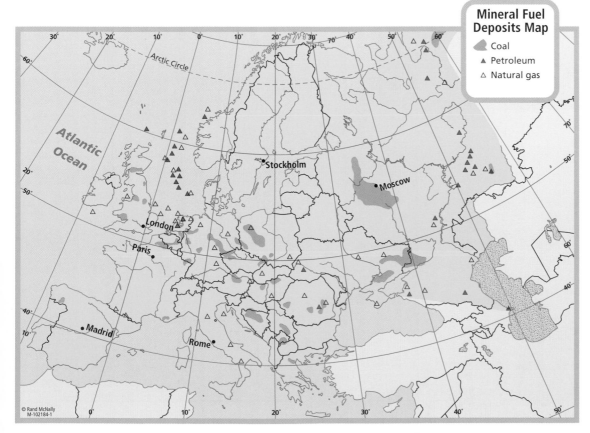

Mineral Fuel Deposits Map
- ◣ Coal
- ▲ Petroleum
- △ Natural gas

© Rand McNally
M-102184-1

North Sea oil and gas are important sources of energy for the United Kingdom and Norway.

Coal was the first fuel for modern factories, but today it is less favored because it is so polluting.

AFRICA

African elephant

Africa is a huge continent. It is larger than every other continent except Asia. More than 1 billion people live in Africa, and the population is growing fast.

The Sahara, the largest desert in the world, covers most of northern Africa. South of the Sahara is the Sahel, an area of dry grasslands. The Sahel expands and recedes with changes in climate.

The tropical rain forests of central Africa provide a natural habitat for gorillas, chimpanzees, and monkeys. North and south of the rain forests and in eastern Africa are vast grassy plains, or savannas. These plains are home to herds of grazing animals, as well as elephants, lions, and other animals most of us see only in zoos.

During the late 19th and early 20th centuries, European countries occupied and governed most of Africa. Today, almost every country in Africa is independent. Africa has 54 countries, the most of any continent.

Many of Africa's people are poor, and they face great challenges in health care, literacy, and life expectancy. Terrible civil wars have torn apart several nations.

Nevertheless, Africa has many possibilities. Hydroelectric power from the Congo and other rivers, minerals such as iron and copper, and improved farming methods offer the hope of better lives to many Africans.

DID YOU KNOW?

Tectonic forces are slowly tearing Africa into two parts. The Rift Valley in eastern Africa marks the dividing line.

A Historical Look At Africa

Circa 140,000 B.C.E.
The first people live in Africa.

Circa 8000 B.C.E
Permanent fishing communities are established along many lakes and rivers.

3000 B.C.E.–400 C.E.
The Nile River valley is home to thriving civilizations.

500–1076
The kingdom of Ghana flourishes in the Sahel.

African Independence

In the late 19th and early 20th centuries, European countries colonized in almost all of Africa. As recently as 1950, only four African countries were independent: Egypt, Ethiopia, Liberia, and South Africa. During the following decades, anti-colonial movements gathered strength across the continent. By the end of the 1970s, a total of 43 countries had become independent. Today, the only African country that is not independent is Western Sahara, which is under the control of Morocco.

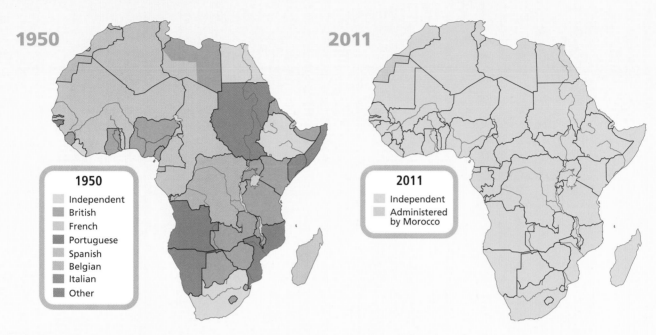

1950

2011

1950
Independent
British
French
Portuguese
Spanish
Belgian
Italian
Other

2011
Independent
Administered by Morocco

The People of Africa

There are more than 800 ethnic groups in Africa. It is estimated that the people of Africa speak between 800 and 1,600 different languages.

Girl from Egypt

Children from Ethiopia

Children from South Africa

Shepherd from the Sahel

1847
Liberia, founded as a refuge for freed slaves returning to Africa, gains independence.

1885
European countries divide Africa into colonies.

1950–1979
Most African countries become independent.

1991
South Africa ends apartheid, the official policy of racial segregation.

2011
South Sudan gains independence.

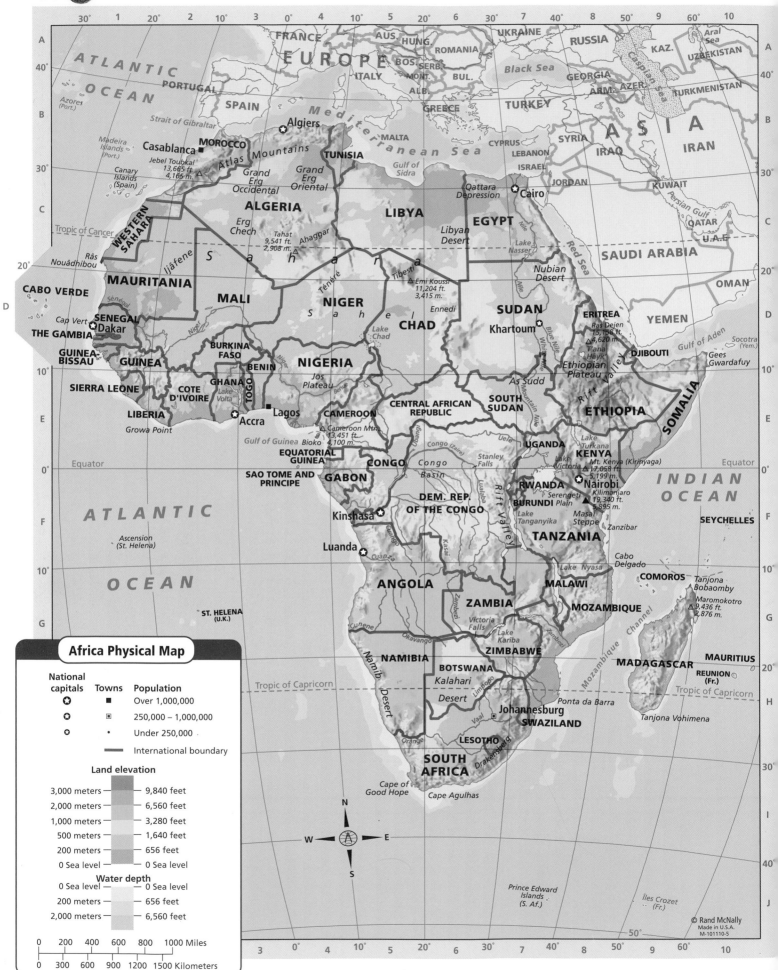

Africa Physical Map

National capitals
⊛ Over 1,000,000
⊛ 250,000 – 1,000,000
⊛ Under 250,000

Towns
■ Over 1,000,000
▣ 250,000 – 1,000,000
• Under 250,000

Population

——— International boundary

Land elevation

3,000 meters	9,840 feet
2,000 meters	6,560 feet
1,000 meters	3,280 feet
500 meters	1,640 feet
200 meters	656 feet
0 Sea level	0 Sea level

Water depth

0 Sea level	0 Sea level
200 meters	656 feet
2,000 meters	6,560 feet

0 200 400 600 800 1000 Miles
0 300 600 900 1200 1500 Kilometers

© Rand McNally
Made in U.S.A.
M-101110-5

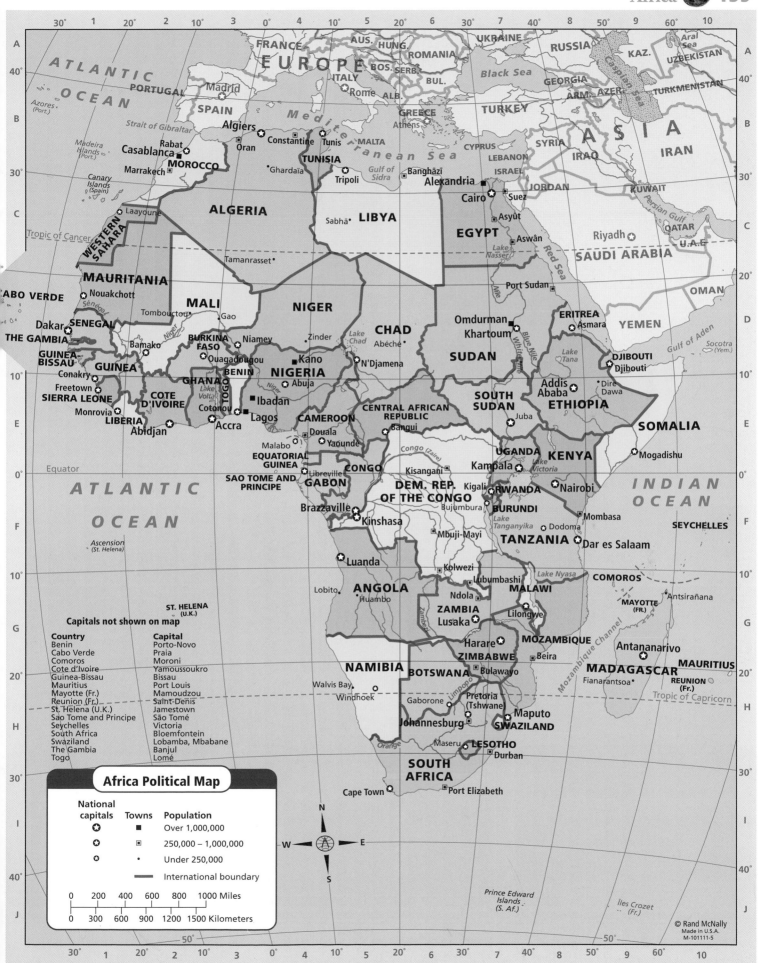

Africa Political Map

National capitals | Towns | Population
- ⊛ | ■ | Over 1,000,000
- ⊙ | ▣ | 250,000 – 1,000,000
- ○ | • | Under 250,000
- ——— International boundary

0 200 400 600 800 1000 Miles
0 300 600 900 1200 1500 Kilometers

Capitals not shown on map

Country	Capital
Benin	Porto-Novo
Cabo Verde	Praia
Comoros	Moroni
Cote d'Ivoire	Yamoussoukro
Guinea-Bissau	Bissau
Mauritius	Port Louis
Mayotte (Fr.)	Mamoudzou
Reunion (Fr.)	Saint-Denis
St. Helena (U.K.)	Jamestown
Sao Tome and Principe	São Tomé
Seychelles	Victoria
South Africa	Bloemfontein
Swaziland	Lobamba, Mbabane
The Gambia	Banjul
Togo	Lomé

© Rand McNally
Made in U.S.A.
M-101111-5

Environments

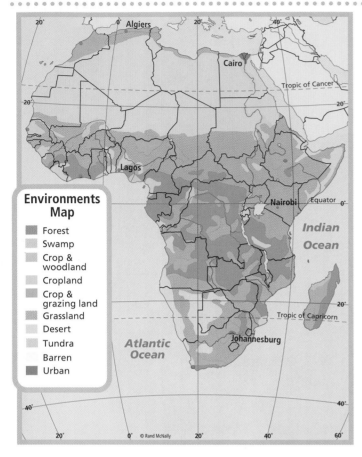

Environments Map

- Forest
- Swamp
- Crop & woodland
- Cropland
- Crop & grazing land
- Grassland
- Desert
- Tundra
- Barren
- Urban

© Rand McNally

Tropical rain forests of central Africa are hot and humid. Jungles are areas of dense, tangled plant growth in these forests.

An erg is a large area of sand dunes in a desert. Deserts cover about one-third of Africa.

Savannas, areas of grassland with few trees, cover about two-fifths of Africa's land area. Similar areas in North America are called prairies.

The region known as the Sahel borders the Sahara on the south. Overfarming, overgrazing, and droughts have caused parts of the Sahel to become desert.

An oasis in a desert is found where underground water comes to the surface.

Although many Africans still live in the countryside, Africa has large, modern cities. This is a view of Johannesburg, South Africa.

Africa's most fertile cropland is found along its rivers. This farm is in Egypt's Nile River valley.

Climate

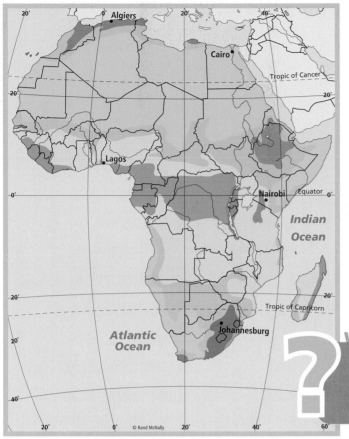

Climate Map

Tropical
- Hot with rain all year
- Hot with seasonal rain

Dry
- Desert
- Some rain

Moderate (Rainy Winter)
- Hot, dry summer
- Hot, humid summer
- Mild, rainy summer

Continental (Snowy Winter)
- Long, warm, humid summer
- Short, cool, humid summer
- Very short, cool, humid summer

Polar
- Tundra – very cold and dry
- Ice cap

Highlands
- Varies with altitude

The Sahara

The Sahara is the largest hot desert in the world. It covers about 3.3 million square miles (about 8.5 million square kilometers). The name *Sahara* comes from the Arabic word for desert.

The highest temperature ever recorded in the world was in the Sahara: 136°F (58°C). But the Sahara can be very cold at night, because the dry air does not hold much heat. The daytime and nighttime temperatures can differ by as much as 100°F (56°C).

On average, rainfall in the Sahara is less than 10 inches (25 centimeters) per year. There may be no rain at all for years at a time.

Besides sand, the Sahara has vast areas of gravel, rocky plateaus, and volcanic mountains.

WHAT IF?

? Scientists believe that the Sahara expands, recedes, and expands again. What happens if people settle on fertile land that turns back into desert?

Animals of the Savanna

African elephants

Lion

Thomson's gazelles

White rhinoceroses

Zebras

Cheetah and cub

Natural Hazards

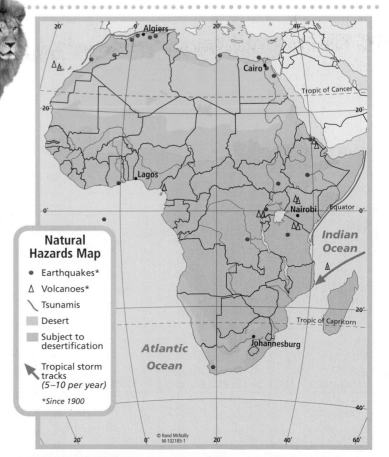

Natural Hazards Map

- • Earthquakes*
- △ Volcanoes*
- Tsunamis
- Desert
- Subject to desertification
- Tropical storm tracks (5–10 per year)

*Since 1900

© Rand McNally
M-102185-1

Population

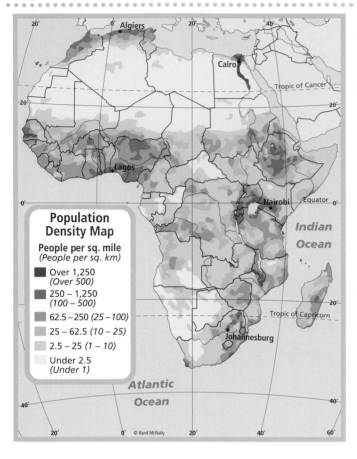

Life Expectancy

Life expectancy varies widely across Africa. In recent decades, the deadly disease AIDS has shortened the average life span of people in many African countries, especially those south of the Sahara Desert.

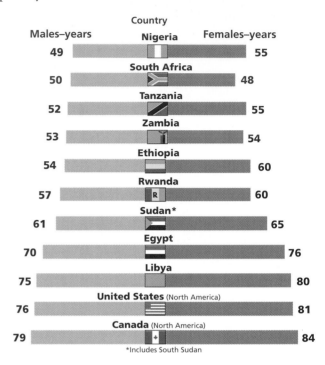

Males–years	Country	Females–years
49	Nigeria	55
50	South Africa	48
52	Tanzania	55
53	Zambia	54
54	Ethiopia	60
57	Rwanda	60
61	Sudan*	65
70	Egypt	76
75	Libya	80
76	United States (North America)	81
79	Canada (North America)	84

*Includes South Sudan

Transportation

DID YOU KNOW?
During the 1967 war with Israel, Egypt sank ships in the Suez Canal to block traffic. The canal stayed closed for eight years.

Fewer than 10% of the roads in Africa are paved.

Camels are still used to transport goods across the desert. Their heavy-lidded eyes and closeable nostrils offer protection in sandstorms, and they can travel long distances without water.

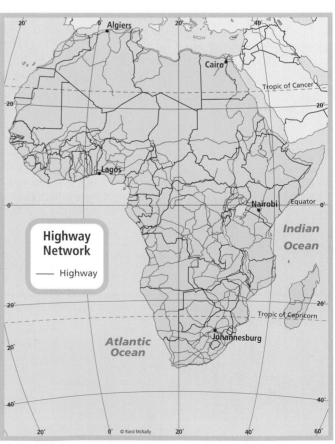

Highway Network
— Highway

Economic Activities

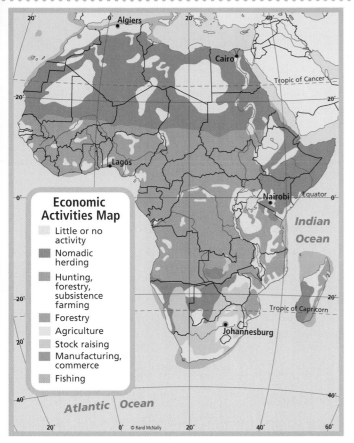

Per Capita Income

Per capita income measures the relative wealth of countries. Most African countries have per capita incomes far below those of the three wealthy non-African countries included in this graph: Canada, Sweden, and the United States.

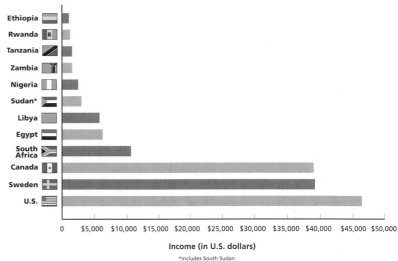

Income (in U.S. dollars)

*Includes South Sudan

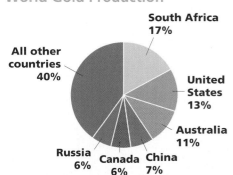

In many parts of Africa, nomadic herding is the way of life for most people.

The monuments of ancient Egypt attract millions of visitors each year. Tourism revenue is an important contributor to Egypt's economy.

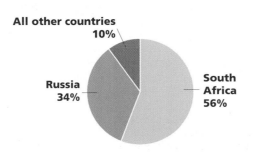

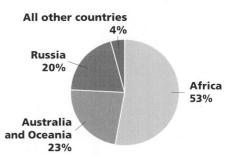

About 65% of all Africans make a living by farming.

World Gold Production

- South Africa 17%
- United States 13%
- Australia 11%
- China 7%
- Canada 6%
- Russia 6%
- All other countries 40%

World Platinum Production

- South Africa 56%
- Russia 34%
- All other countries 10%

World Diamond Production

- Africa 53%
- Australia and Oceania 23%
- Russia 20%
- All other countries 4%

One reason for the high annual per capita income for South Africa is that it is rich in gold, platinum, and diamonds. Discovery of these precious mineral resources in the 1800s brought many Europeans to settle in South Africa.

ASIA

Terraced rice field in Bali, Indonesia

Asia is the world's largest continent, and it is immense. It covers more than 17 million square miles (44 million square kilometers). It stretches from the sands of the Middle Eastern deserts in the west to the island country of Japan in the east. In the north, Siberian Russia extends beyond the Arctic Circle, while in the south Indonesia reaches the equator.

Asia is home to some of the world's oldest civilizations. Farming, cities, and writing began in Mesopotamia, in the Indus River valley, and in China thousands of years ago. Asians also invented many things that we use today, such as the idea of zero, paper, the printing press, and the magnetic compass.

Many countries in Asia are working to develop their economies, and their people still have difficult lives. Other Asian countries such as Japan, Taiwan, and Singapore are economic powers. The fortunes of the oil-rich countries of the Middle East depend on the value of their oil exports.

Asia has more people than any other continent: 4.2 billion, which is about 60% of the world's people. China alone has 1.3 billion people, and India has passed one billion. Eastern China is as densely populated as the New York City urban area.

Oil drums

Mt. Fuji in Japan

Limestone pinnacles along the Li River in China

A Historical Look At Asia

Circa 3500 B.C.E.
Sumerian civilization begins in Mesopotamia (modern Iraq).

C.E. 618-907
The T'ang Dynasty rules China.

403 B.C.E.
Construction of the Great Wall of China begins.

1631-1648
The Taj Mahal is built in India.

The Regions of Asia

Asia has six distinct regions. Use the political map on pages 168 and 169 to determine the countries in each region.

Central Asia
Central Asia is rugged and dry. Farming in most places is difficult, and many people make a living as nomadic herders. The region has large deposits of oil.

Southwest Asia
Most of Southwest Asia is desert and semi-desert. The region has the world's richest deposits of oil.

South Asia
India and neighboring countries make up South Asia. The Himalayas border the northeastern part of this region.

North Asia
North Asia has long, bitterly cold winters. Despite its mineral resources, fewer people live in North Asia than in any other part of the continent.

East Asia
Eastern China and its neighbors make up East Asia. About one quarter of the world's people live in East Asia.

Southeast Asia
The southeast part of the Asian mainland and many islands make up Southeast Asia. Most of the region has a tropical climate.

DID YOU KNOW?
The highest point in the world (Mt. Everest) and the lowest point (the Dead Sea) are both in Asia.

Central Asia

Southwest Asia

South Asia

North Asia

East Asia

Southeast Asia

1854
Japan begins trading with the United States.

Circa 1900
Britain begins developing oil fields in southwestern Iran.

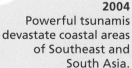

1947
India is divided into two countries, India and Pakistan, and both become independent from British rule.

2004
Powerful tsunamis devastate coastal areas of Southeast and South Asia.

Mt. Everest, which rises along the border between Nepal and China, is the world's highest mountain. It is 29,028 feet (8,848 meters) high.

The Dead Sea, located between Israel and Jordan, is the lowest point on Earth. Its shore is 1,339 feet (408 meters) below sea level.

Lake Baikal in Russia is the deepest lake in the world. Its greatest depth is slightly more than a mile.

Russia's Kamchatka Peninsula is one of the most volcanically active places in the world.

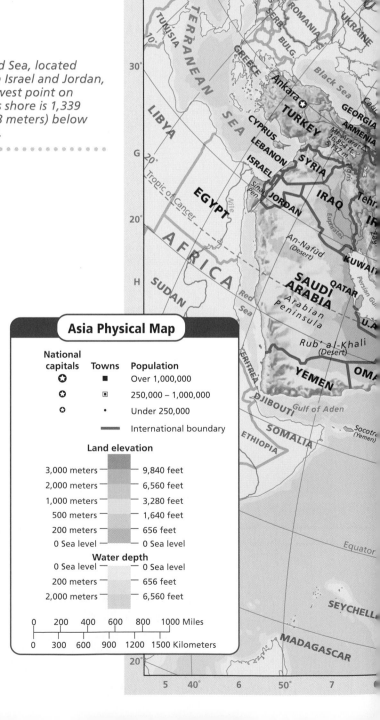

Asia Physical Map

National capitals
- ✪ Over 1,000,000
- ✪ 250,000 – 1,000,000
- ○ Under 250,000

Towns   **Population**
- ■ Over 1,000,000
- ▣ 250,000 – 1,000,000
- • Under 250,000

— International boundary

Land elevation

3,000 meters	9,840 feet
2,000 meters	6,560 feet
1,000 meters	3,280 feet
500 meters	1,640 feet
200 meters	656 feet
0 Sea level	0 Sea level

Water depth

0 Sea level	0 Sea level
200 meters	656 feet
2,000 meters	6,560 feet

0   200   400   600   800   1000 Miles
0   300   600   900   1200   1500 Kilometers

ARCTIC OCEAN

North Pole

BARENTS SEA

KARA SEA

LAPTEV SEA

EAST SIBERIAN SEA

New Siberian Islands

North Siberian Lowland

Central Siberian Plateau

RUSSIA

Verkhoyansk Mts.

BERING SEA

Kamchatka Peninsula

Mys Lopatka

SEA OF OKHOTSK

Yamal Pen.

Severnaya Zemlya

Novaya Zemlya

West Siberian Plain

Ob

Yenisey

S i b e r i a

Stanovoy Mountains

Amur

Lena

Kolyma

Indigirka

Aleutian Islands (U.S.)

Novosibirsk

Angara

Lake Baikal

Yablonovy Range

Sikhote-Alin (Mts.)

Sakhalin

Tatar Strait

Kuril Islands

Hokkaidō

KAZAKHSTAN

Kazakh Hills

Altay Mountains

Sayan Mountains

Selenge

MONGOLIA

Greater Khingan Range

Manchuria

Honshū

JAPAN

Tōkyō

Üstirt (Plateau)

Aral Sea

Lake Balkhash

Dzungarian Basin

Gobi Desert

Bo Hai

NORTH KOREA

SEA OF JAPAN (EAST SEA)

Fuji-san 12,388 ft. 3,776 m.

UZBEKISTAN

Syr Darya

Tien Shan

Beijing

SOUTH KOREA

Korea Strait

Shikoku

Kyūshū

PACIFIC OCEAN

TURKMENISTAN

KYRGYZSTAN

TAJIKISTAN

Pamirs (Mts.)

Amu Darya

Tarim Pendi (Basin)

Qilian Shan (Mts.)

Huang (Yellow)

YELLOW SEA

EAST CHINA SEA

K2 (Qogir Feng) 28,250 ft. △ 8,611 m.

Altun Shan (Mts.)

Qaidam Pendi (Basin)

CHINA

AFGHANISTAN

Hindu Kush

Kunlun Mts.

Qin Ling (Mts.)

Shanghai

Tropic of Cancer

NORTHERN MARIANA ISLANDS (U.S.)

PAKISTAN

New Delhi

Plateau of Tibet

Himalayas

Szechwan Basin

Yangtze

Wuyi Shan (Hills)

Great Indian Desert

Indus

NEPAL

Mt. Everest ▲ 29,028 ft. 8,848 m.

BHUTAN

Brahmaputra

Ganges

Plateau of Yunnan

Nan Ling (Mts.)

Taiwan Strait

Philippine Sea

GUAM (U.S.)

Gulf of Oman

INDIA

Kāthiāwār Peninsula

Mumbai (Bombay)

BANGLA-DESH

Kolkata (Calcutta)

MYANMAR

LAOS

Red

Gulf of Tonkin

Hainan Dao

Luzon Strait

Luzon

Godāvari

Irrawaddy

Salween

Mekong

Indochina

Manila

PHILIPPINES

Deccan (Plateau)

Western Ghats

Eastern Ghats

Bay of Bengal

THAILAND

Bangkok

VIETNAM

SOUTH CHINA SEA

PALAU

ARABIAN SEA

Lakshadweep (India)

Andaman Islands (India)

CAMBODIA

Mindanao

Cape Comorin

SRI LANKA

Andaman Sea

Gulf of Thailand

Mui Ca Mau (Cape)

Sulu Sea

MALDIVES

Dondra Head

Nicobar Islands (India)

MALAY PENINSULA

MALAYSIA

BRUNEI

Celebes Sea

New Guinea

Puncak Jaya △ 16,503 ft. 5,030 m.

Str. of Malacca

SINGAPORE

MALAYSIA

Celebes

Moluccas

Ceram

Banda Sea

Arafura Sea

INDIAN OCEAN

N W E S

Sumatra

Greater Sunda Islands

Java Sea

INDONESIA

Borneo

Lesser Sunda Is.

TIMOR-LESTE

Gulf of Carpentaria

Jakarta

Java

Timor

AUSTRALIA

Timor Sea

© Rand McNally
Made in U.S.A.
M-101114-6

Arctic Circle

Caspian Depression

Volga

Esil

Irtysh

Ob

Equator

Indonesia is an island nation located in Southeast Asia. It has a larger population than all but three of the world's countries: China, India, and the United States.

China is the world's most populous country. It is home to more than 1.3 billion people.

Kyrgyzstan is located in Central Asia. It became a country when the Soviet Union broke up in 1991.

Turkey is Asia's westernmost country. Istanbul, Turkey's largest city, lies along the Bosporus Strait, which divides Asia and Europe.

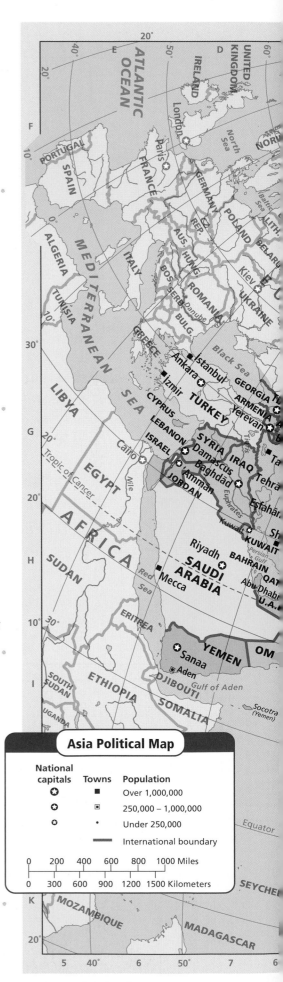

Asia Political Map

National capitals	Towns	Population
✪	■	Over 1,000,000
✪	◻	250,000 – 1,000,000
✪	•	Under 250,000
		International boundary

0 200 400 600 800 1000 Miles
0 300 600 900 1200 1500 Kilometers

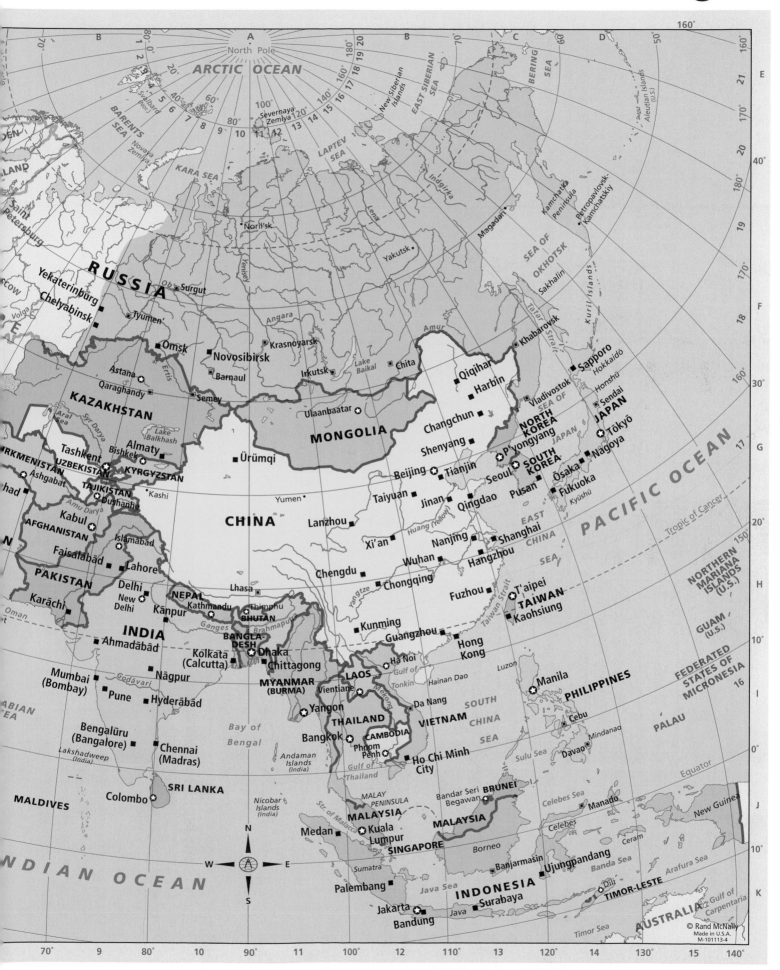

ARCTIC OCEAN

North Pole

BARENTS SEA

KARA SEA

LAPTEV SEA

EAST SIBERIAN SEA

BERING SEA

New Siberian Islands

Aleutian Islands (U.S.)

Severnaya Zemlya

Novaya Zemlya

Saint Petersburg

RUSSIA

Yekaterinburg
Chelyabinsk
Tyumen'
Omsk
Surgut
Nor'l'sk
Krasnoyarsk
Novosibirsk
Barnaul
Irkutsk
Yakutsk
Chita
Magadan
Khabarovsk

SEA OF OKHOTSK

Kamchatka Peninsula
Petropavlovsk-Kamchatskiy

Kuril Islands

Sakhalin

Tatar Strait

Astana
Qaraghandy
Semey
Ulaanbaatar

MONGOLIA

Qiqihar
Harbin
Changchun
Shenyang

Vladivostok

SEA OF JAPAN

Sapporo
Hokkaidō
Sendai
Honshū
Tōkyō
Nagoya

JAPAN

KAZAKHSTAN

Aral Sea
Lake Balkhash
Almaty
Tashkent
Bishkek

KYRGYZSTAN

Ürümqi

NORTH KOREA
P'yongyang
Seoul
SOUTH KOREA
Pusan

Osaka
Fukuoka
Kyūshū

Syr Darya

TURKMENISTAN
UZBEKISTAN
Ashgabat
Dushanbe
TAJIKISTAN

Kashi

Yumen

Beijing
Tianjin

Taiyuan
Jinan
Qingdao

PACIFIC OCEAN

Amu Darya

Kabul
AFGHANISTAN
Islamabad
Faisalabad
Lahore

CHINA

Lanzhou

Xi'an

Nanjing
Shanghai

EAST CHINA SEA

Tropic of Cancer

NORTHERN MARIANA ISLANDS (U.S.)

PAKISTAN
Delhi
New Delhi
Kānpur
Karāchi

Lhasa

NEPAL
Kathmandu
Thimphu
BHUTAN

Chengdu
Chongqing
Wuhan
Hangzhou

Fuzhou

T'aipei
TAIWAN
Kaohsiung

GUAM (U.S.)

Huang (Yellow)

Yangtze

Taiwan Strait

Ahmadābād

INDIA

Ganges
Brahmaputra
BANGLA-DESH
Kolkata (Calcutta)
Dhaka
Chittagong

Kunming

Guangzhou

Hong Kong

FEDERATED STATES OF MICRONESIA

Mumbai (Bombay)
Nāgpur
Pune
Hyderābād

Godāvari

MYANMAR (BURMA)
LAOS
Vientiane
Ha Noi
Gulf of Tonkin

Hainan Dao

Luzon
Manila
PHILIPPINES

Yangon
THAILAND
Bangkok
CAMBODIA
Phnom Penh

Da Nang
VIETNAM

SOUTH CHINA SEA

Cebu
Mindanao
Davao

PALAU

Bengalūru (Bangalore)
Chennai (Madras)

Lakshadweep (India)

Bay of Bengal

Andaman Islands (India)

Ho Chi Minh City

Gulf of Thailand

Sulu Sea

ARABIAN SEA

Gulf of Oman

MALDIVES

Colombo
SRI LANKA

Nicobar Islands (India)

Str. of Malacca

MALAY PENINSULA

Bandar Seri Begawan
BRUNEI

Celebes Sea

Manado

New Guinea

MALAYSIA
Medan
Kuala Lumpur
SINGAPORE

MALAYSIA

Borneo

Celebes

Ceram

Banda Sea

INDIAN OCEAN

Sumatra

Banjarmasin
Ujungpandang

Arafura Sea

Palembang

INDONESIA

Java Sea

Surabaya

Dili
TIMOR-LESTE

Jakarta
Bandung

Java

Timor Sea

AUSTRALIA

Gulf of Carpentaria

N
W E
S

© Rand McNally
Made in U.S.A.
M-101113-4

Middle East Political Map

National capitals	Towns	Population
⊛	■	Over 1,000,000
⊛	▣	250,000 – 1,000,000
⊛	•	Under 250,000
────		International boundary

0   100   200   300   400 Miles

0   200   400   600 Kilometers

ITALY
Adriatic Sea
Sofia
BULGARIA
Skopje
Tirane
MACEDONIA
ALBANIA
Thessaloníki
İstanbul
Bursa
GREECE
Aegean Sea
Eskişehir
Ankara
Athens
İzmir
Ionian Sea
Ionian Islands
TURKEY
Crete
MEDITERRANEAN SEA
Antalya
Konya
Kayseri
İcel
Adana
Gaziantep
Malatya
Diyarbakır
Lake Van
Samsun
BLACK SEA
RUSSIA
GEORGIA
Tbilisi
ARMENIA
Yerevan
AZERBAIJAN
Baku
AZER.
Erzurum
Orūmīyeh
Lake Urmia
Tabrīz
Rasht
CASP
Mosul
Arbīl
As-Sulaymānīyah
Kirkuk
Hamadān
Kermānshāh
CYPRUS
Nicosia
Latakia
Aleppo
SYRIA
Himş
Euphrates
Tigris
LEBANON
Beirut
Damascus
Baghdād
IRAQ
Banghāzī
Gulf of Sidra
Tubruq
ISRAEL
Tel Aviv-Yafo
Gaza
Jerusalem
'Ammān
Dead Sea
Karbalā'
An-Najaf
Alexandria
El-Mansûra
Port Said
Suez Canal
JORDAN
Ahu
Giza
Suez
Cairo
El-Fayoum
Sinai Pen.
Al-'Aqabah
Tabūk
Gulf of Aqaba
Basra
KUWAIT
Kuwait
El-Minya
Nile
Asyût
Suhag
Luxor
Hā'il
Ad-Damn
LIBYA
EGYPT
Al-Jawf
Tropic of Cancer
Aswân
Lake Nasser
Buraydah
Al-Hu
Medina
Riyadh
SAUDI ARABIA
RED SEA
CHAD
SUDAN
N
W   E
S
Port Sudan
Jiddah
Mecca
Aţ-Ţā'if
Khamīs Mushayţ
'Aţbarah
Omdurman
Khartoum
Kassalā
ERITREA
Asmara
DJIBOUTI
Sanaa
YEMEN
Al-Hudaydah
Al-Mu
Al-Fāshir
Wad Madanī
Ta'izz
Al-Ubayyiḏ
Blue Nile
White Nile
ETHIOPIA
T'ana Hāyk'
Aden
Gulf of Aden
Djibouti
SOUTH SUDAN
Addis Ababa
SOMALIA

The Middle East

Africa, Asia, and Europe meet in the Middle East. Since ancient times, great powerful empires have fought to control these lands, their resources, and their trade routes. Today, the oil that many Middle Eastern countries produce is valuable to rich countries. There are also deep-rooted cultural conflicts among the peoples of the region.

Oil pumpjack

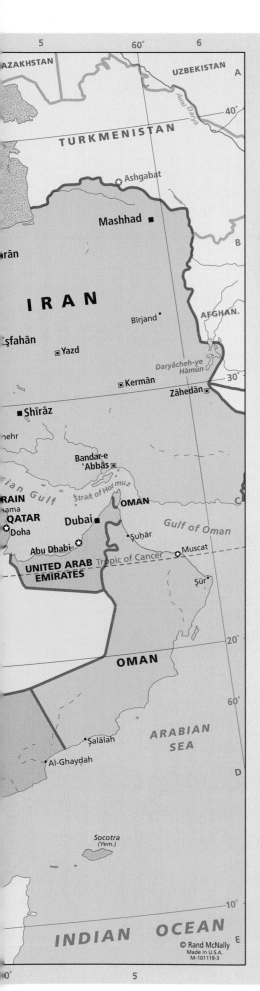

© Rand McNally
Made in U.S.A.
M-101119-3

0   10   20   30   40   50 Miles
0   20   40   60   80 Kilometers

MEDITERRANEAN

SEA

Ⓐ Golan Heights. Occupied and unilaterally annexed by Israel.

Ⓑ West Bank. Controlled by Israel, parts administered by the Palestinian Authority. Permanent status to be determined.

Ⓒ Gaza Strip. Administered by the Palestinian Authority following unilateral withdrawal by Israel in 2005. Permanent status to be determined.

N-CLA61400-P1- -I-1-1

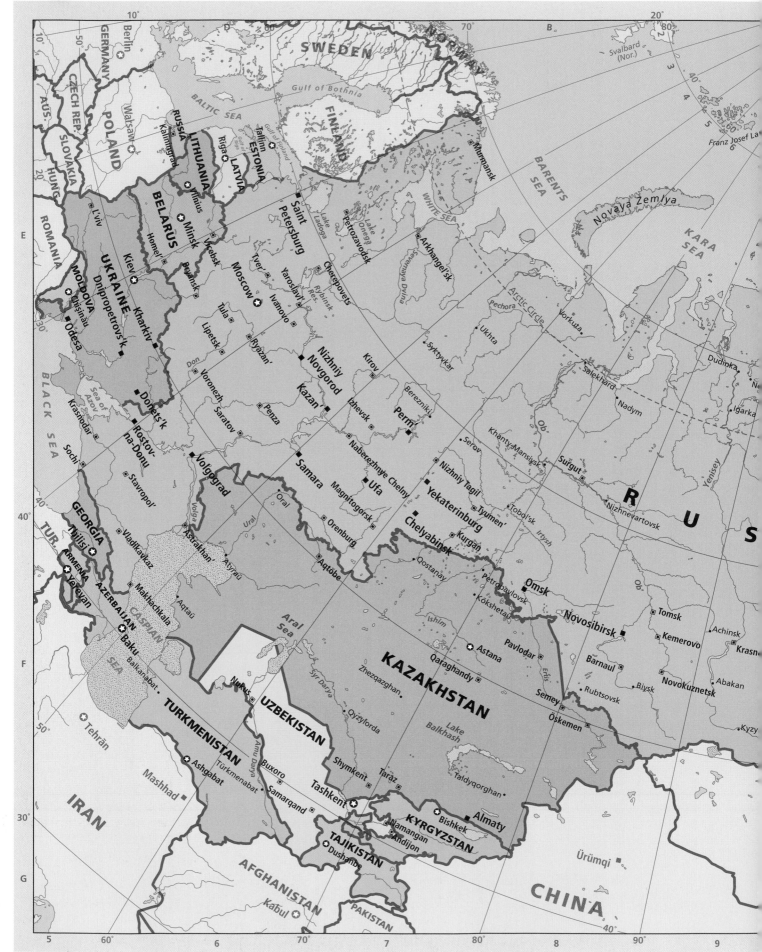

SWEDEN

NORWAY

Svalbard
(Nor.)

Franz Josef Land

GERMANY
Berlin

POLAND
Warsaw

CZECH REP.
AUS.
SLOVAKIA
HUNG.
ROMANIA

BALTIC SEA

Gulf of Bothnia

FINLAND

BARENTS
SEA

KARA
SEA

Novaya Zemlya

Kaliningrad
Riga
LITHUANIA
Vilnius
LATVIA
ESTONIA
Tallinn
Gulf of Finland
Saint
Petersburg
Lake
Ladoga
Lake
Onega
Petrozavodsk
Murmansk
WHITE SEA
Arkhangel'sk
Severnaya Dvina

E

L'viv
UKRAINE
Kiev
Kharkiv
Dnipropetrovs'k
Homel'
BELARUS
Minsk
Hrodna
Vitsebsk
Tver'
Moscow
Yaroslavl'
Ivanovo
Rybinsk
Res.
Cherepovets
Pechora
Arctic Circle
Vorkuta

MOLDOVA
Chişinău
Odesa

Tula
Lipetsk
Ryazan'
Nizhniy
Novgorod
Kazan'
Izhevsk
Perm'
Kirov
Syktyvkar
Ukhta
Salekhard
Dudinka
Nadym
Igarka

BLACK
SEA
Krasnodar
Sochi
Sea of
Azov
Donets'k
Rostov-
na-Donu
Stavropol'
Voronezh
Saratov
Penza
Don
Naberezhnye Chelny
Ufa
Magnitogorsk
Berezniki
Nizhniy Tagil
Yekaterinburg
Serov
Khanty-Mansiysk
Ob'
R   U   S
Nizhnevartovsk
Yenisey

GEORGIA
Tbilisi
TUR.
ARMENIA
Yerevan
Volgograd
Samara
Astrakhan
Oral
Ural
Orenburg
Aqtöbe
Chelyabinsk
Kurgan
Tyumen'
Tobol'sk
Irtysh
Surgut
S

40°
Vladikavkaz
AZERBAIJAN
Makhachkala
Baku
Aqtau
CASPIAN
SEA
Atyraū
Aral
Sea
Qostanay
Petropavlovsk
Kökshetau
Omsk
Tomsk
Achinsk
Krasn
Kemerovo

Balkanabat
TURKMENISTAN
Ashgabat
Mashhad
Nukus
UZBEKISTAN
Syr Darya
Zhezqazghan
Qyzylorda
Ishim
Astana
Qaraghandy
Pavlodar
Ertis
Novosibirsk
Barnaul
Biysk
Rubtsovsk
Novokuznetsk
Abakan

IRAN
Tehrān
Türkmenabat
Anu Darya
Buxoro
Samarqand
KAZAKHSTAN
Shymkent
Taraz
Lake
Balkhash
Taldyqorghan
Semey
Öskemen
Kyzy

AFGHANISTAN
Kābul
PAKISTAN
Tashkent
TAJIKISTAN
Dushanbe
Namangan
Andijon
KYRGYZSTAN
Bishkek
Almaty
Ürümqi
CHINA

5   6   7   8   9

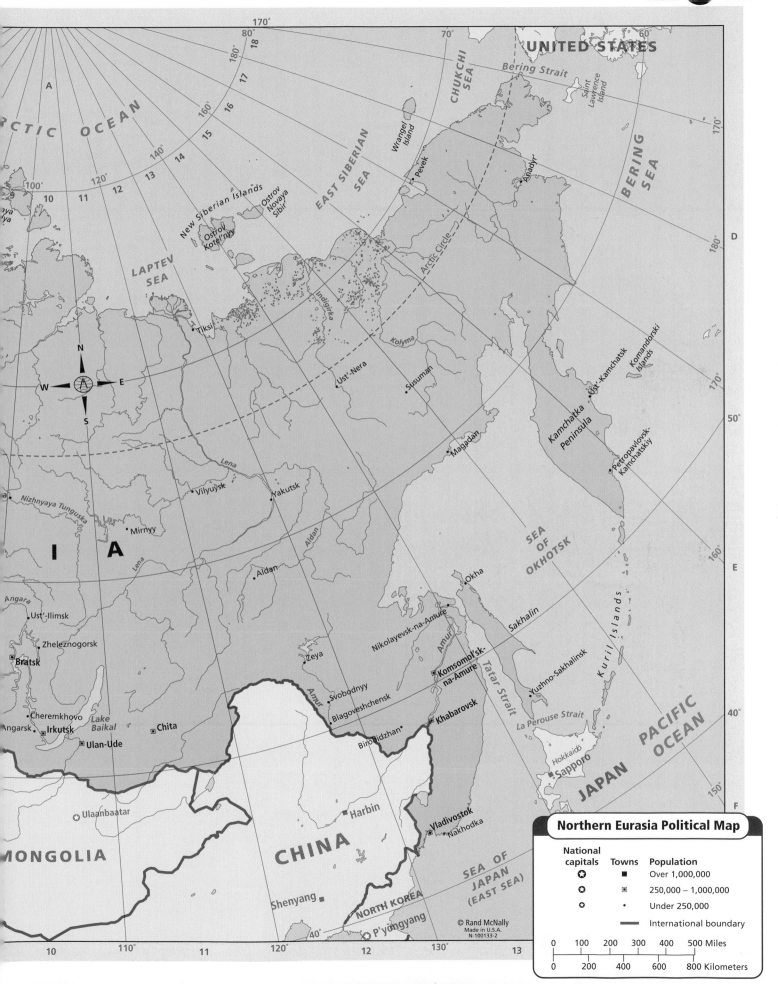

170°
180°
18
17
16
15
14
13
12
11
10

80°
70°
60°

ARCTIC OCEAN

A

UNITED STATES

Bering Strait

CHUKCHI SEA

Saint Lawrence Island

160°
140°
120°
100°

9

10

11

12

13

14

BERING SEA

170°

D

180°

New Siberian Islands

Ostrov Novaya Sibir'

Wrangel Island

Pevek

Anadyr'

LAPTEV SEA

Ostrov Kotel'nyy

EAST SIBERIAN SEA

Arctic Circle

N
W E
S

Tiksi

Indigirka

Kolyma

Susuman

Ust'-Nera

Magadan

Komandorski Islands

Ust'-Kamchatsk

170°

50°

Lena

Vilyuysk

Yakutsk

Kamchatka Peninsula

Petropavlovsk-Kamchatskiy

Nizhnyaya Tunguska

Mirnyy

Aldan

Lena

Aldan

SEA OF OKHOTSK

160°

E

I   A

Angara

Ust'-Ilimsk

Zheleznogorsk

Bratsk

Zeya

Amur

Svobodnyy

Blagoveshchensk

Okha

Nikolayevsk-na-Amure

Amur

Komsomol'sk-na-Amure

Sakhalin

Kuril Islands

Yuzhno-Sakhalinsk

Tatar Strait

La Perouse Strait

PACIFIC OCEAN

40°

Cheremkhovo

Lake Baikal

Chita

Khabarovsk

Angarsk

Irkutsk

Ulan-Ude

Birobidzhan

Hokkaidō

Sapporo

JAPAN

150°

F

Ulaanbaatar

Harbin

Vladivostok

Nakhodka

MONGOLIA

CHINA

SEA OF JAPAN (EAST SEA)

Shenyang

NORTH KOREA

P'yongyang

40°

© Rand McNally
Made in U.S.A.
N-100133-2

10
110°
11
120°
12
130°
13

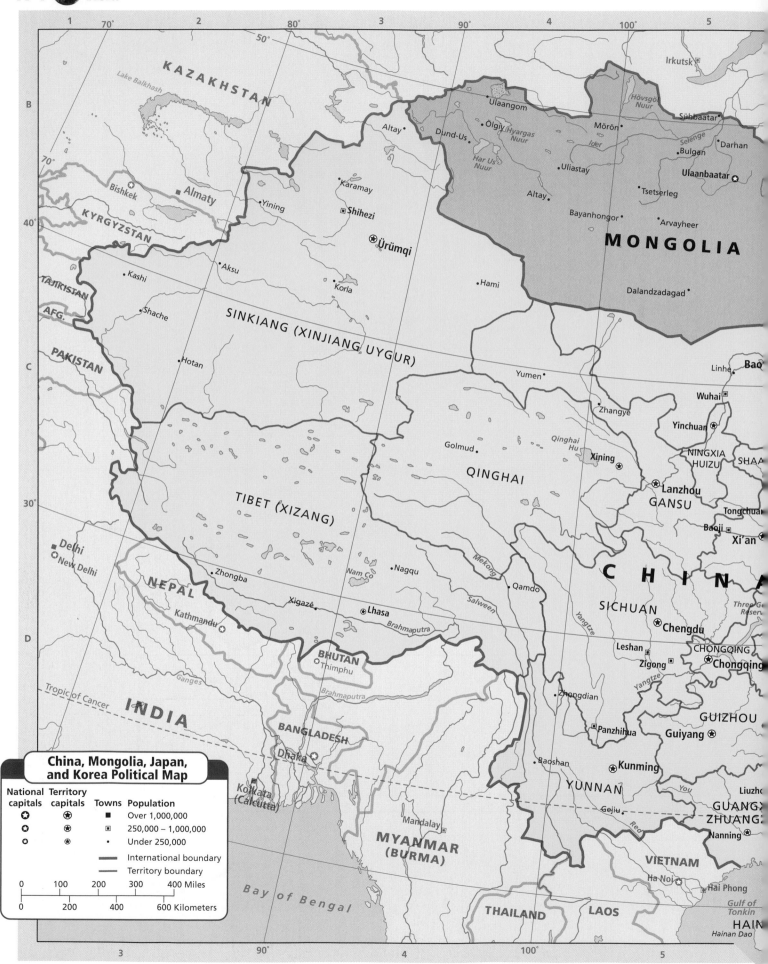

KAZAKHSTAN

Lake Balkhash

Bishkek

KYRGYZSTAN

TAJIKISTAN

AFG.

PAKISTAN

■ Almaty

• Yining

• Karamay

☉ Shihezi

⊕ Ürümqi

• Kashi

• Aksu

• Korla

• Shache

• Hotan

SINKIANG (XINJIANG UYGUR)

Altay •

Dund-Us •

Ulaangom •

Ölgiy Hyargas Nuur

Har Us Nuur

Altay •

• Uliastay

Hövsgöl Nuur

Mörön •

Selenge

Sühbaatar •

Iger

• Bulgan

Darhan •

⊛ Ulaanbaatar

• Tsetserleg

Bayanhongor •

• Arvayheer

MONGOLIA

• Hami

Dalandzadagad •

Linhe • ☐ Bao

Wuhai ☐

Yinchuan ☐

NINGXIA HUIZU

SHAA

Yumen •

• Zhangye

Qinghai Hu

Xining ☉

⊛ Lanzhou

GANSU

Tongchuan

Baoji ☐

Xi'an ☐

Golmud •

QINGHAI

TIBET (XIZANG)

Nam Co

• Nagqu

Mekong

Salween

Yangtze

C H I N A

SICHUAN

Three G Reser

⊛ Chengdu

Leshan ☐

CHONGQING

Zigong ☐

Chongqing

• Zhongba

Delhi ■

⊕ New Delhi

NEPAL

Kathmandu ☉

Xigazê •

⊛ Lhasa

Brahmaputra

Ganges

BHUTAN

Thimphu ☉

• Qamdo

Brahmaputra

• Zhongdian

GUIZHOU

• Panzhihua

Guiyang ☉

YUNNAN

• Baoshan

Kunming ☉

Liuzho

GUANGX ZHUANG

Gejiu •

Nanning •

You

Red

VIETNAM

Ha Noi ⊛

Hai Phong •

Gulf of Tonkin

Tropic of Cancer

I N D I A

BANGLADESH

Dhaka ⊕

Kolkata (Calcutta) ☐

Mandalay •

MYANMAR (BURMA)

Bay of Bengal

THAILAND

LAOS

HAIN

Hainan Dao

China, Mongolia, Japan, and Korea Political Map

National capitals	Territory capitals	Towns	Population
✪	✪	■	Over 1,000,000
☉	☉	☐	250,000 – 1,000,000
✪	✪	•	Under 250,000

International boundary

Territory boundary

0   100   200   300   400 Miles

0   200   400   600 Kilometers

RUSSIA

6 120°   7 130°   8 140°   9 150°   10

SEA OF OKHOTSK

B

Ergun Zuoqi

Heihe

Ergun

Hailar   Yakeshi

Hulun Nur

Choybalsan

HEILONGJIANG

Bei'an

Hegang

Shuangyashan

Kerulen

Baruun-Urt

Qiqihar   Daqing   Suihua   Jixi

Harbin

Songhua

Sakhalin

La Perouse Strait

Asahikawa

Sapporo

Hokkaidō

150°

40°

Ulaan-Uul

Baicheng

JILIN

Mudanjiang

Changchun   Jilin

Liaoyuan

Vladivostok

Ch'ŏngjin

Hakodate

Aomori

Morioka

NEI MONGGOL

Chifeng

Fushun

Shenyang   Benxi

Jinzhou   Anshan

LIAONING   Dandong

Sinŭiju

Fuxin

Kimch'aek

NORTH KOREA

Akita

Honshū

Sendai

SEA OF JAPAN (EAST SEA)

Niigata

JAPAN

Iwaki

C

Hohhot   Zhangjiakou

Datong

Baoding

Shijiazhuang   HEBEI

Yangquan

SHANXI

Handan

Beijing   Tangshan

Tianjin

Dalian

Yalu   Wŏnsan

Namp'o   P'yŏngyang

Bo Hai   Korea Bay

Seoul

SOUTH KOREA

Toyama

Kanazawa

Nagano   Tōkyō

Yokohama

Nagoya   Shizuoka

Hamamatsu

Utsunomiya

Oki-shotō

Yantai

Huang (Yellow)

Zibo

Jinan

SHANDONG

Qingdao

YELLOW SEA

Ch'ŏngju

Taejŏn

Chŏnju

Kwangju

Taegu

Ulsan

Pusan

Masan

Kyōto

Kōbe   Ōsaka

Hiroshima

Matsuyama

Anyang

Xinxiang

Kaifeng

Zhengzhou

Xuzhou

JIANGSU

Yancheng

Kitakyūshū

Fukuoka

Ōita

Kumamoto

Shikoku

HENAN   ANHUI

Huainan

Nanjing   Nantong

Cheju-do (S. Korea)

Nagasaki

Korea Strait

Miyazaki

Xiangfan

Hefei

Wuhu

Wuxi

Suzhou   Shanghai

Kyūshū

Kagoshima

EAST

Huangshi

Wuhan

Yangtze

Hangzhou

Ningbo

CHINA

Yaku-shima   Tanega-shima

PACIFIC OCEAN

30°

N

W   E

S

D

Jingdezhen

Dongtiog Hu

Nanchang

Poyang Hu

ZHEJIANG

Wenzhou

SEA

Amami-Ō-shima

Tokuno-shima

Changsha

Pingxiang

Hengyang

JIANGXI

HUNAN

Fuzhou

FUJIAN

Ryukyu Islands (Japan)

Okinawa-jima

130°

Naha

20°

140°

8

ASIA

140°

Chilung

T'aipei

T'aichung

Chiai

T'ainan   TAIWAN

Kaohsiung

Iriomote-jima   Miyako-jima

Ishigaki-shima

Tropic of Cancer

PHILIPPINE

SEA

MONGOLIA

CHINA

NORTH KOREA

JAPAN

SOUTH KOREA

TAIWAN

Shaoguan

GUANGDONG

Xiamen

Shantou

Taiwan Strait

Guangzhou

Hong Kong

Macau

Pratas Island
(Occupied by Taiwan, claimed by China)

SOUTH CHINA SEA

PHILIPPINES

Luzon Strait

E

6   120°   7

Climate

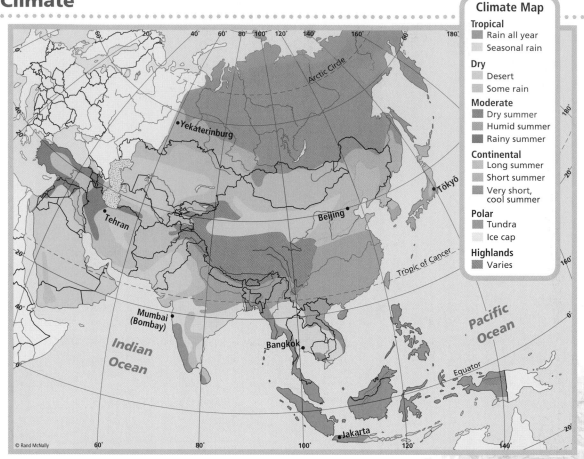

Climate Map

Tropical
- Rain all year
- Seasonal rain

Dry
- Desert
- Some rain

Moderate
- Dry summer
- Humid summer
- Rainy summer

Continental
- Long summer
- Short summer
- Very short, cool summer

Polar
- Tundra
- Ice cap

Highlands
- Varies

© Rand McNally

Rain forests thrive in the hot, rainy climate of Southeast Asia.

Eastern China has a moderate climate with humid summers. This is like the climate of the eastern United States.

Economic Activities

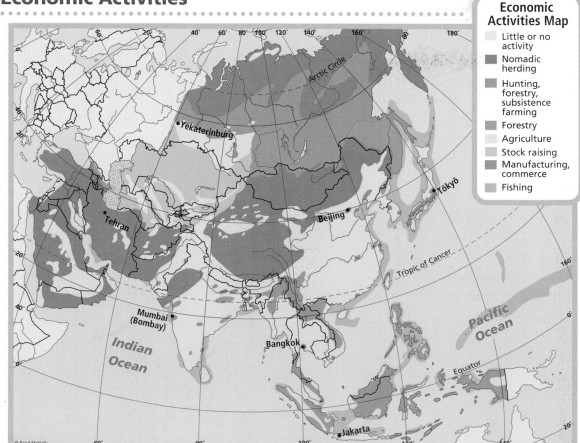

Economic Activities Map
- Little or no activity
- Nomadic herding
- Hunting, forestry, subsistence farming
- Forestry
- Agriculture
- Stock raising
- Manufacturing, commerce
- Fishing

© Rand McNally

Rice is the most important food crop in Southeast Asia.

Japan sends many of its exports to the United States, but it trades with other countries, as well. Trading with many countries helps a country continue to earn money if one trading partner has economic problems.

Populations

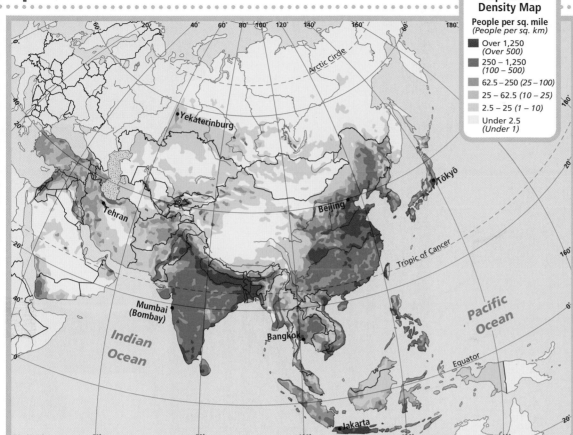

Population Density Map
People per sq. mile
(People per sq. km)

■	Over 1,250 *(Over 500)*
■	250 – 1,250 *(100 – 500)*
■	62.5 – 250 *(25 – 100)*
■	25 – 62.5 *(10 – 25)*
■	2.5 – 25 *(1 – 10)*
□	Under 2.5 *(Under 1)*

Seoul, South Korea, is home to more than 9.7 million people.

Bangladesh is one of the most densely populated countries in the world.

Much of Mongolia is sparsely populated.

India and China

China and India are the world's population giants. Both have populations of more than one billion people. India's population, however, is growing faster. By 2040 it will be larger than China's. Since about 1980, China has brought down its rate of population growth by strictly limiting how many children a family may have.

India and China Population Growth

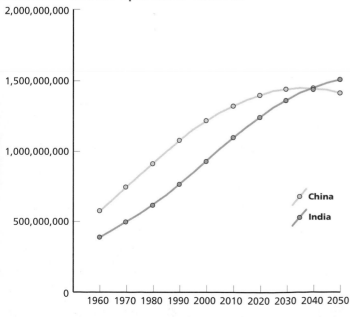

● China
● India

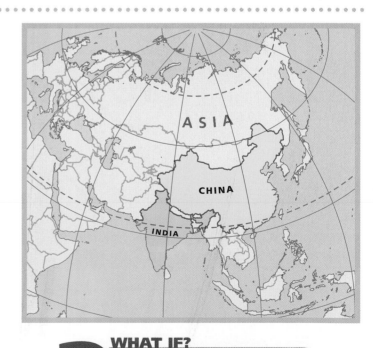

WHAT IF?

? What do you think life in India will be like if the population continues to grow rapidly?

Transportation

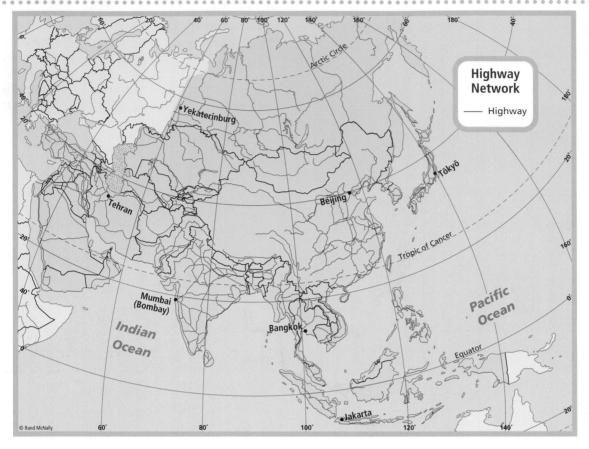

Highway Network

— Highway

Yekaterinburg

Tehran

Tōkyō

Beijing

Mumbai
(Bombay)

Bangkok

Indian
Ocean

Pacific
Ocean

Equator

Tropic of Cancer

Arctic Circle

Jakarta

© Rand McNally

Japan's bullet trains can travel at speeds of up to 155 miles per hour (249 kilometers per hour).

Mountainous terrain makes road-building difficult in many parts of Asia.

The country of Nepal lies along the southern edge of the Himalayas. Thick woodlands cover some of the lower elevations.

Environments

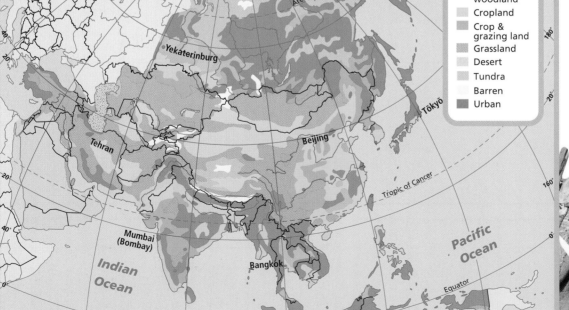

Environments Map

- Forest
- Swamp
- Crop & woodland
- Cropland
- Crop & grazing land
- Grassland
- Desert
- Tundra
- Barren
- Urban

Yekaterinburg

Tehran

Tōkyō

Beijing

Mumbai
(Bombay)

Bangkok

Indian
Ocean

Pacific
Ocean

Arctic Circle

Tropic of Cancer

Equator

Jakarta

© Rand McNally

Grasslands called steppes cover much of Central Asia.

Camel

Natural Hazards

Natural Hazards Map
- • Earthquakes*
- △ Volcanoes*
- ╲ Tsunamis
- ➤ Tropical storm tracks (over 5 per year)

*Since 1900

Tsunamis

Tsunamis are huge ocean waves caused by underwater earthquakes or volcanoes. They usually travel at speeds of about 300 miles per hour (500 km/hr).

Tsunamis that reach the shore can cause terrible damage to coastal areas. On December 26, 2004, a strong earthquake off the coast of Sumatra in Indonesia caused a tsunami that destroyed huge coastal areas in Indonesia, Thailand, India, and Sri Lanka and also hit Madagascar and continental Africa. More than 200,000 people were killed. Most other tsunamis have occurred in the Pacific Ocean.

Energy

On the Mineral Fuel Deposits map, note the cluster of symbols indicating petroleum deposits around the Persian Gulf, which is near the left edge of the map. This area is part of the Middle East, which produces one-third of the world's oil.

Mineral Fuel Deposits Map
- ◣ Coal
- ▲ Petroleum
- △ Natural gas

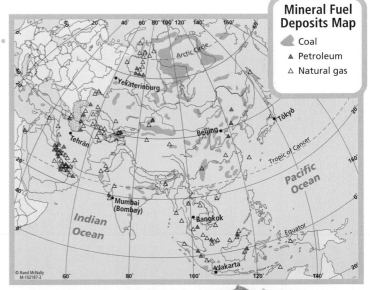

Oil exporting has brought great wealth to the countries in the Persian Gulf region of the Middle East. This photo shows an oil refinery in the United Arab Emirates.

A pipeline delivers oil to an oil tanker in Saudi Arabia.

China produces more than 45% of the world's coal.

AUSTRALIA AND OCEANIA

Uluru, also known as Ayers Rock, in central Australia

Sydney, Australia

A dairy farm on New Zealand's South Island

Australia is the only continent except Antarctica that lies completely in the Southern Hemisphere. Oceania consists of New Zealand, part of the island of New Guinea, and thousands of other islands in the Pacific Ocean. Many of these islands are tiny coral atolls where no one lives. Others are the tops of volcanoes.

Australia is the smallest continent. It is about the size of the conterminous 48 U.S. states. It has a drier climate than every other continent except Antarctica. Because Australia is in the Southern Hemisphere, it is warmer in the north than in the south.

Australia's vast, dry interior is called the Outback. Few people live there. Much of the land is used for grazing cattle and sheep on huge ranches called "stations." For many years, children on stations have "gone to school" by two-way radio connection with their teachers and other students called the School of the Air. Today, computers also provide connections for such children.

Australia's first people are the Aborigines. They came to Australia from Asia thousands of years before the first Europeans came. People from Asia also settled other islands of Oceania. New Zealand was the last place they reached. English people started coming to Australia and New Zealand in the late 1700s. People from the British Isles still make up most of the population, but Asians and people from the Pacific Islands have joined them. In both Australia and New Zealand, most people live along the coasts in modern cities.

Kangaroos

A Historical Look At Australia

Circa 40,000 B.C.E.–30,000 B.C.E.
Aborigines arrive in Australia from Asia.

1788
The British establish the first Australian penal colony in Sydney.

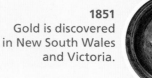

1800s
Chinese settlers arrive in Northern Territory

1851
Gold is discovered in New South Wales and Victoria.

Australia's Extremes

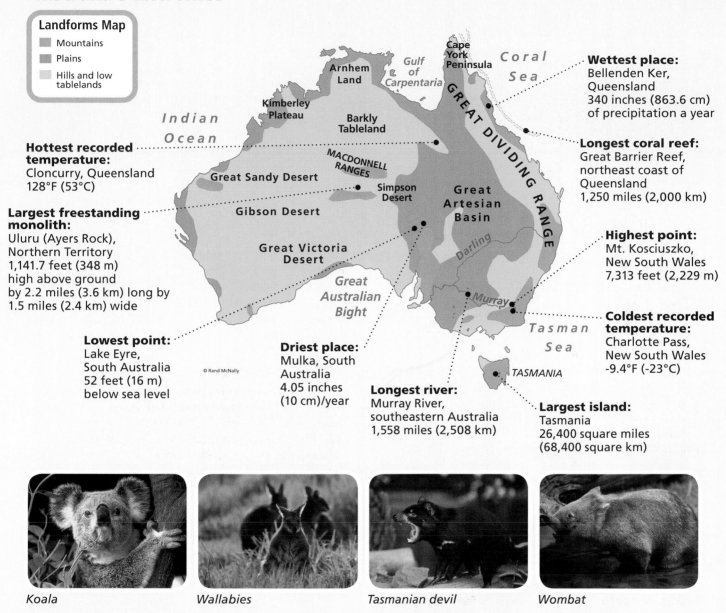

Landforms Map
- Mountains
- Plains
- Hills and low tablelands

Indian Ocean

Gulf of Carpentaria

Coral Sea

Cape York Peninsula

Arnhem Land

Kimberley Plateau

Barkly Tableland

MACDONNELL RANGES

Great Sandy Desert

Simpson Desert

Gibson Desert

Great Victoria Desert

Great Artesian Basin

GREAT DIVIDING RANGE

Darling

Murray

Great Australian Bight

Tasman Sea

TASMANIA

© Rand McNally

Hottest recorded temperature:
Cloncurry, Queensland
128°F (53°C)

Largest freestanding monolith:
Uluru (Ayers Rock),
Northern Territory
1,141.7 feet (348 m)
high above ground
by 2.2 miles (3.6 km) long by
1.5 miles (2.4 km) wide

Lowest point:
Lake Eyre,
South Australia
52 feet (16 m)
below sea level

Driest place:
Mulka, South
Australia
4.05 inches
(10 cm)/year

Longest river:
Murray River,
southeastern Australia
1,558 miles (2,508 km)

Wettest place:
Bellenden Ker,
Queensland
340 inches (863.6 cm)
of precipitation a year

Longest coral reef:
Great Barrier Reef,
northeast coast of
Queensland
1,250 miles (2,000 km)

Highest point:
Mt. Kosciuszko,
New South Wales
7,313 feet (2,229 m)

Coldest recorded temperature:
Charlotte Pass,
New South Wales
-9.4°F (-23°C)

Largest island:
Tasmania
26,400 square miles
(68,400 square km)

Koala

Wallabies

Tasmanian devil

Wombat

1893
New Zealand is the first
country to give women
the right to vote.

1901
Australia becomes
a self-governing dominion
within the British Empire.

1976
The First Aboriginal
Land Rights Act is passed.

2000
Sydney hosts the
summer Olympic
Games.

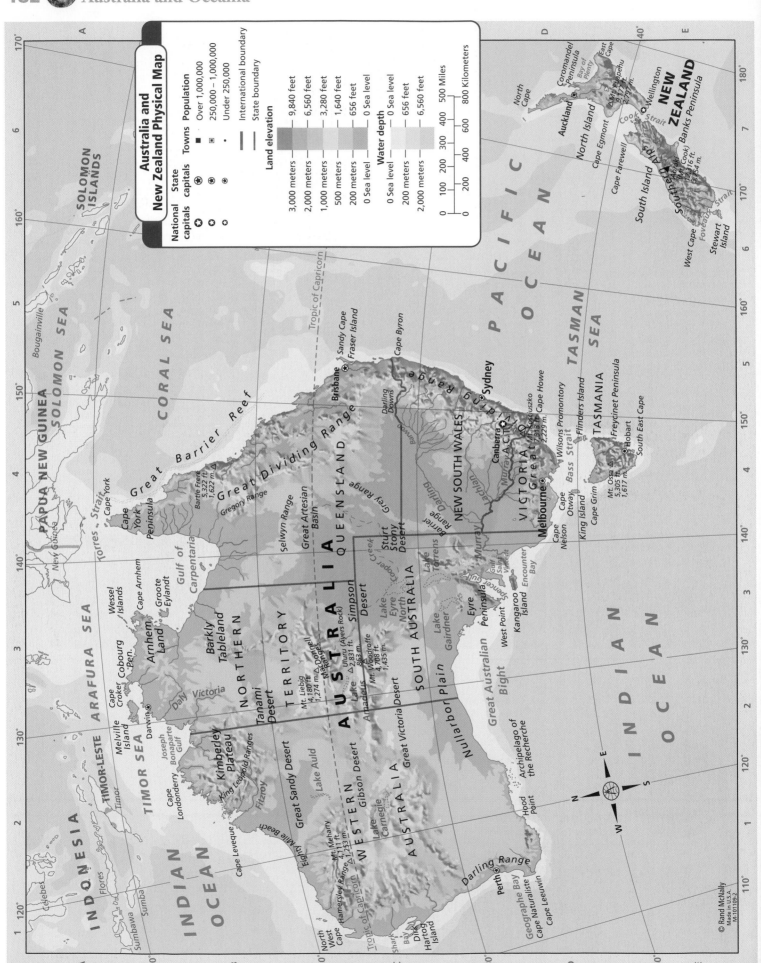

**Australia and
New Zealand Physical Map**

Towns | **Population**
Over 1,000,000
250,000 – 1,000,000
Under 250,000

National capitals | **State capitals**

International boundary
State boundary

Land elevation
3,000 meters — 9,840 feet
2,000 meters — 6,560 feet
1,000 meters — 3,280 feet
500 meters — 1,640 feet
200 meters — 656 feet
0 Sea level — 0 Sea level

Water depth
0 Sea level — 0 Sea level
200 meters — 656 feet
2,000 meters — 6,560 feet

500 Miles
800 Kilometers

INDONESIA
PAPUA NEW GUINEA
New Guinea
Torres Strait

SOLOMON ISLANDS
SOLOMON SEA
Bougainville

CORAL SEA

ARAFURA SEA
TIMOR SEA
Timor
TIMOR-LESTE
Flores
Celebes
Sumba
Sumbawa

Melville Island
Cape Croker
Cobourg Pen.
Cape Arnhem
Wessel Islands
Groote Eylandt
Arnhem Land
Darwin
Joseph Bonaparte Gulf
Cape Londonderry
Kimberley Plateau
King Leopold Ranges
Fitzroy
Cape Leveque

Cape York
Cape York Peninsula
Gulf of Carpentaria
Barkly Tableland
NORTHERN TERRITORY
Tanami Desert
Daly
Victoria
Lake Auld

Great Barrier Reef
Bartle Frere 5,322 ft. 1,622 m.
Gregory Range
Selwyn Range
Great Dividing Range

Sandy Cape
Fraser Island
Brisbane
Darling Downs
Cape Byron

Grey Range
Great Artesian Basin
QUEENSLAND

Sturt Stony Desert
Simpson Desert
Cooper Creek
Lake Eyre North
Lake Eyre South
Lake Eyre
Barcoo

SOUTH AUSTRALIA
Lake Torrens
Lake Gairdner
Lake Eyre

Sydney
NEW SOUTH WALES
Barrier Range
Darling
Murray
Murrumbidgee
Macquarie

Canberra A.C.T.
Mt. Kosciuszko 7,313 ft. 2,229 m.
Cape Howe
VICTORIA
Great Dividing Range
Melbourne
Cape Otway
Cape Nelson
King Island
Wilsons Promontory
Bass Strait
Flinders Island
TASMANIA
Mt. Ossa 5,305 ft. 1,617 m.
Freycinet Peninsula
Hobart
Cape Grim
South East Cape

WESTERN AUSTRALIA
Great Sandy Desert
Hamersley Range 4,111 ft. 1,253 m.
Mt. Meharry
Gibson Desert
Lake Carnegie
Great Victoria Desert
Mt. Liebig 4,180 ft. 1,274 m.
Uluru (Ayers Rock) 2,831 ft. 863 m.
Lake Amadeus
Mt. Woodroffe 4,708 ft. 1,435 m.
Macdonnell Ranges

Nullarbor Plain
Great Australian Bight
West Point
Eyre
Eyre Peninsula
Kangaroo Island
Spencer Gulf
Gulf Saint Vincent
Encounter Bay
Yorke Peninsula

North West Cape
Tropic of Capricorn
Eighty Mile Beach
AUSTRALIA
Darling Range
Perth
Geographe Bay
Cape Naturaliste
Cape Leeuwin
Archipelago of the Recherche
Hood Point
Shark Bay
Dirk Hartog Island

INDIAN OCEAN

PACIFIC OCEAN

TASMAN SEA

NEW ZEALAND
North Cape
Coromandel Peninsula
Bay of Plenty
East Cape
Auckland
North Island
Cape Egmont
Mt. Egmont
Mt. Ruapehu 9,175 ft. 2,797 m.
Wellington
Cook Strait
Banks Peninsula
Cape Farewell
South Island
Southern Alps
Aoraki (Mt. Cook) 12,316 ft. 3,754 m.
West Cape
Foveaux Strait
Stewart Island

© Rand McNally
Made in U.S.A.
M-101109-2

Australia and New Zealand Political Map

Towns Population
- ■ Over 1,000,000
- ◻ 250,000 – 1,000,000
- • Under 250,000

National capitals	State capitals
✪	✪
◌	◌

International boundary
State boundary

0   100 200 300 400 500 Miles
0   200 400 600 800 Kilometers

Oceans and Seas
- INDIAN OCEAN
- PACIFIC OCEAN
- CORAL SEA
- SOLOMON SEA
- ARAFURA SEA
- TIMOR SEA
- TASMAN SEA
- Celebes Sea
- Bass Strait
- Torres Strait
- Cook Strait
- Foveaux Strait
- Great Australian Bight
- Gulf of Carpentaria
- Joseph Bonaparte Gulf
- Spencer Gulf
- Shark Bay
- Geographe Bay
- Encounter Bay
- Halifax Bay
- Bay of Plenty

Countries / Regions
- INDONESIA
- TIMOR-LESTE
- PAPUA NEW GUINEA
- SOLOMON ISLANDS
- VANUATU
- NEW ZEALAND

Australian States / Territories
- WESTERN AUSTRALIA
- NORTHERN TERRITORY
- SOUTH AUSTRALIA
- QUEENSLAND
- NEW SOUTH WALES
- VICTORIA
- A.C.T.
- TASMANIA

Cities — Australia
- Darwin
- Katherine
- Derby
- Broome
- Port Hedland
- Karratha
- Exmouth
- Carnarvon
- Meekatharra
- Newman
- Geraldton
- Perth
- Bunbury
- Albany
- Esperance
- Kalgoorlie-Boulder
- Tennant Creek
- Alice Springs
- Weipa
- Normanton
- Mount Isa
- Cairns
- Townsville
- Mackay
- Longreach
- Emerald
- Rockhampton
- Bundaberg
- Charleville
- Toowoomba
- Brisbane
- Southport
- Coffs Harbour
- Taree
- Newcastle
- Sydney
- Wollongong
- Penrith
- Dubbo
- Bourke
- Broken Hill
- Canberra
- Wagga Wagga
- Albury
- Bendigo
- Ballarat
- Geelong
- Melbourne
- Mildura
- Adelaide
- Port Augusta
- Whyalla
- Mount Gambier
- Launceston
- Hobart

Cities — New Zealand
- Whangarei
- Auckland
- Hamilton
- Tauranga
- Rotorua
- Napier
- New Plymouth
- Palmerston North
- Wellington
- Nelson
- Christchurch
- Timaru
- Dunedin
- Invercargill

Physical Features
- Cape York Peninsula
- New Guinea
- Bougainville
- Groote Eylandt
- Dirk Hartog Island
- Fraser Island
- Kangaroo Island
- King Island
- Flinders Island
- Norfolk Island (Austl.)
- Archipelago of the Recherche
- North Island
- South Island
- Stewart Island
- Lake Carnegie
- Lake Amadeus
- Lake Eyre North
- Lake Torrens
- Lake Gairdner
- Cooper Creek
- Darling
- Lachlan
- Murray
- Fitzroy
- Daly
- Tropic of Capricorn

Other labels
- Honiara
- Port Moresby
- Port Vila
- Bay of Plenty

Climate

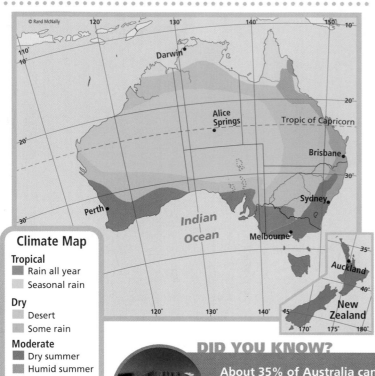

Climate Map

Tropical
- Rain all year
- Seasonal rain

Dry
- Desert
- Some rain

Moderate
- Dry summer
- Humid summer
- Rainy summer

Continental
- Long summer
- Short summer
- Very short, cool summer

Polar
- Tundra
- Ice cap

Highlands
- Varies

DID YOU KNOW?

About 35% of Australia can be classified as desert. In fact, Australia is the driest continent in the world after Antarctica.

Transportation

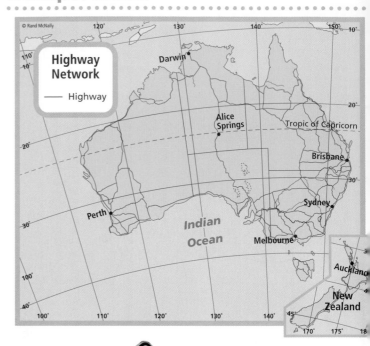

Highway Network
— Highway

Australia's highways provide important links between widely separated towns and cities, especially in the Outback.

Environments

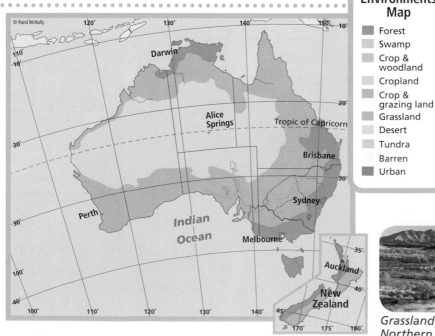

Environments Map
- Forest
- Swamp
- Crop & woodland
- Cropland
- Crop & grazing land
- Grassland
- Desert
- Tundra
- Barren
- Urban

Pinnacles Desert in Nambung National Park, Western Australia, Australia

Grassland in Northern Territory, Australia

Rain forest in Queensland, Australia

Grazing sheep, South Island, New Zealand

Economic Activities

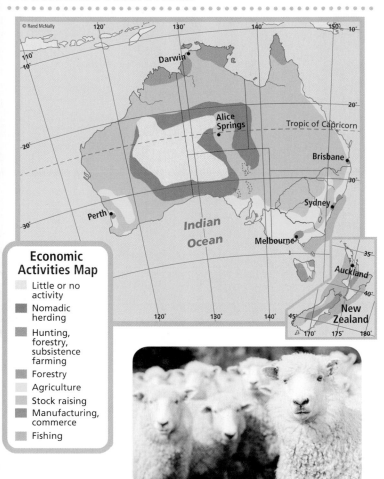

Economic Activities Map
- Little or no activity
- Nomadic herding
- Hunting, forestry, subsistence farming
- Forestry
- Agriculture
- Stock raising
- Manufacturing, commerce
- Fishing

In Australia, sheep outnumber humans four to one. In New Zealand, the ratio is seven to one. Together, the two countries produce nearly 30% of the world's wool.

The Great Barrier Reef

The Great Barrier Reef stretches for roughly 1,429 miles (2,300 km) along the northeast coast of Queensland, Australia. It is made up of more than 3,000 separate coral reefs. Together, they cover 132,974 square miles (344,400 square kilometers). The Great Barrier Reef is the largest group of coral reefs and islands in the world.

Scientists believe that the reef began forming millions of years ago. More than 600 types of soft and hard corals, in a great variety of colors, form the reef. In addition, about 1,500 species of fish live in the warm waters around the reef. Scientists warn that some human activities are causing serious damage to the reef.

Population

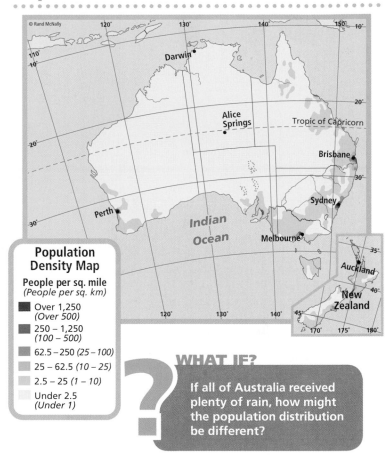

Population Density Map
People per sq. mile
(People per sq. km)
- Over 1,250 *(Over 500)*
- 250 – 1,250 *(100 – 500)*
- 62.5 – 250 *(25 – 100)*
- 25 – 62.5 *(10 – 25)*
- 2.5 – 25 *(1 – 10)*
- Under 2.5 *(Under 1)*

WHAT IF?
If all of Australia received plenty of rain, how might the population distribution be different?

More than 600 islands are found along the Great Barrier Reef. Some of them have been developed as tourist resorts, but many are uninhabited.

Green turtle

A whale shark

Acropora plate coral

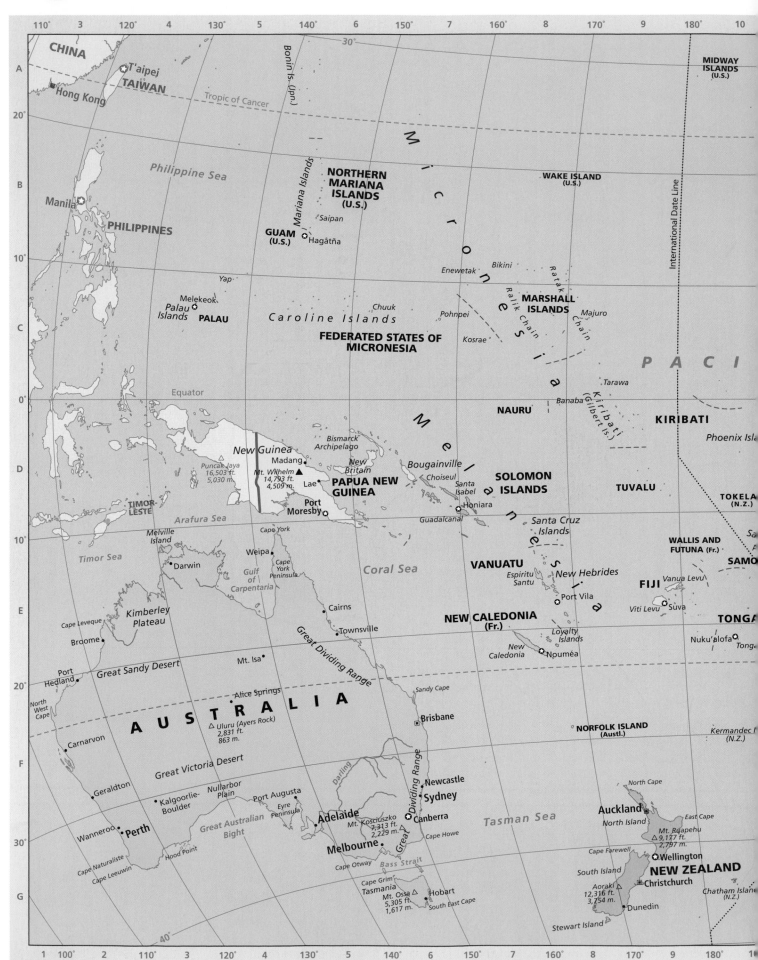

CHINA

T'aipei
TAIWAN
Hong Kong

Tropic of Cancer

Philippine Sea

Manila

PHILIPPINES

Bonin Is. (Jpn.)

30°

Mariana Islands

NORTHERN
MARIANA
ISLANDS
(U.S.)

Saipan

GUAM
(U.S.)
Hagåtña

MIDWAY
ISLANDS
(U.S.)

WAKE ISLAND
(U.S.)

Micronesia

International Date Line

Yap

Melekeok
Palau
Islands   PALAU

Caroline Islands

Enewetak   Bikini

Chuuk

Pohnpei

FEDERATED STATES OF
MICRONESIA

Kosrae

Ralik Chain

Ratak Chain

MARSHALL
ISLANDS

Majuro

P A C I

Equator

Tarawa

Banaba

Kiribati
(Gilbert Is.)

NAURU

KIRIBATI

Phoenix Isla

Puncak Jaya
16,503 ft.
5,030 m.

New Guinea

Madang

Mt. Wilhelm
14,793 ft.
4,509 m.

Lae

PAPUA NEW
GUINEA

Port
Moresby

Bismarck
Archipelago

New
Britain

Bougainville

Choiseul

Santa
Isabel

SOLOMON
ISLANDS

Honiara

Guadalcanal

Melanesia

TUVALU

TOKELA
(N.Z.)

TIMOR-
LESTE

Arafura Sea

Melville
Island

Darwin

Cape York

Weipa

Cape
York
Peninsula

Gulf
of
Carpentaria

Coral Sea

Santa Cruz
Islands

VANUATU

Espiritu
Santu

New Hebrides

Port Vila

Vanua Levu

FIJI

Viti Levu   Suva

WALLIS AND
FUTUNA (Fr.)

SAMO

Timor Sea

Kimberley
Plateau

Cape Leveque

Broome

NEW CALEDONIA
(Fr.)

Loyalty
Islands

TONGA

Cairns

Great Dividing Range

Townsville

New
Caledonia   Nouméa

Nuku'alofa

Tong

Port
Hedland

North
West
Cape

Great Sandy Desert

Mt. Isa

Sandy Cape

Alice Springs

A U S T R A L I A

Brisbane

NORFOLK ISLAND
(Austl.)

Kermandec I
(N.Z.)

Carnarvon

Uluru (Ayers Rock)
2,831 ft.
863 m.

Great Victoria Desert

Geraldton

Kalgoorlie-
Boulder

Nullarbor
Plain

Darling

Dividing Range

Newcastle

Sydney

North Cape

Auckland

North Island

East Cape

Wanneroo   Perth

Cape Naturaliste

Great Australian
Bight

Port Augusta

Eyre
Peninsula

Adelaide

Melbourne

Mt. Kosciuszko
7,313 ft.
2,229 m.

Canberra

Cape Howe

Tasman Sea

Mt. Ruapehu
9,177 ft.
2,797 m.

Cape Farewell

South Island

Wellington

NEW ZEALAND

Cape Leeuwin

Hood Point

Cape Otway

Bass Strait

Cape Grim

Tasmania

Mt. Ossa
5,305 ft.
1,617 m.

Hobart

South East Cape

Aoraki
12,316 ft.
3,754 m.

Christchurch

Chatham Islan
(N.Z.)

Stewart Island

Dunedin

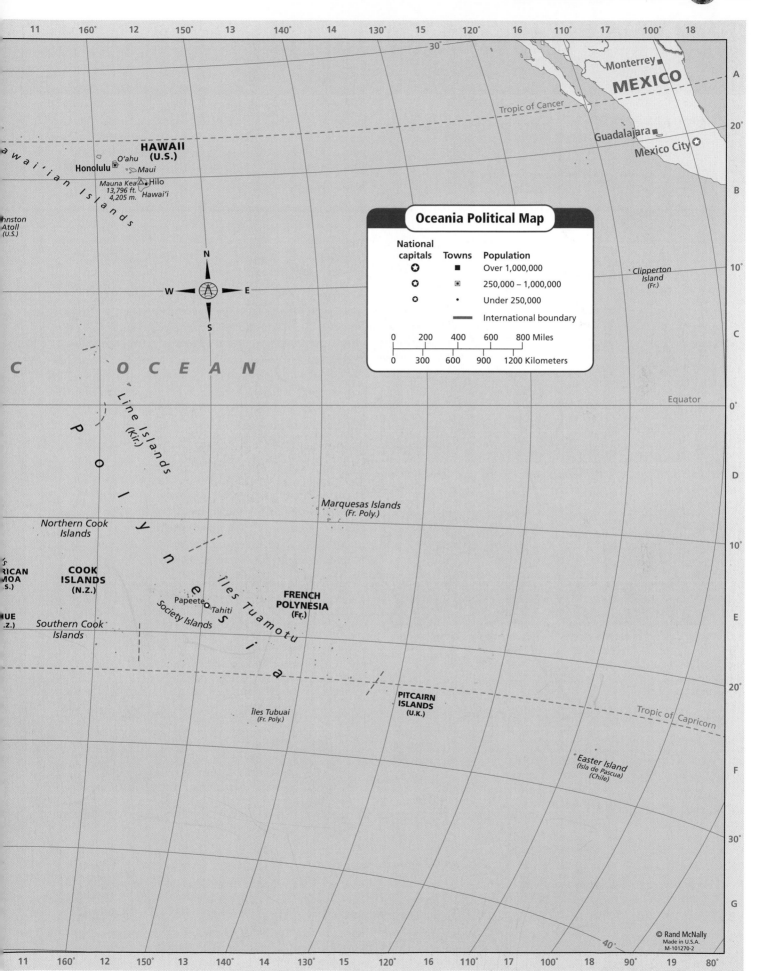

Oceania Political Map

National capitals	Towns	Population
✪	■	Over 1,000,000
✪	▣	250,000 – 1,000,000
✪	•	Under 250,000
	—	International boundary

0   200   400   600   800 Miles
0   300   600   900   1200 Kilometers

Monterrey
MEXICO
Tropic of Cancer
Guadalajara
Mexico City

HAWAII (U.S.)
O'ahu
Honolulu
Maui
Mauna Kea △ Hilo
13,796 ft.
4,205 m.   Hawai'i

awai'ian Islands

hnston
Atoll
(U.S.)

Clipperton
Island
(Fr.)

N
W   E
S

C   O C E A N

Equator

Line Islands
(Kir.)

P

O

l

y

Marquesas Islands
(Fr. Poly.)

Northern Cook
Islands

n

e

s

RICAN
MOA
(S.)

COOK
ISLANDS
(N.Z.)

Îles Tuamotu

NUE
.Z.)

Southern Cook
Islands

Papeete
Tahiti
Society Islands

FRENCH
POLYNESIA
(Fr.)

i

a

PITCAIRN
ISLANDS
(U.K.)

Tropic of Capricorn

Îles Tubuai
(Fr. Poly.)

Easter Island
(Isla de Pascua)
(Chile)

© Rand McNally
Made in U.S.A.
M-101270-2

ANTARCTICA

Antarctica is the world's fifth-largest continent. Most of it lies within the Antarctic Circle. It is the world's most isolated landmass. The nearest land is the southern tip of South America, about 769 miles (more than 1,238 km) from the Antarctic Peninsula.

All the land within the Antarctic Circle has days in winter when the sun never rises and days in summer when the sun never sets. At the South Pole, between March 20 and September 21 the sun never rises, and between September 21 and March 20 it never sets.

Antarctica is the coldest place on earth. Average summer temperatures may reach only about 0° F (-18° C). Such a cold, frozen landmass produces cold winds that collide with warmer air around the coast and form a belt of storms. Antarctica receives very little precipitation. What precipitation does fall produces ice, which accumulates into thick ice sheets that gradually push toward the coast and form ice shelves over the edge of the land.

People discovered Antarctica only about 200 years ago. Exploration on land started a little more than 100 years ago. No people live on Antarctica permanently. More than a dozen countries have established scientific stations where scientists study such things as global climate change, the atmosphere's thinning ozone layer, and plant and animal life. A growing number of tourists visit the continent each year.

Scientists know that the continent has such resources as coal, but an international agreement prohibits exploiting these resources. Perhaps the most important resource is the abundant life in the cold waters off the coast.

Kayaking along the Antarctic coast

Passengers crowd the deck of an icebreaker ship as it plows through pack ice.

Explorer in a wind tunnel

Snow petrel

A Historical Look At Antarctica

1918–1821
Fabian von Bellingshausen, a Russian, is the first European to see Antarctica.

1911
Roald Amundsen is the first person to reach the South Pole.

1895
A Norwegian expedition is the first to land on Victoria Land.

1929
Richard Byrd flies over the South Pole.

Scientific Stations in Antarctica

Frozen and isolated as it is, Antarctica offers some important advantages for researchers. Its darkness makes it a good place to study the stars. Its clean air allows studies of air quality. Scientists can see the effects of human activity. Antarctica has no borders—although seven countries have made territorial claims—so scientists from different countries can share the information they find.

Palmer Station
The only U.S. station north of the Antarctic Circle

Argentina
Brazil
Chile
China
Korea
Poland
Russia
Uruguay

United States
Chile
Ukraine
Argentina
United Kingdom
Argentina
Argentina

Halley Station
The site of important ozone research

Argentina
United Kingdom

Germany
South Africa

India

SANAE IV
Built on poles, since 60-80 inches (150 to 200 cm) of snow piles up in winter

McMurdo Station
Home to Antarctica's largest community and capable of supporting up to 1,200 people

United States
New Zealand

United States
South Pole

Amundsen-Scott South Pole Station
Located about 1,150 feet (350 m) from the geographic South Pole

ANTARCTICA

Russia

Russia

Japan

Russia

Mawson Station
The oldest continuously inhabited station south of the Antarctic Circle

France

Dumont d'Urville Station
Built in 1956 to replace a station that burned down

Vostok Station
The coldest recorded temperature on Earth, -128° F. (-89.2° C), was measured here on July 21, 1983.

China
Russia

Australia

Australia

Mirny Station
Opened in 1956

Australia

Davis Station
The southernmost Australian station

Russia

A scientific station operated by Argentina

Telecommunications equipment at a scientific station

Animals in Antarctica

Orcas, also known as killer whales

Wandering albatross

Emperor penguins

Leopard seal

1957-1958
The International Geophysical Year (IGY) focuses on the scientific study of Antarctica.

1959
The Antarctic Treaty is signed. It provides for peaceful scientific cooperation in Antarctica.

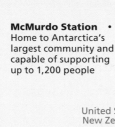

1991
The Protocol on Environmental Protection to the Antarctic Treaty bans commercial mining operations in Antarctica.

2000
An iceberg 170 miles long and 25 miles wide breaks off the Ross Ice Shelf.

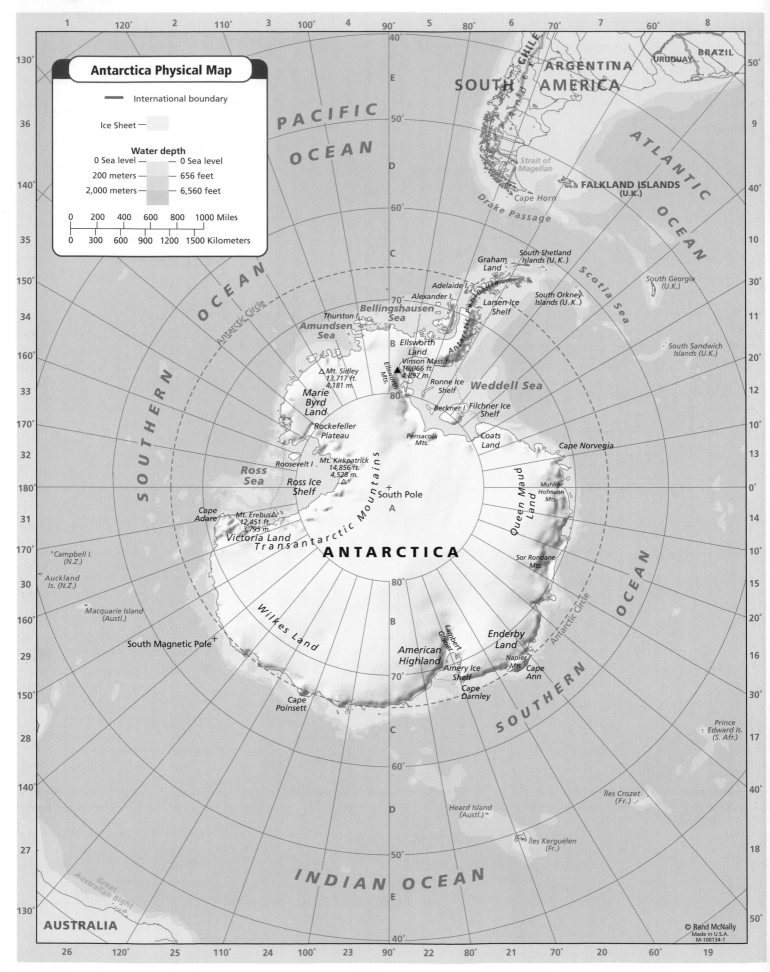

Antarctica Physical Map

— International boundary

Ice Sheet —

Water depth

0 Sea level —	— 0 Sea level
200 meters —	— 656 feet
2,000 meters —	— 6,560 feet

0 200 400 600 800 1000 Miles

0 300 600 900 1200 1500 Kilometers

PACIFIC OCEAN

SOUTH AMERICA

CHILE

ARGENTINA

URUGUAY

BRAZIL

Strait of Magellan

Drake Passage

Cape Horn

FALKLAND ISLANDS (U.K.)

ATLANTIC OCEAN

SOUTHERN OCEAN

Antarctic Circle

South Shetland Islands (U.K.)

Graham Land

Adelaide I.

Alexander I.

Larsen Ice Shelf

South Orkney Islands (U.K.)

Scotia Sea

South Georgia (U.K.)

Thurston I.

Bellingshausen Sea

Antarctic Peninsula

Amundsen Sea

Ellsworth Land

Vinson Massif 16,066 ft. 4,897 m.

South Sandwich Islands (U.K.)

Mt. Sidley 13,717 ft. 4,181 m.

Ellsworth Mts.

Ronne Ice Shelf

Weddell Sea

Marie Byrd Land

Berkner I.

Filchner Ice Shelf

Rockefeller Plateau

Pensacola Mts.

Coats Land

Cape Norvegia

Roosevelt I.

Mt. Kirkpatrick 14,856 ft. 4,528 m.

Queen Maud Land

Muhlig-Hofmann Mts.

Ross Sea

Ross Ice Shelf

South Pole

Transantarctic Mountains

Cape Adare

Mt. Erebus 12,451 ft. 3,795 m.

ANTARCTICA

Sor Rondane Mts.

Victoria Land

Campbell I. (N.Z.)

Auckland Is. (N.Z.)

SOUTHERN OCEAN

Antarctic Circle

Macquarie Island (Austl.)

South Magnetic Pole

Wilkes Land

Lambert Glacier

American Highland

Enderby Land

Napier Mts.

Cape Ann

Prince Edward Is. (S. Afr.)

Cape Poinsett

Amery Ice Shelf

Cape Darnley

SOUTHERN OCEAN

Îles Crozet (Fr.)

Heard Island (Austl.)

Îles Kerguélen (Fr.)

INDIAN OCEAN

Great Australian Bight

AUSTRALIA

© Rand McNally
Made in U.S.A.
M-100134-1

Thematic Content Index

This index makes it easy to compare different continents and regions of the world in terms of climate, economies, and other major themes covered in the atlas.

State	Population	Rank in Population	Area in Square Miles	Rank in Area	Year Admitted to the Union	Order Admitted to the Union	State Capital	Largest City
Alabama	4,779,736	23	50,645	28	1819	22	Montgomery	Birmingham
Alaska	710,231	47	570,641	1	1959	49	Juneau	Anchorage
Arizona	6,392,017	16	113,594	6	1912	48	Phoenix	Phoenix
Arkansas	2,915,918	32	52,035	27	1836	25	Little Rock	Little Rock
California	37,253,956	1	155,799	3	1850	31	Sacramento	Los Angeles
Colorado	5,029,196	22	103,642	8	1876	38	Denver	Denver
Connecticut	3,574,097	29	4,842	48	1788	5	Hartford	Bridgeport
Delaware	897,934	45	1,949	49	1787	1	Dover	Wilmington
Florida	18,801,310	4	53,625	26	1845	27	Tallahassee	Jacksonville
Georgia	9,687,653	9	57,513	21	1788	4	Atlanta	Atlanta
Hawaii	1,360,301	40	6,423	47	1959	50	Honolulu	Honolulu
Idaho	1,567,582	39	82,643	11	1890	43	Boise	Boise
Illinois	12,830,632	5	55,519	24	1818	21	Springfield	Chicago
Indiana	6,483,802	15	35,826	38	1816	19	Indianapolis	Indianapolis
Iowa	3,046,355	30	55,857	23	1846	29	Des Moines	Des Moines
Kansas	2,853,118	33	81,759	13	1861	34	Topeka	Wichita
Kentucky	4,339,367	26	39,486	37	1792	15	Frankfort	Lexington
Louisiana	4,533,372	25	43,204	33	1812	18	Baton Rouge	New Orleans
Maine	1,328,361	41	30,843	39	1820	23	Augusta	Portland
Maryland	5,773,552	19	9,707	42	1788	7	Annapolis	Baltimore
Massachusetts	6,547,629	14	7,800	45	1788	6	Boston	Boston
Michigan	9,833,640	8	56,539	22	1837	26	Lansing	Detroit
Minnesota	5,303,925	21	79,627	14	1858	32	St. Paul	Minneapolis
Mississippi	2,967,297	31	46,923	31	1817	20	Jackson	Jackson
Missouri	5,988,927	18	68,741	18	1821	24	Jefferson City	Kansas City
Montana	989,415	44	145,546	4	1889	41	Helena	Billings
Nebraska	1,826,341	38	76,824	15	1867	37	Lincoln	Omaha
Nevada	2,700,551	35	109,781	7	1864	36	Carson City	Las Vegas
New Hampshire	1,316,470	42	8,953	44	1788	9	Concord	Manchester
New Jersey	8,791,894	11	7,354	46	1787	3	Trenton	Newark
New Mexico	2,059,179	36	121,298	5	1912	47	Santa Fe	Albuquerque
New York	19,378,102	3	47,126	30	1788	11	Albany	New York
North Carolina	9,535,483	10	48,618	29	1789	12	Raleigh	Charlotte
North Dakota	672,591	48	69,000	17	1889	39	Bismarck	Fargo
Ohio	11,536,504	7	40,861	35	1803	17	Columbus	Columbus
Oklahoma	3,751,351	28	68,595	19	1907	46	Oklahoma City	Oklahoma City
Oregon	3,831,074	27	95,988	10	1859	33	Salem	Portland
Pennsylvania	12,702,379	6	44,743	32	1787	2	Harrisburg	Philadelphia
Rhode Island	1,502,567	43	1,034	50	1790	13	Providence	Providence
South Carolina	4,625,364	24	30,061	40	1788	8	Columbia	Columbia
South Dakota	814,180	46	75,811	16	1889	40	Pierre	Sioux Falls
Tennessee	6,346,105	17	41,235	34	1796	16	Nashville	Memphis
Texas	25,145,561	2	261,231	2	1845	28	Austin	Houston
Utah	2,763,885	34	82,169	12	1896	45	Salt Lake City	Salt Lake City
Vermont	625,741	49	9,217	43	1791	14	Montpelier	Burlington
Virginia	8,001,024	12	39,490	36	1788	10	Richmond	Virginia Beach
Washington	6,724,540	13	66,455	20	1889	42	Olympia	Seattle
West Virginia	1,852,994	37	24,038	41	1863	35	Charleston	Charleston
Wisconsin	5,686,986	20	54,158	25	1848	30	Madison	Milwaukee
Wyoming	563,626	50	97,093	9	1890	44	Cheyenne	Cheyenne

States Ranked by Land Area
(largest land area to smallest)

1	Alaska
2	Texas
3	California
4	Montana
5	New Mexico
6	Arizona
7	Nevada
8	Colorado
9	Wyoming
10	Oregon
11	Idaho
12	Utah
13	Kansas
14	Minnesota
15	Nebraska
16	South Dakota
17	North Dakota
18	Missouri
19	Oklahoma
20	Washington
21	Georgia
22	Michigan
23	Iowa
24	Illinois
25	Wisconsin
26	Florida
27	Arkansas
28	Alabama
29	North Carolina
30	New York
31	Mississippi
32	Pennsylvania
33	Louisiana
34	Tennessee
35	Ohio
36	Kentucky
37	Virginia
38	Indiana
39	Maine
40	South Carolina
41	West Virginia
42	Maryland
43	Vermont
44	New Hampshire
45	Massachusetts
46	New Jersey
47	Hawaii
48	Connecticut
49	Delaware
50	Rhode Island

States Ranked by Population
(largest population to smallest)

1	California
2	Texas
3	New York
4	Florida
5	Illinois
6	Pennsylvania
7	Ohio
8	Michigan
9	Georgia
10	North Carolina
11	New Jersey
12	Virginia
13	Washington
14	Massachusetts
15	Indiana
16	Arizona
17	Tennessee
18	Missouri
19	Maryland
20	Wisconsin
21	Minnesota
22	Colorado
23	Alabama
24	South Carolina
25	Louisiana
26	Kentucky
27	Oregon
28	Oklahoma
29	Connecticut
30	Iowa
31	Mississippi
32	Arkansas
33	Kansas
34	Utah
35	Nevada
36	New Mexico
37	West Virginia
38	Nebraska
39	Idaho
40	Hawaii
41	Maine
42	New Hampshire
43	Rhode Island
44	Montana
45	Delaware
46	South Dakota
47	Alaska
48	North Dakota
49	Vermont
50	Wyoming

States Ranked by Population Density
(highest density to lowest)

1	New Jersey
2	Rhode Island
3	Massachusetts
4	Connecticut
5	Maryland
6	Delaware
7	New York
8	Florida
9	Ohio
10	Pennsylvania
11	California
12	Illinois
13	Hawaii
14	Virginia
15	North Carolina
16	Michigan
17	Indiana
18	Georgia
19	New Hampshire
20	Tennessee
21	South Carolina
22	Kentucky
23	Louisiana
24	Wisconsin
25	Washington
26	Alabama
27	Texas
28	Missouri
29	West Virginia
30	Vermont
31	Minnesota
32	Mississippi
33	Arkansas
34	Iowa
35	Arizona
36	Oklahoma
37	Colorado
38	Maine
39	Oregon
40	Kansas
41	Utah
42	Nebraska
43	Nevada
44	Idaho
45	New Mexico
46	South Dakota
47	North Dakota
48	Montana
49	Wyoming
50	Alaska

States Ranked by Order of Statehood
(first to last)

1	Delaware
2	Pennsylvania
3	New Jersey
4	Georgia
5	Connecticut
6	Massachusetts
7	Maryland
8	South Carolina
9	New Hampshire
10	Virginia
11	New York
12	North Carolina
13	Rhode Island
14	Vermont
15	Kentucky
16	Tennessee
17	Ohio
18	Louisiana
19	Indiana
20	Mississippi
21	Illinois
22	Alabama
23	Maine
24	Missouri
25	Arkansas
26	Michigan
27	Florida
28	Texas
29	Iowa
30	Wisconsin
31	California
32	Minnesota
33	Oregon
34	Kansas
35	West Virginia
36	Nevada
37	Nebraska
38	Colorado
39	North Dakota
40	South Dakota
41	Montana
42	Washington
43	Idaho
44	Wyoming
45	Utah
46	Oklahoma
47	New Mexico
48	Arizona
49	Alaska
50	Hawaii

Index Abbreviations

The following abbreviations are used
in the index.

Afr.	Africa
Austr.	Australia
cap.	capital
Can.	Canada
dep.	dependency
dist.	district
Eur.	Europe
Mex.	Mexico
mtn.	mountain
mts.	mountains
N.A.	North America
Terr.	Territory or Territories
S.A.	South America
U.A.E.	United Arab Emirates
U.K.	United Kingdom
U.S.	United States

Map Abbreviations

The following abbreviations are used
in the maps.

ALB.	Albania
ARK.	Arkansas
ARM.	Armenia
AUS.	Austria
AZER.	Azerbaijan
BEL.	Belgium
BHU.	Bhutan
BNGL.	Bangladesh
BOS.	Bosnia and Herzegovina
BUL.	Bulgaria
CONN.	Connecticut
CRO.	Croatia
CZ.	Czech Republic
D.C.	District of Columbia
DEM. REP.	Democratic Republic
DEN., Den.	Denmark
DOM. REP.	Dominican Republic
EL SAL.	El Salvador
EST.	Estonia
FED.	Federated
Fr.	France
ft.	feet
GEO.	Georgia
GUAT.	Guatemala
HOND.	Honduras
HUNG.	Hungary
ILL.	Illinois
Is.	Islands
KAN.	Kansas
KS.	Kosovo
KY.	Kentucky
KYRG.	Kyrgyzstan
L.	Lake
LAT.	Latvia
LEB.	Lebanon
LITH.	Lithuania
MA.	Macedonia
MASS.	Massachusetts
MD.	Maryland
MICH.	Michigan
MOLD.	Moldova
MONT.	Montana
MT.	Montenegro
Mt.	Mount
MTN.	Mountain
MTS., Mts.	Mountains
NAT'L	National
NEBR.	Nebraska
NETH.	Netherlands
NEW HAMP.	New Hampshire
NIC.	Nicaragua
Nor.	Norway
NP	National Park
N.Y.	New York
N.Z.	New Zealand
OKLA.	Oklahoma
PA.	Pennsylvania
PENN.	Pennsylvania
Port.	Portugal
RA.	Range
R.I.	Rhode Island
ROM.	Romania
SERB.	Serbia
SLVK.	Slovakia
Sp.	Spain
St.	Saint
Ste.	Sainte
SWITZ.	Switzerland
TAJIK.	Tajikistan
TENN.	Tennessee
U.A.E.	United Arab Emirates
U.K.	United Kingdom
U.S.	United States
W.	Western
WYO.	Wyoming

Introduction to the Index

This index is an alphabetical list of many of the places
that appear on the maps in this atlas. Each entry in the
index includes:

- the place name
- a description of the type of feature it is
- its location
- its map key, or letter-number grid location
- the number of the page on which it appears

Some places appear on more than one map in the atlas,
but each place is indexed to just one map.

Names that are abbreviated on the maps are generally spelled
out in the index. The names of physical features, such as
mountain peaks and lakes, are alphabetized under the proper
part of the name; for example, Lake Michigan is indexed as
"Michigan, Lake". Places in the United States are followed by
the name of the state in which they are located. If they extend
beyond a single state, they are indexed to the country. Places
outside of the United States are indexed to the country and
continent in which they are located.

If they extend beyond a single country, they are indexed to
the continent.

The map key, or letter-number grid location, indicates the
location of the symbol. For features (such as mountain ranges)
that cover large areas, and for features (such as rivers) that are
lines, the map key indicates the location of the feature's name
(not its symbol) on the map.